The God of All Grace

J. Douglas MacMillan
Preacher and Teacher

Christian Focus

© Christian Focus Publications
ISBN 1 85792 240 9
Published in 1997 by
Christian Focus Publications,
Geanies House, Fearn, Ross-shire,
IV20 1TW, Great Britain

CONTENTS

ARTICLES

Foreword

There is a general recognition that the reading of sermons, even the best, does not make the same impact upon the reader that the hearing of them does upon the listener. The immediacy of personal encounter is lacking – an immediacy that owes much to the personality of the preacher and to the nuances of voice and manner. In his study of John Knox as a preacher, Douglas MacMillan argued that 'all students of the subject acknowledge that even verbatim reporting seldom captures the power and the thrill that accompany the hearing of truly great preaching. That kind of preaching has a dimension to it, a chemistry in it, which cannot be transferred to the permanence of writing'. But there are exceptions to most generalisations and we come as near as possible to such an exception in the sermons collected in this volume. Of course those who knew and delighted in the preaching of Douglas MacMillan will pine for the days when they heard the warm, loving, persuasive and passionate voice that sometimes trumpeted and sometimes whispered, that counselled, pleaded and commanded. If some of the intimacies of the living voice are lacking, the sincerity and passion are here as vividly as ever. Moreover the reading requires more direct attention to what was said rather then to the incidentals of voice and manner that reinforced the utterances. That, I think, is how Douglas would have wanted it. Attend to what is said and you cannot fail to be aware of the urgency and passion of the preacher who, above all things, wants you to respond positively to the God of all grace as He bids you believe and rest in His Son Jesus Christ for salvation.

In all these sermons the grace of God that brings salvation is the theme, and no-one who reads is left in doubt that issues of life and death turn upon the reception or rejection of that grace. The reward of positive reception is infinitely gladsome. The consequence of rejection is infinitely dire. The message is directly to you, the reader, yes you in your distinct individuality, in your precise circumstances, to you here and now. All the time the word is personally applied. These are not just academic disquisitions. These are the heart-breaking pleadings of a man who cannot bear the thought that you might lose out on God's greatest gift. Here you are aware of the Son of God, the holy and just One stooping low for the rescue of sinners: stooping lower than we would ever have dared to ask. When He wore the crown of thorns – 'We would never have asked Him to stoop so low, would we?' asks the preacher. Here is a vivid description of what Jesus suffered for sinners. 'His labour was soul labour and it was whole souled labour.' And now that you have heard what God has done in Christ you must recognise that 'no other person can put you to hell but yourself. Not even God can send you to hell if you are willing to be saved.'

These are examples of the passionate will to convince that always marked the preaching of Douglas MacMillan. If you have an unconverted friend, you'll do him a great service if you persuade him to read even some of these sermons.

The theme of grace and the preaching of the grace of God is continued and developed more formally in the lectures which are included in the book. The primacy of preaching, the necessity of evangelism are re-emphasised in the studies of the nature and operation of grace. 'Grace is just God acting graciously' says our author, 'When grace comes, God comes.' The importance of evangelism as the proclamation and offer of grace, is demonstrated in reflections upon the lives of men who, under God, shaped the course of the Reformation – Calvin and Knox.

'He being dead, yet speaks'. How often do we say that even when all we have are echoes of the voices of those who have gone home. Here, however, we have more than echoes. Read and you will be astonished by the vibrancy and strength of the voice that proclaims so gloriously the grace of God that brings salvation.

Clement Graham

I was born in the County of Argyll, in the Parish of Western Ardnamurchan on the last day of September, 1933. I had the great
privilege of being born into a Christian home and was the youngest of six children, two girls and four boys. The most westerly
point of mainland Britain, Ardnamurchan is a peninsula running
into the Atlantic ocean with the island of Skye lying to the North
and the island of Mull to the South. It was, in many ways, an
idyllic place in which to be brought up and fostered in me a great
love for the countryside, and in particular, for the sea and the
mountains.

When I was a little boy, my father was a building-contractor
but also ran a croft, or small farm on which the family did the
work. From the earliest time I can remember, the croft animals,
cows and calves, sheep and lambs, horses, and of course, collie
dogs were part of our rich and varied everyday life. We did not
realise it at the time, but it was a kind of life fast fading into the
obscurity of history.

My father was a very hard-working, upright, honest, able man
with a fine mind and a very skilful pair of hands. A deeply exercised Christian, his heart was open to all kinds of people and he
was a helper of every needy person and cause. I don't think I have
ever met anyone whom I have respected in quite the same way as
I respected him. He was converted in middle life, in the year 1921,
when a visiting preacher held meetings in our village. He went
through a long, trying period under great conviction of sin and
was hugely troubled for a time over the doctrine of election. His
deliverance from all this came by way of a powerful experience
of God's grace in Christ when reading a sermon on that very subject by C. H. Spurgeon.

I have counted it as a fortunate thing that, being the son of a
bardic family and endowed with a fine command of good, fluent
Gaelic, he has left some of his early spiritual experiences on record
in the form of a few fine Gaelic spiritual songs and hymns. After

This personal testimony was written by Douglas shortly before he was
taken to heaven on 3rd August, 1991. It originally appeared in *He Found
Me*, a collection of personal testimonies published by Christian Focus
Publications.

his conversion he began to preach, and along with other young Christian converts of that period to hold Cottage meetings in the villages surrounding his home. My mother, Jessie MacLachlan, was also of Ardnamurchan people on both sides of her family, but had been born and brought up in Glasgow. She came to Ardnamurchan to care for an elderly uncle and soon afterwards was converted through hearing my father preach.

Memories of my childhood are happy ones and many of them centre around the gospel and the love which the gospel always brings into a home. I still recall very vividly our worship times as a family, my father's prayers, and his carrying me on his shoulders as we went through the woods and over the hill tracks to the lovely, white-sanded bay where the people of four little hamlets met for worship and preaching at three o'clock on Sunday afternoons. Our home often entertained the preachers or other Christians and so I think I always knew that the Lord's people were happy and greatly enjoyed each others' fellowship.

I remember, on one occasion, sitting in that small church at Sanna Bay listening to our minister preaching on the Judgment and describing how people on that Day would call on the mountains to fall on them and cover them from the face of God. At one point in his sermon, he tiptoed, very gently, over to the windows of this little church and, pointing upwards to where we could all see the huge, rugged, granite rocks and boulders perched on the steep slopes of the hills as they towered above us, he said, in a voice filled in awe, 'People will be calling on those very rocks and hills to hide them from God, if they are not ready to meet him on that great day.' I was probably only three or four years old at the time, but I can still remember feeling the power of that moment and the still, solemn hush that came over us all.

I can remember something else which had an even more vivid and lasting effect on my life and which took place when I was eight years old. In our times of family worship we used to sing some verses of a Psalm; and, one Sunday evening when we were singing the opening verses of Psalm 40 I had a very powerful sense of the nearness and the love of God. As we sang, I felt something very special in these words which speak about God taking us out of the miry clay, setting our feet upon a rock, and putting a new song in our mouths. My heart was touched and melted, and I really felt that God loved me and had come to me; so I told my parents and my friends at school that I had been converted. For quite a long time after I tried to live like a Christian, at home and at school.

Outgrowing religion

When I was nearly twelve I had to leave home to attend secondary school at Tobermory on the island of Mull. Here, two things worked against my continuing to think and act as a Christian. First of all, there were no other believers of my own age. Secondly, one of my new teachers positively undermined my faith in the Bible. By the time I was thirteen, I felt I had outgrown religion. I put behind me the impressions I had had from early childhood. Religion was all right for the likes of my parents, whom I regarded as old and old-fashioned, but it was not something which I needed.

Before I was fourteen, I had to leave school. Two years earlier my father had moved to quite a large farm which he ran with my two older brothers and, at certain times, help from an uncle with the sheep. My oldest brother was leaving home that Autumn to study at Veterinary College in Glasgow and, at the same time, I ran into difficulties finding accommodation near my school. Just as these were being overcome, in the month of January 1948, my uncle died very suddenly and so with pressure of work in looking after his croft with its horse, cows and sheep, as well as the sheep on our own farm, I was, to my own entire satisfaction, allowed to abandon any further thought of returning to school almost a year before attaining the minimum leaving age and, in the event, never went back at all.

I had just got settled into this new situation and the beginning of a working teenage life when my mother, who had had surgery a year or so earlier, began to be very unwell and finally became ill with a painful, terminal cancer. Strangely enough, despite her own faith and cheerfulness, her illness and especially the long, dragged out, closing year of her life confirmed me in the anti-religious, anti-Christian attitudes I had begun to adopt during my last year at school.

Another influence in my life at this time was the books I used to borrow from a man with communist views (a red Clydesider) who came to live not far away. As I read these books, especially

through the long wintry nights, I felt confirmed in my rejection of
Christianity.

Will I meet you in heaven?
I also recall something which happened one night in the early
springtime of that final year of mother's life. My brother and I
had been out at a ceilidh and dance, singing and playing accordi-
ons in a village about thirty-five miles away. We got home in the
wee, small hours of the morning – just as a new day was beginning to break. I opened the back door of our house and immediately heard a strange, but beautiful sound. It was my mother's
voice. She had had some training in voice production when young
and had, at one time, sung with some groups in Glasgow. But
here she was now, just months before her death and at a time
when her days were often filled with great pain, awake in the
middle of the night with the stress of her illness, and my father
sitting with her, softly singing a glorious testimony of faith in the
verses of one of her favourite Psalms:

> I shall not die, but live, and shall
> The works of God discover:
> The Lord hath me chastised sore,
> But not to death giv'n over.
>
> O set ye open unto me
> The gates of righteousness;
> Then will I enter into them,
> And I the Lord will bless.   (Psalm 118:17-19)

She was singing the second verse just as my hand was on the
handle of the back door. I was so overcome I could not go in. I
went away up into the hills to cry. Here I was full of youthfulness
and with everything opening out before me, and there she was, so
weak and in such pain, yet singing with triumph about what was
opening out before her. There was something about that, and about
her whole life, that touched even my hard heart.

Three months later, one hot day in July, I was in my mother's
room and she asked me to read a few verses for her from the
Bible.

'Where would you like me to read?'
'In John chapter 14.'

I took up the Bible and began to read: Let not your heart be troubled: ye believe in God, believe also in me. In my Father's house are many mansions: if it were not so, I would have told you. I go to prepare a place for you. And if I go and prepare a place for you, I will come again, and receive you unto myself; that where I am, there ye may be also.

'That's enough.'

'But, Mam, would you not like me to read a bit more? I could read the whole chapter.' (I was actually feeling quite proud that I could do this for my mother.)

But she said, 'No, Douglas, that's enough. That's everything.' Then she turned to me and said, 'Douglas, there is something I want to say to you. I may never talk to you again. In a short time I am going to be with Jesus. But I want to ask you, *Will you meet me there?*'

Four days later, she died. So seven days after that last conversation, I was standing beside my mother's grave. It was as if I could hear her voice ringing in my ears, 'Will I meet you in Heaven?' I knew that, if there was a Heaven, I was not walking on the road that led to it. I felt I had to harden my heart against my mother's appeal, and I did.

Were you in church last Sunday?

However, there were many things which began to get to me and leave me very uneasy with my life and outlook. For example, in my work as a shepherd I was closely in touch with nature. Especially in lambing time I had to get up when it was dark and climb the hills as day was dawning. From the height of the mountains behind our house, the beauty of nature was staggering. I remember sitting down on the top of a mountain, early one morning, and looking out to the west I could see the nearer islands and beyond them, the Outer Hebrides. Beyond that, there was nothing between me and America. The beauty and immensity of everything made my hair stand on end. I could not get the question out of my head – *Where did all this come from?*

To cut a long story short, six or seven years of atheism came to an end as I found it actually easier to accept the existence of God than to go on believing that all this beauty and order came from nothing.

But now a new struggle started. What if the God who made the world was the same God as my parents believed in? What if the Bible was true? What if there was a Heaven and a Hell? I remember that, as I was out drinking one evening, I was suddenly overcome by the seriousness of a question from which I could not escape. *What if all I had been taught about the Bible was true?*

One night, when I was in a local pub, a man asked me, 'Douglas, were you in church last Sunday?'

I said, 'No – not me! These fellows just put me to sleep.'

A week later I was playing my accordion at a dance. I got up to dance with a girl and, as we moved round the floor together, she suddenly asked me, 'Douglas, were you in church last Sunday?' I was beginning to feel persecuted! But she went on: 'There's a wonderful young preacher. You must go and hear him.' I'll not repeat what I said to her.

The mask removed

My older brother used to drive my father to the midweek service in the church six or seven miles away. But one Wednesday around that time my brother was away at a cattle sale and I got the job of driving my father to the church. I intended, while he was in the church, going to the pub for a drink and then going to visit a girl. However, as we came near to the church I had an idea. I asked my father, 'Who will be preaching tonight? Is it that young preacher?'

'Yes.'

I thought, 'This is my chance to find out what they are all talking about.' I went in with my father, but as soon as I sat down in the church amongst these old people I began to wonder if I was going mad. What if my mates found out that I spent my Wednesday evening in a church!

Then the door behind the pulpit opened and I got quite a shock. I thought that all preachers were old men, ready to crumble and fall into the grave. They were religious because there was nothing better for them to do. But this young man was just a little older than I was myself. He looked as if he had a broken nose – in fact his whole appearance reminded me of my hero Freddie Mills, the British cruiserweight boxer who was then champion of the world.

At first I was disappointed when he began to speak. His voice was low, as if he was afraid of all the old ladies in black. His text was: 'Because thou sayest, I am rich, and increased in goods, and have need of nothing; and knowest not that you are wretched, and miserable, and poor, and blind and naked: I counsel you to buy from me gold tried in the fire...' (Revelation 3:17-18). To this day I am amazed that he chose to speak on a text like that when he must have expected to address a group of old Christians. Anyway he described what he found in the text – the spectacle of a soul worshipping itself. What took my breath away was – he gave an exact description of me, and of my life. I was living for myself, for pleasure and for what I could accomplish. I drank, I enjoyed the company of the lassies, but there were also hard ambitions which had taken over my life. I lived for money, and there was another thing. I used to do the round of the Highland Games, and often featured in the prize lists for the 'Heavy Events'. I was especially keen on hammer throwing. I had been doing it since I was fifteen and thought that in about four years I could reach the top.

But, as I listened to the preacher in that quiet country church, all these things lost their dazzle. The very things which had become the focal point for my driving ambition began suddenly to look pathetic and empty. What was the point in giving over my life to these things? The mask was being removed from my life.

I began to wonder – 'Did my old man tell this preacher about me? But no; I did not even know myself I would be listening to this until I stopped at the door.'

I was not converted that night, though I promised the preacher that I would come to the church again. It was three weeks before I saw him. I was driving along beside the sea in the old lorry we used at the farm when I spotted him walking beside the road, carrying a Calor gas cylinder. He had about a mile to go yet. I said to myself, 'Will I stop, or will I go roaring past him? If I give him a lift, he'll ask me why I haven't been back in church.' In the end I stopped and said quite roughly to him, 'Want a lift, Jock?' he wanted a lift all right. He threw the cylinder in the back and climbed up beside me. Just as I thought, the first thing he said to me was, 'You never came back to church.'

'No – I've been busy.'

'You are a liar.'

'That's a terrible thing for a preacher to say.'

'But you are a liar; it wasn't because you were busy – am I
right?'

'I suppose you are.'

He shouted, above the sound of the old engine, 'You know
what I think? I think you are running scared. I think you are scared
that you will get converted.'

'No, I am not scared. Actually, I would like to be converted,
but I don't think I can be.'

'What do you mean?'

'Well, since that night, I have asked God two or three times to
convert me and nothing has happened.'

By this time we had reached where he was staying. He said,
'Why don't you come in?'

It can't be as simple as that!
I went in with him, and he talked to me as no-one had ever talked
before. Then he said to me, 'If you are really serious about this,
what about going down on your knees and we will ask God to
change you.'

I wasn't very keen. I was embarrassed, but then I said to myself, 'I want this if I can get it,' so I went down on my knees. At
first he wanted me to pray, but there was no way I was going to do
that with him there. I said, 'You are the one who is paid to do the
praying. You pray!'

He began to talk to God as if he really knew him and as he
continued he quoted John 3:16: 'God so loved the world that he
gave his only begotten Son, that whosoever believeth in him should
not perish but have everlasting life.' I had known these words all
my life, but as he quoted them it was as if someone drew aside
curtains so that light came into a dark room. I understood these
words in a new way. I saw that Christ had finished all that was
necessary for my salvation. I didn't have to do anything to save
my soul. I got a hold of the preacher's arm and said, 'Say that
again.'

He stared at me. 'Say what again?'

'That bit about God loving the world: say that again.'

He repeated the text.

I said, 'Does that mean that, if I really believe that Jesus is the
Son of God and that he died on the Cross at Calvary to save us

from our sins, and trust him because of that, I will be saved?'

He said, 'Yes – that's just what it means.'

I said, 'It can't be as simple as that!'

But, although I was arguing like that, I felt I was understanding the way of salvation for the first time in my life. What I had known in one way for so long now seemed so new! And as I believed it for the first time, a great peace began to flood into my heart, and a stillness came over me.

Then I thought, 'That's all right, but you know how a Christian is supposed to live.' I began thinking of all the things I would have to stop. He saw my face changing and asked, 'What's wrong now?'

I said, 'I don't think I could live like a Christian. I would have to give up too much.'

'Listen, Douglas,' he said. 'You think through everything you feel you would have to give up. Think about it very carefully.' Then he said, 'In this hand, (holding out his right hand) I'll give you everything you are afraid of losing; and in this hand (holding out his left hand) I'll give you Christ.'

He didn't make it easy for me. I'm sure I must have sat there for ten minutes (he said afterwards it felt like an eternity) thinking deeply about all that was involved. Then at last I absolutely knew which one I had to take. I said, 'If I can really have Christ as my Saviour, I'll take him.' As soon as I had said that, my heart was filled with joy and love.

Then I suddenly remembered my father. I had dropped him off in the village at two o'clock. He was going to collect his pension and visit a friend, and I was to have picked him up at four o'clock. By this time it was twenty past seven. I said to the preacher, 'Man, I've forgotten my old man. He has been waiting on me for three and a half hours.'

I jumped into the old lorry and went roaring off back to the little bungalow where my father had said he would be. The lady came to the door and let me in. I hurried ahead of her into the living room. My father was sitting opposite the door. As soon as I came in he got up, crossed the room, took me in his arms and said, 'Douglas, thank God.'

'Why?'

'You've been converted.'

'How do you know?'

'I could see in your face, as soon as you came in the door, that my prayer had been answered.'

Call to the ministry

By the time I had been a Christian for two years I was quite sure that the Lord was calling me to preach the gospel. I tried to satisfy this demanding heart-urge by applying for, and getting acceptance as a Lay Preacher with my local Presbytery. Having spoken at one or two of the little, weekly Prayer Meetings conducted by my father, I preached my first sermon in Lochgilphead Free Church, in March 1957. My father died in June of that year and it was in the days following that momentous – but in some ways marvellous – event, I knew that I would have to seek entrance to the ministry of the gospel.

At the end of August 1958, I left home to take up full time study at Skerry's College, Edinburgh, with a view to entering the ministry of the Free Church of Scotland. I had, of course, at least four years of secondary school studies to make up and knew that I was facing an uphill task. Over the next two years, my time was spent in studying for University Preliminary Entrance exams.

My only source of income, once I stopped work, was an annual grant of £70 from the church, so to make ends meet I drove a lorry in the afternoons for a Haulier who used to camp on our farm over the Summer holidays. He and his wife were tremendously kind to me at that time and were a great help during a period when I felt very homesick and missed my dogs, my sheep and my hills.

Throughout that period, though, the Lord was really good to me. I enjoyed listening to fine preaching, made many new Christian friends and, within two years, gained passes which enabled me to enter Aberdeen University. I enjoyed my time there enormously, marrying at the end of my first Session, and graduating MA in 1963. I then returned to Edinburgh to pursue my theological studies at the Free Church College.

Places of service

I was ordained to the gospel ministry, and inducted to my first pastorate in St. Columba Free Church, Aberdeen, on 3rd September, 1966. The congregation was not large but both Mary and I knew it well from our student days and over the last few years of my predecessor's very faithful ministry it had not only grown in numbers but it had increased in spiritual vigour as well and there was a fine tone and quality to its life. We knew that during the University Sessions there would be quite a number of students amongst us.

During my time in the Dee Street Church, as it was most popularly known, my ministry was quite varied with a lot of hospital visiting, evangelism amongst lapsed churchgoers, open-air meetings, street tracting and work amongst College and University students. We saw the Lord at work amongst the people there and over the years quite a number of young people were converted. This was one of the happiest periods of my life and I enjoyed the work tremendously. I was quite heartbroken when I felt the time had come to leave for another church.

In 1974 I was given and, after much heart-searching, accepted a call to St. Vincent Street Free Church in Glasgow. The work there was different from Aberdeen but I also enjoyed it a great deal. There I saw quite a number of older people being converted – indeed, the first person and the last which I knew to be definitely converted to Christ there were both over seventy years of age, something which I always regarded as quite unusual. Anyway, I ministered very happily there until 1982 when I was appointed to the chair of Church History and Church Principles in the Free Church College, Edinburgh.

I had eight years at the College and much enjoyed working with the men studying for the ministry of our own and various other churches. I was able to speak and preach in many places outwith Scotland and came to know the Lord's work on a wider scale than formerly.

I had just indicated acceptance of a call to a congregation in Edinburgh, where I am now ministering, when I took ill with coronary disease in the late Spring of 1990. That eventuated in open heart surgery and a triple bypass in July of that year. It was my first ever experience of hospital or of serious illness and it is a great joy for me to say that through all this rather traumatic experience I was very deeply aware of the Saviour's presence and felt my heart fortified by his peace.

I was very humbled by the large number of calls and letters we received – from all around the world, almost – assuring us of continued prayer both from churches and individuals. And those prayers were wonderfully answered. It was a marvellous experience to feel myself absolutely cushioned with the love and power of Christ on the evening before my operation and not merely to know, but actually to feel that I was on the receiving end of a huge battery of Christian love and Christian prayer.

Over the months since then, I have made steady progress back to health and have been able to pick up the beginnings of a new ministry amongst a people from whom, and in whom, I receive many tokens of the Lord's love and graciousness. On the medical side of things I have also received great kindness as well as dedicated and attentive care. I have marvelled at the skill, patience and sheer professionalism of all the people involved in this ministry of healing and, under God, owe them a great deal.

Gratitude to God

I feel that I owe a special debt of gratitude to the Lord for the help and support I have had from my wife, Mary, in our thirty years together as well as during this last year and its times of illness and utter weakness. As I have indicated, she is also a graduate of Aberdeen University, was a teacher prior to our marriage, and is the daughter of a well-known Free Church minister and writer, the late Rev Murdoch Campbell, Resolis. Mary has been a great help right through my ministry and has made our home a place where people feel welcome.

We have five children; Eilidh (Gaelic for Helen); Murdo; Mhairi (Mary); Neil and Douglas. All of them are grown up now and are deeply committed Christians. The first is a Social Worker in Inverness; the second works with the Department of Agriculture; the third is a Clinical Psychologist; the fourth is studying for the ministry of our church; and the youngest is a student in Cardiff.

Looking back over my life the greatest thing which ever happened to me was, without a shadow of a doubt, my conversion in 1955. I have never regretted that the Lord sought and found me, a lost, unworthy sinner, and changed my heart and life with his grace and power. The Lord has been very gracious and good to me down through the years and has never failed me.

My only regrets lie along the line of my own many failures to be all that I should have been for him. But despite the sins and disobedience and the imperfect service I have been able to give to the Lord I would not want to change any of it. My life has been full and happy, and every day has been rich with his love and mercy.

I would like to guard against the thought that I am in any way special, or that my experience, although so uniquely personal, is any different in principle from that of other Christians. It is not so. I am a very ordinary person who was found and saved by a very extraordinary Saviour, and I owe him a debt that can never be repaid either in this world or in the world to come. The wonder that filled my heart the night I first found Jesus in June 1955 is still there – the complete wonder that, as Paul put it long ago, *he loved me, and gave himself for me.*

GRACE

1

What Grace Is

It is often said, and with perfect truth, that the central theme of the Bible is salvation. Had there been no salvation planned and put into operation by God for the redemption of sinful men, then it is highly unlikely that there would have been a biblical revelation to man at all. The existence of biblical revelation itself implies a prior purpose of salvation and indicates to us that the Bible has been given, quite literally, as a Manual of Salvation. So it is not strange that salvation should be the central theme, the great burden, of the Bible's message to man.

But the salvation of the Bible is of a unique and special kind. There is nothing among men, not even in their religions, which compares with it. To know this salvation is to learn that, strictly speaking, it belongs to an order all its own. There is nothing which gives us a perfect comparison; nothing of which it can be said with total truth, '*That* is what it is like!'

We are not surprised to learn therefore that the Bible uses a very special family of words to describe and define various aspects of salvation; the uniqueness of salvation requires it to be so. What may surprise us is that there is *one* particular word frequently used in the Bible to convey to the reader the nature and character of salvation. Without this word – the word 'grace' – the true nature of biblical salvation would never be understood properly. So crucial is this one word to the understanding of salvation that it provides a 'seed bed' out of which grows the Bible's theology of salvation. All the major doctrines of the faith root back into it. It is, in many ways, the keyword of Christianity. Without some understanding of it the gospel of salvation remains an enigma. If it is used as the interpretive key, the gospel unfolds itself with perennial freshness and penetrating power. The word *grace* carries with it solemn implications for our destiny and therefore demands our close attention.

The gospel of the grace of God is the central message of the

Bible, and the key factor in the Christian's experience of salvation. There can be absolutely no question but that the love of God for sinners is the mainstay of every Christian life as it is nourished and directed by the teaching of the Bible.

This is reflected by the place that the saving love of God holds amongst Christians everywhere. Wherever they have fellowship together their speech is, simply and naturally, strongly seasoned with the assurance of this great and precious fact. It is with texts which state this truth and elaborate its theme that every true child of God strengthens his soul.

'For God so loved the world that he gave his only begotten Son' (John 3:16).

'Behold, what manner of love the Father has bestowed upon us that we should be called the sons of God' (1 John 3:1).

'Greater love has no man than this, that a man lay down his life for his friends' (John 15:13).

It is with the glorious realities of which such texts assure us, that God the Father loves us and that Christ the Saviour died for us, that we comfort one another in times of darkness and trial and establish our souls in times of doubt and dismay.

The whole burden of this amazing love, its essential nature, its ultimate achievement, finds its focus for us in this word *grace*, one of the best-known and best-loved words in the New Testament. As J. I. Packer writes, 'It is a commonplace in all the Churches to call Christianity a religion of grace.'[1] In fact, wherever we meet with the semblance of biblical religion, whether in books, individuals, groups or churches, we encounter a frequent usage of the word. We must not be deceived. This does not mean that all is well in the world of religion. Packer continues, 'It is repeatedly pointed out in books and sermons that the Greek New Testament word for grace (*charis*), like that for love (*agape*), is a wholly Christian usage, expressing a notion of spontaneous self-determined kindness which was previously quite unknown to Graeco-Roman ethics and theology. It is staple diet in the Sunday School that grace is God's Riches at Christ's Expense. And yet, despite these facts, there do not seem to be many in our churches who actually believe in grace.'

That comment of Packer's, along with his earlier observation

---

1. J. I. Packer, *Knowing God* (Hodder and Stoughton, 1973) p. 142.

about the widespread homage paid to the word *grace* by varied and sometimes contradictory beliefs, alerts us to the urgent need for definition and clarification.

Importance of our understanding

It is clear that where such a basic and essential word as grace is misunderstood, the great realities of which it speaks will also be misunderstood. There will be a gap between our understanding and the true reality. In some areas of life or even in some areas of doctrine this kind of gap may not matter a great deal, but in this particular instance it is absolutely crucial. A mistaken view of grace will inevitably lead to a distorted view of salvation and we will be in real danger of 'turning to a different gospel – which is really no gospel at all' (Gal. 1: 6,7).

Here we are concerned with a word that bears directly on the very nature of the gospel and upon the kind of salvation held out to us there. Our correct understanding of the word *grace* is critical or it will not bring us the message which God, in his love, intends it to convey. Knowledge of truth is essential to belief in it, and what we know obviously has a powerful effect on what we believe. However, knowing a truth does not necessarily mean that we will believe it. One of the rather sad features of our present-day religious scene is that the basic meaning of the word grace is not only misunderstood but tends not to be believed.

The failure on the part of so many people to believe in grace is probably because our explanations and definitions of what grace really is are not always clear or adequate. But it also reflects the fact that there is an element in grace and in the living experience of grace which ultimately defies total analysis and complete understanding. To experience grace is to experience an utterly undeserved kindness from an unexpected source and this attitude is so alien to our sinful, selfish natures and our modern lifestyle that it is difficult for us to understand it, or accept it.

The Bible does contain a doctrine and theology of grace and there are three important strands of teaching on the subject, each of which must be given due emphasis if we are to understand the Bible's teaching about salvation.

Grace is power

This is the first element in the teaching on grace. Grace is power.
We can go a step further here and say that grace is the power of
God which is made available to helpless individuals. In fact, we
may go as far as to say that it is the power of the Father, the Son
and the Holy Spirit exerted in complete unity of purpose and harmony of action for our salvation.

The element of power is an absolute essential in our understanding of the grace that brings salvation. If grace did not include a power great enough to achieve the salvation of sinners
then we could never be totally certain of any sinners being saved.
We could not say as the Bible does, that 'it is by grace you have
been saved' (Eph. 2:5) if the word did not convey the notion of
power and the ability to achieve all that is involved in salvation.

It becomes ever more certain that grace must contain this element of power when we reflect on the nature of sin and the actual
condition of those who are held in its grip. The Bible makes no
attempt to hide or obscure the havoc, the damage that sin has
brought into our lives: 'As for you, you were dead in your transgressions and sins' (Eph. 2:1); 'By the trespass of one man death
reigned' (Rom. 5:17). The Bible describes in graphic terms this
state of complete spiritual death common to us all. Only grace
can bring life where there was death, can make us alive again, can
change this condition. That is exactly the kind of power which is
attributed to grace in the Scriptures: 'God ... made us alive with
Christ even when we were dead in transgressions; it is by grace
you have been saved' (Eph. 2:5)

This gives a realistic picture of what grace has to do in the
salvation of real people, real sinners, like ourselves. It lays hold
of those who are spiritually dead, and imparts new life. It comes
to one who was an enemy of God and gives instead a new heart
that is full of love for him. In irresistible power, it transforms a
sinner into a saint, an enemy into a child of God.

The power involved here is power of a unique and special order.
The Bible compares it, in its results and effects, to the power of
God exercised in creating all things. It is a life-giving, quickening,
creative power: 'For God, who said, "Let the light shine out of
darkness," made his light shine in our hearts to give us the light of
the knowledge of the glory of God in the face of Jesus Christ' (2

Cor. 4:6). To grasp this is to have the key to understanding many other biblical truths of a similar kind. In describing the deep-seated, radical nature of the change that Christian conversion involves, Paul actually declares, 'If anyone is in Christ, he is a new creation; the old has gone, the new has come' (2 Cor. 5:17).

There can be no question but that the graphic language used to describe the condition of sinners and the nature of conversion is there to emphasise for us our spiritual helplessness when it comes right down to the mechanics of how we are turned from death to life. Death is a very intense, a very strong word. Applied as it is to the spiritual state of the natural man (i.e. man apart from grace) it excludes any thought of self-help at all. It highlights both our helplessness and the urgent and crucial necessity for us to experience the life-giving power of God. It is only because grace is power, that it can save those who are 'dead in sins' (Eph. 2:1).

If this helplessness was not spiritual, then perhaps salvation might come through something other than power. For example, it might come by wise counsel or by powerful exhortation. Both of these are important and if based on biblical revelation, they should, we might think (as many people do) be quite adequate for the task. But the hard facts disallow the effectiveness of such a strategy altogether – it would be quite useless. Death puts men beyond the reach of good advice. It is sheer folly to ask a dead person to *do* anything. That would be asking for the impossible. It would be asking for a definitive, positive course of action in the face of complete inability to respond. A dead man does not need instruction or exhortation: he needs life! In the matter of salvation it is exactly the same. The sinner does not only need good advice or reasonable exhortation in order to become a Christian. Something far more effective is needed; something that no preacher or counsellor or adviser can ever give; something without which he will remain forever dead in his sins. He needs the quickening, life-giving power of God. He needs grace.

This is one of the reasons why the New Testament disciples gloried in the gospel message they had been sent to preach and teach. They knew it was good news, but they knew that it was more. They knew the gospel as a tremendously effective and transforming power which, when it began to work in the hearts of men and women, brought about a radical, lasting change in their

lives. 'Our gospel,' writes the apostle Paul, 'came to you not simply
with words, but also with power' (1 Thess. 1:5); and to the Romans
he wrote: 'I am not ashamed of the gospel: it is the power of God
for salvation' (Rom. 1:16). This is how Dr. Martin Lloyd-Jones
states the matter in one of his powerful sermons on Ephesians:

> We are spiritually dead by nature, and no one can do anything
> until he has been quickened, raised, given life and created anew.
> According to the New Testament, no category is adequate to
> describe what we are in Christ save this conception of the re-
> birth, regeneration; and no man can give birth to himself. The
> power of God is the beginning and end of salvation; all is of him
> and his power.[2]

Grace is love

The second idea conveyed by the word grace is that of love. Yes,
grace is power. It is not, however, a random power, operating
without purpose or direction. Rather, it is power harnessed and
directed by love, a love which acts for the good of all on whom it
sets its kindness and affection. The American theologian, Dr. B.B.
Warfield wrote: 'Power, in itself considered, may blast as well as
bless. The power that grace is always blesses, because grace is
love.'[3]

Recently we have had an awe-inspiring demonstration of the
havoc that power, uncontrolled, can cause. Huge areas of the
United States and of Canada were devastated by a tornado. Our
daily newspapers and television screens have vividly portrayed
the wreckage for us. In a matter of moments the work of years has
been laid waste. Sheds, houses, gardens, roadways, bridges, whole
towns were uprooted and broken and smashed. People lost their
property. Some people lost their lives. What is a tornado? From
one point of view it is immense power gone completely out of
control – power gone mad, unleashing an energy that destroys
everything in its pathway. That is a power to be feared. But brought
under the control and direction of purpose and usefulness how
beneficial the energy of power can be. It can be used, even in the

---

2. Martin Lloyd-Jones, *God's Ultimate Purpose* (Banner of Truth,
1978), p. 396.
3. B. B. Warfield, *Selected Shorter Writings*, Volume 1, p. 287.

case of the wind, to warm our homes and add comfort and help to many aspects of our lives.

Now this is the way it is with grace and this second element in our definition of what grace means is vitally important to a correct understanding of the gospel. Grace is an exertion of God's power, but it is always his power being exerted in kindness and tenderness. It is the love of God acting according to its nature. It is God himself acting graciously, acting in the way of positive blessing. Here we have nothing less than the power of omnipotence acting under the direction and dictation of infinite love – a power which can touch us in our weakest places and in our darkest moments with all the tenderness of a great love.

There is a very beautiful example of this in the ministry of Jesus. We read in the Gospels of a mighty, powerful work of Jesus which is known as The Raising of Jairus' Daughter. The narrative as we have it from Mark 5:22-43 gives one interesting detail which none of the other Evangelists mention. Mark records the very words that Jesus used to call the little girl back to life: 'Talitha, cumi.' These words were, of course, from the everyday language of the people concerned and they had a very lovely meaning and usage. Literally they meant 'Rise, little lamb' and they were the morning call of a mother to her child or, as we would say nowadays, 'Time to be up, love.' As the Lord Jesus exercised his power in bringing this little girl back to life, as he reunited the bond between soul and body which death severs, he used the ties of early familiarity and motherly affection to temper that power and to suit it to the needs and circumstances of a bewildering experience. That, I would suggest, is very like our Lord Jesus and very like the grace that is involved in our salvation. It is power exercised in tender love.

Paul in his letter to the church at Ephesus conveys the same idea to his readers. When speaking of the grace which saves sinners, he attributes it all to its real source and speaks very beautifully of the riches of God's mercy and 'his great love wherewith he loved us' (Eph. 2:4). This element of love in grace is basic and essential to our understanding and appreciation of the nature of grace. When we are saved by grace our salvation traces right back to the love of God as its single, ultimate source.

Grace is a gift

The third idea contained in the word *grace* is the thought that it comes freely and costs nothing at all. The New Testament makes it quite clear that the love of God is not earned by us. It brings us a sharply pointed contrast between grace and works, as the basis on which sinners can be saved and does so in order to teach us that God's saving of sinners is always on the basis of grace. If salvation could be earned in any way it would no longer be of grace (Rom. 11:6).

Now a gift is usually an act of kindness which is prompted by love. This is exactly like the lovingkindness that flows through the grace of God. Grace is more than kindness, it is kindness to those who are ill-deserving.

At one time, the educational system ensured that young people who made the grade could go on to study at College or University at no cost to the family. They were 'grant eligible' and so qualified for free education. It came, not at a price, but as a gift. In the same manner the sinner, unable to pay the debt he owes to the broken law of God becomes, by his very sinnership, 'grant eligible'. If he is to be saved at all his salvation must be funded and gifted out of 'the exceeding riches of his grace in his kindness towards us through Christ Jesus' (Eph. 2:7).

Finally, on this matter of the freeness with which grace comes or is bestowed, we must not overlook the fact that it is the freedom of God himself which lies at the heart of the issue. Is God free to act in the way which most pleases him and which he wills to take? God does not need any one of us in order to have the perfect felicity and blessedness that is his continually – nor does that felicity depend on anything external to himself. It is also the case that since we have sinned and have become enemies of God (Rom. 5:10) he is in no way compelled to show us any favour. We cannot even on the basis of our 'rights' ask him for mercy; the highest claim we can make on him is a claim for justice, and justice being what it is, that would mean condemnation and rejection by God. God is not in any way obliged to pardon sinners; the very fact that he is God means that he is just as free to act in condemnation as he is in salvation. The very fact that we are sinners means that no blame could attach to him should he decide to act only for condemnation.

James Packer sums up this idea of the freeness of grace when he writes, 'Grace is free in the sense of being self-originated, and of proceeding from One who was free not to be gracious.'[4]

How amazing and how wonderful is God's grace in its freeness. Had that freeness not involved the pure, inherent, moral right not to be gracious towards sinners, then grace would not be the totally free and spontaneous love which the Bible proclaims it to be and of which Calvary is the ultimate proof (Rom. 5:8).

These then are the basic elements which blend into our understanding of what grace is. When we accept the biblical teaching that we are 'saved by grace' then we accept that we are saved by power – the omnipotent power of God. We accept that we are saved by love; amazing, undeserved, infinite love. And we accept that we are saved by a God who was absolutely free to have dealt with us, not in mercy, but in justice. That he has not done so, we owe totally to the fact that he freely chose to deal with us in grace.

---

4. Packer, *Knowing God*, p. 146.

2

What Grace Does

We have already seen that the doctrinal and theological meaning of grace must be understood in terms of power, love and gift. We must now look at what this implies for us on a practical level. This may be done by examining the context and biblical setting of the word. What grace is may often become clearer for us if we look at what grace does. When we are studying an idea, a word or a doctrine, it is always helpful to examine it in terms of what it does, how it functions and what it achieves.

I can recall vividly the first occasion on which I saw a farm tractor. Born and bred in the countryside and reared within a farming community, I had heard a good deal about tractors. Until the Spring of 1947 I had never actually seen one – up till then all our farm work had been done with horses. Now, when I had my first glimpse of a tractor it was not working in a field but was powering its way along the road pulling a trailer full of agricultural machinery. From that moment on, if asked what a tractor was like, I would have been able to describe it in some detail. A tractor, I could have said, is a compactly designed machine which has large traction wheels at the rear and smaller wheels at the front. It has an engine, a gearbox, a steering wheel, hydraulic lifting equipment and various other things which add to its impressive appearance. But, and this is the important point, I was soon to see that tractor hard at work in our fields – ploughing, harrowing, sowing, drilling and so on; in fact, doing all the jobs around the farm for which a tractor is specifically designed and equipped. From then on I could describe a tractor, not merely by the various bits and pieces which had gone into its construction, nor merely by its appearance; I could now understand a tractor in terms of abilities and practical achievements.

This illustrates one way in which the Bible teaches us what grace is. It lets us understand it in terms of demonstration and performance. A powerful instance of this is to be found in Acts 11. In this chapter we are told about the beginnings of the first church among the Gentiles at Antioch. Believers who had been forced to flee Jerusalem because of persecution reached there and began to preach. They won many Gentile converts. When the home church in Jerusalem heard about this they chose a wise, godly man called Barnabas and sent him to Antioch to assess and report on the situation. The basic question was whether those non-Jewish people at Antioch were really being converted. Barnabas was sent to find out if God was doing a genuine work of grace among the Gentiles. To follow Barnabas is thrilling. We read that 'when he arrived and saw the evidence of the grace of God, he was glad and encouraged them all to remain true to the Lord with all their hearts' (Acts 11:23).

Now what Barnabas actually saw, as a literal rendering of the words shows, was the 'grace of God'; that is what it says. However, the NIV translation highlights the fact that it was *not* grace in isolation. As such, grace cannot be seen. Power, love and freedom are entities which must be 'embodied' in order to be seen. What Barnabas saw was people *in whom* grace had been at work. He looked at them and he saw what grace had accomplished and achieved. It had produced results and effects which he recognised as being characteristic evidence of saving grace. As Barnabas talked with those new converts and as he had fellowship with them, he saw evidence, conspicuous signs, which amounted to nothing less than proof for Barnabas that grace had been at work. Grace was, quite literally, observable; it was made visible in the lives which it gripped and changed. Here is an instance of grace known in its effects.

The important lesson to learn is that a genuine work of grace leaves its mark. It has a stamp, a hallmark all of its own, that it imprints deeply into every life it renews in Christ. Its own unique characteristics mark its presence and trace out its power. In essence, we are being taught here that the saving grace of God, by its very nature, signals its own presence wherever it comes; it advertises itself by its own power; it demonstrates its reality and its effectiveness by what it does. It is to be known and understood, not only from its theological definitions or its doctrinal formulations, important as those are, but from its practical achievements. Then it becomes something which can be seen by all who, like Barnabas, have eyes with which to see it.

One of the earliest and most famous of many postwar Hydro-Electric schemes in Scotland was the one known as Loch Sloy. Its power station is a well-known landmark on the scenic, twisting tourist route that wends its way along the 'Bonnie Banks of Loch Lomond'. Out from behind this power station there emerge two banks of huge pipes which stretch themselves up the steeply rising hill until, disappearing over the first crest, they are lost to view. I have never actually climbed that hill to see for myself where those pipes go, but I don't need to do that to know that they climb their way right up into the mountains until, at last, they tap the waters of Loch Sloy. How do I know that? Well, it is a fact that advertises itself very simply, by a superbly conceived method. The outstanding feature in the frontage of the power station is the series of high, tall windows, which give the impression that it is a glass-fronted building. Those high windows are always brilliantly illuminated by a powerful wattage and through them may be seen the evidence that an ample volume of water is thundering down those pipes to turn the enormous dynamos and thus generate electricity. In this way the project is advertised for what it is by a demonstration of its own power! In the same way, the power of grace, the source of which is so largely hidden from us, signals its presence wherever it comes to do its work.

The first time I saw the Loch Sloy power station we were being driven down Loch Lomondside by one of my brothers. As we passed he said, 'They light the streets of Glasgow with water from a loch up the hill there.' That was a light-hearted but true way of stating the matter. Had he gone into a detailed technical explanation of the process of harnessing water power I should have forgotten it long ago but his graphic description of the facts have remained in my memory. In the same way, Acts 11 contains a simple straightforward statement of grace at work. It does not discuss the larger question of *how* grace had worked its achievements but instead, speaks of it in a way that leaves a profound impression that grace is able to achieve great things when it works in people like ourselves. Just as the power station with its blazing light advertised and accredited the Loch Sloy scheme for what it really is, so the power of grace is advertised and accredited for what it is.

There are many similar passages in the Bible which illustrate that grace can be known by what it does. In addition, there are

thrusts and trends of a general kind right through the Bible where
we may see one or other of these elements of love or power or
freeness stand out with particular clarity. Let us look at some
instances where those elements of grace can be traced and where
we may discern each in its own way, achieving the work of grace
in human experience.

Grace working as power

In this context we will consider one man in particular. Out of the
very detailed knowledge we have of him we are able to gain a
very vivid impression of the power of grace.

He is a sensitive, determined and very religious Jew, well-
bred, well-connected, well-educated. Being one of the great
academics of his day he was heading for the top in Jewish religious
and national life. As a rising theological star, who was outstripping
his companions in terms of scholarship, erudition and prestige,
he had a total and fanatical hatred of all things Christian. It is in
connection with this that his name is mentioned for the first time
in the New Testament. He is introduced to us as a man who gave
wholehearted approval to the slaughter of the very first martyr of
the early church – the stoning of Stephen. There is a simple but
convincing description of the entire scene in Acts chapter 7. At
the conclusion of the story we read, 'and Saul was there, giving
approval to his death' (Acts 8:1). These words imply that Saul
was there in an official capacity, ensuring that the deed was
properly done.

The next time we read of him, he is still of the same mind:
'Saul was still breathing out murderous threats against the Lord's
disciples. He went to the high priest and asked for letters to the
synagogues in Damascus, so that if he found any there who belonged to the Way, he might take them as prisoners to Jerusalem'
(Acts 9:1,2).

To put the matter bluntly, Saul of Tarsus does not seem to be
a very likely candidate for conversion to Christ, does he? If we
were to make up a list of people likely to respond to the message
of the gospel, he and those of a similar outlook would be right at
the bottom. We would think it very unlikely that they would be
suitable candidates for evangelism. They would probably not be
very high in our prayer list of those whom we ask God to bring

salvation and forgiveness in Christ Jesus. Most of us would say of Saul, 'He's hopeless. He's a vicious, murderous man and a blasphemer as well – he's beyond redemption. Let's concentrate our evangelistic effort on a more likely prospect than Saul.' Although all this could be said with some conviction, was Saul a hopeless renegade?

As far as obedience to and faith in Jesus was concerned he was a renegade, but he was not beyond the reach or the power of the grace of God. Where we, on our own, might have failed miserably in persuading this man to become a Christian, the grace of God, in all its power, humbled him in the dust in less time than it takes to tell the story.

The wonderful story of the conversion of Saul is told in Acts 9. Although there is an unusual and a startling vision of the Risen Christ at the very heart of his experience, in later years he describes the event in terms of God's grace: 'I am the least of the apostles and do not even deserve to be called an apostle, because I persecuted the church of God. But by the grace of God I am what I am, and his grace to me was not without effect' (1 Cor. 15:9,10). No, indeed – it had the most powerful effect on this unlikely prospect. It revolutionised his mind and his heart and his life in such a way that the persecutor of the Christians became the greatest promoter of the Christian gospel that the world has seen. Saul became Paul the apostle who has been loved by every Christian in every generation since.

The fact that Paul's conversion did have such an unusual vision at its heart has, sometimes, made some Christians and some preachers identify this dramatic aspect of his experience with the power of grace. We must not confuse things which differ. Paul was right to single out and to trace his conversion back not merely to a vision but to the grace of God. Let us look at another illustration of the power of grace at work.

In Acts 16 we read of another conversion – this time the conversion of a woman. She was a Gentile but became a follower of the Jewish religion and was described as a worshipper of God (verse 14). This linked her with a group of praying women and when Paul reached Philippi, where she lived, he went to this group and preached to them. While Paul was preaching, the woman, Lydia, was converted. Her conversion is described in moving, helpful and informative language. The words should encourage Christians who have not had dramatic experiences at their conversion and should be helpful to those who think of, or look for conversion in terms of a vivid, dramatic event. This is how Lydia's conversion is described: 'The Lord opened her heart to receive Paul's message.' Here, in a very quiet and undemonstrative way, the same power of grace that had transformed Paul was at work in the heart of this woman and she believed in and responded to the gospel. Although their conversion experiences were very different, both were converted by the same power and Lydia could have echoed Paul's words: 'By the grace of God I am what I am, and his grace to me was not without effect' (1 Cor. 15:10).

In terms of the effectiveness of the power of grace, every true Christian is a true demonstration of what grace can do. In every age there have been those whose conversion, like Paul's own, graphically illustrates one of the great Pauline statements of gospel power: 'Where sin abounded, grace did much more abound' (Rom. 5: 20).

Grace working as love

The Bible first introduces us to the nature of grace in the account of man's sin and his Fall. This is done, not incidentally, but in a positive and deliberate manner. The link between sin and grace is thus firmly established in our minds and a good foundation is laid for all we will be taught in subsequent revelation.

Because of its nature, characteristics and qualities, grace could only be revealed and only become known, over against the presence, the work and the effects of sin. Grace is unmerited favour – it is love in the face of demerit and disqualification. It took the fact of man's sin to bring grace out into the light. Pre-fallen man had enjoyed the goodness of God. When that same goodness comes out to post-fallen man it is no longer merely goodness. It is grace. When sinners are being dealt with in a way they do not deserve – with goodness, kindness and love – that is grace at work.

It is the practice, apparently, of those who trade in precious jewels that, when they have particularly fine specimens for sale, they are very careful to exhibit them to possible purchasers against a special background. In the case of pearls, black or very dark, fine velvet is chosen. Set against this sombre-hued backdrop, the

lustre and sheen of the pearl is seen to the very best advantage
and its beauty is enhanced.

This is exactly the way in which God has chosen to demonstrate and exhibit the lustre and the love of his grace to us. It
shines out against the dark, sombre background of sin and the
heart-rebellion that sin involves. The coming of sin into the experience of man brought the existence of grace into the light. It displayed openly a characteristic of the divine nature which had always been there but which, until then, had been hidden from man.

In Genesis 3 we have an account of the facts which disclose
the beginnings of sin and grace in the history of mankind. Here
we have the initial revelations of grace as the undeserved, unmerited love of God. In this chapter we read these words addressed to
the serpent, the Evil One, after he had tempted and led the woman
and the man into sin: 'I will put enmity between you and the
woman, and between your offspring and hers; he will crush your
head, and you will strike his heel' (Gen. 3:15).

These words are familiar to every reader of the Bible and are
the climax of the account of the Fall. The ancient Latin theologians called them the *Proto-evangelicum* (the first good news)
and they are recognised by scholars as the very first prophecy and
promise of a coming Saviour. The emphasis is all upon what God
will do. What he says he will do is quite clearly based upon what
he has already decided to do. He outlines a complete strategy
which speaks of a preconceived and carefully prepared plan of
action. The outstanding fact in this whole interview between God
and the serpent and sinners is that once God appears it is his authority, his sovereignty, his royal, majestic will that is stamped
on the entire scene.

As early as this, the biblical doctrine of God confronts us with
a God with whom we must not trifle – a God who knows what he
is doing and is doing it in a sure and decisive manner. Also, the
biblical doctrine of salvation is already shaping in the direction
of its ultimate distinctiveness. There can be no doubt about the
thrust of it. It is salvation by grace, for if God had not taken the
initiative in Eden, there would have been no salvation at all.

Yet another feature to notice is that God plants enmity between the serpent and the woman. What does this mean? The
woman's values, her sense of truth, her perspective on reality,

had all been given a serious and terrible twist and here God is taking action that will make her deeply and personally aware that the serpent is her enemy and that God is her friend. There was to be a fresh adjustment of her understanding and of her perspective on life and reality; there was to be a reversal of her mental belief and her emotional attitude, and she was to learn that the serpent had never been a friend at all. He had been seeking the destruction of her soul all along. This complete turnaround in her experience is rooted in the initiative and action of God. It all flows from his grace – grace which is determined to save the object of its love and affection. What grace proposes to do when it talks of putting 'enmity' against the serpent into the heart of the woman, is to create a change of heart – a gracious change of heart, for only grace can make sin appear as an enemy to the sinner. It also implies a change of nature very similar to the New Testament doctrine of the new birth. In other words, the love involved here is going to do something which only God can do. This is love allied to favour. This is grace.

It is not surprising to find similar indications of grace in earlier verses in the same chapter of Genesis. It is an interesting and, I think, very instructive fact that the first words of God to fallen man come as a question – 'Where are you?' (Gen. 3:8). It indicates that man is hiding, that he feels his guilt, that wrongdoing has made him afraid of God. His hiding is a sign that he knows he now deserves and expects to be punished. The question is surely designed to do more than bring man out into the open; it is calculated to bring home to his heart just how far away from God his sin has really driven him and to make him feel the separation between himself and God. It will bring conviction of what sin is and what sin does. This conviction is the kind that stamps itself out as the hallmark of the Holy Spirit: 'he will convict the world of guilt in regard to sin and righteousness and judgement' (John 16:8). That is one of the first acts of grace in the Spirit's saving work in man.

Our interest in the form of the first words to Adam is heightened when we notice that God's first words to Eve also come in the form of a question: 'What is this you have done?' (Gen. 3:13). This seems to be a part of a deliberate pattern which it would be helpful to study more closely.

If a person who is anxious and guilt-ridden seeks the help of a pastor or Christian counsellor there will not only be explanation and advice given but searching questions will be asked which may lead to painful self-examination. What is the function of such questioning? What was the purpose of the question Eve was asked? Why did God ask Adam and Eve these questions?

The answer is that God was probing their minds and searching their hearts. He was showing them themselves, stirring their consciences, touching their emotions. The process exemplifies for us the lines along which God still deals with sinners. It may well be that what we see here, even at this early point in the history of sin and grace, is God doing that work which brings men and women into his blessing – the blessing which, in its full-orbed New Testament form, says: 'If we confess our sins, he is faithful and just to forgive us our sins and purify us from all unrighteousness' (1 John 1: 9).

The forgiveness of sins, however, requires sacrifice and atonement. We must not overlook the fact that the grace which was seen at work in the Garden of Eden is the same grace which roots and grounds itself in the great reality of Christ's coming. The grace emerging into view in God's questions to the man and the woman is grace which has already formed the purposes and informed promises revealed in the Messianic references in Genesis 3:15. Already grace, in its amazing love, has decided that from the line and seed of the woman there will arise a Man who will destroy the serpent. This initial unveiling of grace sets a clear, definite and distinctive pattern for us. It is a pattern that is to run its way so powerfully through all subsequent revelation that it provides us with one of the great, sublime, unifying themes of Scripture, a theme which weaves the sixty-six books of the Bible into a unique and specific entity. There we have a library of books which all carry one basic message to us.

This theme which has emerged is simply the theme that God always takes the initiative in salvation. It runs on through biblical revelation until it finds its most luminous and cogent expression in Jesus and his mission. Christ's own expression of it is simple and superb: 'The Son of Man is come to seek and to save that which was lost' (Luke 19:10). It should not surprise us that perhaps those very words could have been written over God's visit to the very first sinners in Eden – and, in one sense they were.

As we sum up this brief study of grace at work in Eden the essential factor is that God has intruded himself into the picture and has stamped his authority all over it. This stamp of authority is not merely the authority of divine judgement – it is also the authority of divine grace. The hard facts about sin are a vital dimension of the entire scene but so too are the first disclosures of grace. Man is brought out of his hiding-place to an encounter, not merely with the justice he anticipated, but with a love he had not expected; a love he had no right to expect and which he could not have imagined; the love of God to an undeserving sinner.

The principle which we have isolated from the whole narrative should be quite clear by now. It is present all through the Scriptures and it finds its most memorable utterance in the words of Paul in his letter to the Romans, 'Where sin abounded, grace did much more abound' (Rom. 5:20).

Before leaving the subject of the love which is at work in grace, I want to illustrate it further, and to do so from the teaching of Jesus in the parable of the Prodigal Son. In this parable, the love which is grace is shown to be like a father's love. From one point of view this story could be known as the Parable of the Patient Father. There is no doubt that the father it pictures for us was patient as only a father who greatly loved his boy could be. The high point of the parable, its great climactic moment, is reached when we read, 'But while he was still a long way off, his father saw him – he ran to his son, threw his arms around him and kissed him' (Luke 15:20). We must keep it firmly in mind that this is not just a superb piece of dramatic storytelling on the part of Jesus. Here we have his theology, as well as his portrait of the Father's patient love and warm welcome to a returning, penitent sinner. It is our Saviour's description of the love that flows at the heart of saving grace.

Some time ago, the tremendous depth and power of a father's love was given vivid, tragic illustration on our TV screens. A jetliner had come down in the sea off Ireland and all on board were lost. Some of the relatives, who had flown into Britain to claim the bodies of their loved ones, were being interviewed. One man did his best to explain how he felt. 'I have lost my wife, I have lost my daughter, and I have lost my only son.' Breaking down completely, with great tears brimming in his eyes, he looked away into the distance and whispered, 'I loved my little son; I loved him very much.' In the face of that father we had, at that moment, a very moving testimony to the power of a father's love.

In the parable Jesus taught that this is the kind of love, multiplied by infinity and eternity, which is poured out in the grace of God. 'For God so loved the world that he gave his only begotten Son, that whosoever believeth on him should not perish but have everlasting life' (John 3:16).

Now we will look at the third strand which we traced in grace.

Grace working as a free gift

Of equal importance with the ideas of grace as power and grace as love is this thought, that grace comes to us as a free gift – or as some theologians used to say, a 'donation'. Its freeness lies in the fact that it comes to us although it is in no way merited.

This is forcefully brought home to us in the Bible's teaching and continual emphasis on the fact that sinners do not and cannot, in any way or by any means, earn grace or the salvation that grace holds out to them. Paul is a striking illustration of this truth. His own experience must have reinforced his theological insight into the free nature of grace. The grace which took hold of him (Phil. 3:12) did so while he was intent on stamping out Christianity altogether and while he was in a murderous mood towards Jesus' followers. He must have been very deeply conscious that if grace was not free and totally undeserved, then his chances of ever sharing in it were abysmally small. In some measure at least, every true Christian believer will feel the same.

Let us look at one text which sets out the freeness of grace in the strangest possible terms: 'Now when a man works, his wages are not credited to him as a gift, but as an obligation' (Rom. 4:4). The thought here is very simple but it is vitally important to grasp it, lay hold of it and understand what the apostle is saying. If a man works for wages, if he earns them, then he has a right to them. His employer is obligated to pay him and there is no semblance or thought of gift in it at all. The thought would have been clearly understood by everyone who read these words in Paul's day and it can be just as clearly understood today. However, on the basis of that statement he goes on to make an important ob-

servation about the way in which salvation comes to a sinner:
'However, to the man who does not work but trusts God who
justifies the wicked, his faith is credited to him as righteousness
.... Therefore the promise comes by faith, so that it may be by
grace' (Rom. 4:5, 16).

If salvation were to come to us because of our work, then it
would come to us as an obligation – as if God was obliged to save
us. It would no longer be salvation on the basis of grace alone. It
would no longer be free. It would no longer be a gift. It is really
insulting to speak in such a case as if it had anything to do with
grace.

Many Scripture texts give assent to the truth that salvation
comes by way of grant, or free gift. For example, Paul wrote to
Christian believers at Ephesus and said: 'It is by grace you have
been saved through faith ... not by works, so that no one can boast'
(Eph. 2:8,9). To his friend and helper, Timothy, he wrote: 'God,
who has saved us and called us to a holy life ... not because of
anything we have done but because of his own purpose and grace'
(2 Tim. 1:9).

The uppermost thought in these texts, and there are many more
like them, is that of gift. The notion of works as a basis of salvation, or as meriting the grace of God, is so totally at variance with
this whole concept that the two, grace and works, are completely
contrary to each other in this context. They belong to two different camps. As far as our acceptance with God, our justification,
our salvation are concerned, grace and works cancel each other
out completely. The Bible places a strong emphasis on this: 'If by
grace, then it is no longer by works; if it were, grace would no
longer be grace' (Rom. 11:6).

Paul's exaltation of grace to this supreme place in our salvation
is stated and elaborated by him with unremitting logic. It cannot,
must not be misunderstood. Whatever is of *works* is not of grace
at all. If salvation is of works, it cannot be by grace. Equally,
whatever is of grace is not of works in the slightest degree. Grace
and works are as mutually exclusive as light and darkness, as
different as day to night.

The amazing stories of what grace has done, of how grace has
worked and of the lives that grace has changed provide us with a
lifetime study, and even then we would not have explored or un-

derstood all that grace involves. However, we see enough, we are told enough, we are taught clearly enough and we learn enough about grace to humble us before its love, assure us before its power and make us debtors for evermore to its free, unmerited bestowal.

One of the most satisfying definitions of grace that I have heard is one that I heard from a preacher friend who is now with the Lord. Preaching on the words, 'My grace is sufficient for you', he said: 'What is God actually saying to his servant in these words? Surely he is just saying, "Paul, I the living, eternal, unchanging God, I am enough for you," because grace cannot be separated from God himself; grace is just God acting graciously. When grace comes, God comes. Where grace is, there is God in all the plenitude of his power. And to the Christian, no matter the need or the circumstances, to have God is enough, because to have God is everything.'

These words eloquently define for us the nature of grace. They tell us that the love and the power and the gift are all found, ultimately, to be inseparable from God acting graciously in order to save us.

When we look at grace then we are looking at what God has revealed and exposed to us of his own heart. In the face of such revelation, we must feel as the Psalmist did long ago: 'Such knowledge is too wonderful for me; it is high, I cannot attain unto it' (Ps. 139:6). But even where we are conscious that we do not understand we may still bless God for what he has taught us and shown us in his Word about grace. We can bless him because, in unveiling something of his grace to us, he has, ultimately, been unveiling himself. Above all, we can bless him because he is 'the God of all grace'.

3

The Sovereignty of Grace

If grace really is 'God acting graciously' then it will not surprise us that it reflects the freedom, distinctiveness and authority with which God carries out his works.

This, in essence, is what is meant when our preachers and theologians talk about grace being 'sovereign'. In no way should the use of this word, in the context of God's grace, cause us to fear. It should not alarm us or make us suspicious of those who love to use it. There is no reason to back off mentally or to withdraw from anything the word implies about God and his dealings with us. To use this term in connection with grace is to say that the grace which works in salvation is a regal, majestic, kingly grace; that it is, in short, divine grace; and, as such, is always invested with the highest authority and always exercised in omnipotent power.

The truth involved here should be very precious to every Christian believer. It spells out the message that the grace which has worked in salvation is grace which belongs to the King of kings, the One who is God from everlasting to everlasting. Our salvation flows out from the God who is the font of all life and being; Creator and Redeemer, both, he is also the one, only living God.

We must beware of regarding grace as a mere power or influence; something which can be abstracted or isolated from God himself, and which acts or operates in separation from God. This would be to cut directly across the biblical teaching and would do very grave injustice to the whole doctrine of grace which the Bible unfolds. To be true to that doctrine, our thought and conception of grace must never exclude God or try to shut out his action and his love.

When grace comes into operation for the salvation of a sinner it has a lot to contend with, much to accomplish, much to overcome. It has to contend with all that goes into making us sinners; it has to contend with, not our own favourable view of ourselves

but, the very unfavourable view that the Bible gives of every sinner, the true view. Our situation before God is seldom, if ever, as
favourable as we reckon it to be – indeed if we are unconverted it
is always dangerously unsafe. Grace has to come and deal with us
where we really are, and as we really are.

It is at this very point that one of the great barriers to grace and
its work raises its opposition. Quite simply, this is the desire of
the natural heart to improve its standing before God and to do
something – anything – which will attract or merit his favour.
Biblical teaching is firmly opposed to any such notion. The grace
which comes to save never comes because we have attained some
ideal of behaviour – perhaps in prayer or in spiritual obedience to
the divine commands; perhaps in gospel hearing or by attaining
some peak of moral or spiritual achievement. The very opposite
is the case. Whenever grace comes, it always comes, not on the
basis of our own efforts or our own righteousness, but on the
unmerited favour of God.

This point cannot be emphasised too strongly – that when grace
sets out to save a sinner it has a great deal to contend with, a great
deal to overcome. From a strictly human point of view it has to
accomplish an impossible task! One thing I have learned in almost thirty years of preaching the gospel – and every gospel
preacher learns the same lesson – is how utterly useless all my
efforts in preaching, teaching and counselling can be. Experience
has confirmed what the Bible says. The conversion of sinners to
Christ in true, heart-humbling repentance and a Christ-exalting,
living faith is the work, not of man, but of the Holy Spirit.

Sin dominates the unconverted

In describing the relationship between unconverted, unregenerate people and God, the Bible absolutely refuses to use any flat-
tery or to compromise the truth by soft-pedalling of any kind.
Paul describes his own pre-conversion state, and that of fellow
Christians, in strong, blunt language. He speaks of a time 'when
we were God's enemies' (Rom. 5:10), and a state in which 'sin
reigned unto death' (Rom. 5:21).

It shocks and startles us to think of sin in such terms: sin ruling,
reigning, becoming master, exercising a lordship, imposing its
wishes as it pleases. Yet those are the very terms which Paul uses.

It is in his words of counsel and advice to a young friend and preacher that we find one of Paul's most vivid statements of this truth. Speaking out of a deep, lasting experience of grace he says: 'This is a faithful saying, and worthy of all acceptation, that Christ Jesus came into the world to save sinners' (1 Tim. 1:15). Even with that tremendous affirmation of the purpose and motive of Christ's work in the world, Paul's statement of the issue is not yet complete. He adds a phrase to that statement which is very significant: 'of whom I am chief.' That is Paul's punchline – do we today realise what he was saying? This man, who had been very religious, self-satisfied and self-righteous in his pre-conversion days, had learned a lasting lesson from the grace that had saved him and made him a humble follower of Jesus. He had learned that grace can never be earned, merited or deserved. Grace had not let him forget what it felt like to be the worst of men; grace does not exalt men but humbles them and keeps them humble. It is the authority of that unmerited grace, which rescued Paul in the face of his every effort to disparage and despise and destroy it, which kills pride in the heart and makes us feel debtors to grace to the end of our days. There should be no place given to selfish pride in the Christian life. In the words of 1 Corinthians 4:7: 'For who makes you different from anyone else? What do you have that you did not receive?'

When we pause to reflect on the fact that man, although 'dead in sins' (Eph. 2:1), is not passive or indifferent to God but is really at enmity with God, then it is easy to see that this is not merely a doctrinal matter but a realistic and practical description of man in his fallenness and sinfulness. Far from being neutral and quiescent in relation to God and the claims of God's law, the unconverted person is really an enemy of God. People can remain apparently indifferent to God until, perhaps, some claim of his is laid upon them or they are made to feel his authority in the circumstances of their lives. Then enmity and dislike of God rise to the surface.

The authority and sovereignty which sin exerts over people is a biblical doctrine which is verified in everyday life, sometimes in ways that are sad and heartbreaking. We need only look around us, or within us, to gather a host of illustrations of how sin dominates and enslaves. There are times when the sway of sin may actually prosecute its reign right into physical destruction and death. Sadly, the teaching of Scripture on this controlling power of sin over man is given practical manifestation all around us.

The alcoholic, the drug-addict, the gambler – the list would be endless – provide pathetic examples and proofs of the grip of sin on our lives. Any preacher, or minister, or social worker, indeed any person who cares deeply about the needs of the people around him or her sees the illustration of this truth over and over again depicted in the lives of their daily contacts. Sin, in its hold over men and women, is a treacherous and destructive force and all too often can be seen to 'reign in death'.

The Lord Jesus warned of the same peril – the terrible sway and sovereignty of evil over the mind of every person. His language was so strong that today there are many who slide away from his words in their belief and in their teaching, but they are the words of Jesus, the One who knew the hard facts about sin as no other ever has, or ever will. 'You belong to your father, the devil, and you want to carry out your father's desires' (John 8:44). Again, he said: 'No one can serve two masters. Either he will hate the one and love the other, or he will be devoted to the one and despise the other. You cannot serve both God and Money' (Matt. 6:24).

Jesus did not deal with the outward and the superficial. He reached in to the deep places of the soul that were twisted and wrong and hurting. He never gave a shallow diagnosis of what was wrong, but homed in on the basic problem. We too must be alert and refuse to be content with any gospel that offers us an easy, cheap, or shallow solution to the deep-seated problems that sin brings into our lives. We must allow the teaching of Jesus – and all the other relevant biblical data – to inform our minds and dictate our beliefs. That is as essential in the area of the authority and dominion of sin as it is for any other aspect of the gospel's teaching.

In the light of Scripture we have to face the fact that we are either serving God and living obediently under the authority and rule of his grace, or we are serving Satan and are under the dominion and sway of his evil power.

Now, it is over against this entire background of what sin is that the Bible puts forward the grand, comforting truth of the sovereign authority of grace. Is it not a truth to warm the heart and encourage our hope? Is it not a strain of Bible teaching for which we should humbly thank God? I would suggest that it is. I would go further and boldly assert that the Christian who does not search his Bible to learn more of this truth, or the Christian who sets it aside for any reason whatsoever, is deprived by neglecting a truth which leads to a strong, healthy, robust faith.

Think of it this way. Is there a power at work in the world and in the hearts of humans which threatens and achieves the destruction, temporal and eternal, of multitudes of men and women? Is there a tyranny and a slavery attached to sin which has frequently so wrecked and enfeebled them that they are helpless to throw it off or overcome it by their own unaided efforts? Is sin so strongly enthroned in the hearts of sinners that they do not even wish it off the throne? If these things are so, and both the Bible and experience teach us that they are, what a blessing that there is grace. The grace that sets out to save such sinners, is sovereign and authoritative; the grace of a royal, majestic God. This is the grace that real sinners, in this real world, truly need and it is the only kind of grace that the Bible holds out to them.

Where a person is dominated by a power, freely accepted and obediently served, it takes a greater power to supplant and replace it. That is why Thomas Chalmers, the great Scottish preacher and theologian of last century, entitled one of his greatest sermons, 'The Expulsive Power of a New Affection'. Grace comes freely in its love and power and subdues sin until it actually reigns in righteousness. The sovereignty of sin in the human heart demonstrates and demands the sovereign authority of the grace which works salvation in the heart.

In pinpointing and highlighting the marvellous nature and character of grace Paul emphasises its power to achieve its effects and carry through its purposes in the very places where sin has most blatantly reigned – in the heart, in the home, in the community: 'Where sin abounded, grace did much more abound; that as sin hath reigned unto death, even so might grace reign through righteousness unto eternal life by Jesus Christ our Lord' (Rom. 5:20,21).

This is the marvel of the gospel. It comes into the very place, the situation, the circumstance where it is most urgently needed as the only thing in the world equipped and able to do the very work required. It comes as a living reality into this sad, weary, old world that Christians and evangelists are sent to claim for God. The world over which God's people pray, for which they work and over which they sometimes despair, is that very world into which grace comes in love and saving power.

Every preacher of this gospel has stories to tell of the way grace comes, sometimes unexpectedly, to save the most unlikely people. Again and again throughout my own ministry I have seen grace set to work in people of whom, humanly speaking, I had very slender hope as far as salvation was concerned. I have seen such people soundly converted while others for whom I cherished high hopes have never been savingly dealt with at all. This is one of the wonderful aspects of being a minister of the gospel – one just never knows what grace is going to do next. Every Christian who has seen the miracle of God's grace at work in life-changing experiences, knows what it is to go home and kneel in thankfulness to God for the authority of his wonderful, powerful, loving works of grace.

Sovereignty makes grace irresistible

We should never be surprised when grace appears clothed in the majesty which belongs to it, for it is always and ever the grace of God. This means that it has strength and power and freeness and authority which do not belong to sin, even where sin exercises its reign in the most open and blatant fashion. It means also that grace comes armed with the beauty of holiness, equipped with invincible power, acting in truth and in accordance with the most perfect righteousness, but touched also with feelings of compassion, imbued with great love and tenderness. It means that when grace works, its exercise and use is always under the direction of infinite wisdom and mercy as well as under the dictates of infinite power and infinite authority.

One summer, while on holiday in my home area of Ardnamurchan, I spent a morning with my brother. On that particular day, he had a young man in on the farm with a huge mechanical digger to shift and clear some tons of fallen rock. It was a rather awe-inspiring experience to stand and watch the ease with which the mechanical arm of that digger could snatch and lift and swing those enormous blocks of rock. Some of these huge slabs were actually being used to form part of a picturesque garden wall at the back of my brother's house. The way in which that machine could swing the rocks, sometimes at roof-level, and place them exactly where they were wanted – the inch-perfect, delicate precision with which such power could be exercised was very impressive. Of course, the skill did not belong, strictly speaking, to the machine. It came from a quick mind and clever hands; knobs were pushed, levers were nudged, gears were moved – and all with a dexterity and artistry that spoke of years of experience. Behind the massive machine and its awesome feats of power was another form of power and energy – a form which we often take for granted – the power of personality and mental appreciation and moral understanding. So it is with the work of grace in human experience; it is the action and influence of the living and personal God, not the action of an impersonal energy. Just as the real authority in the movement of those huge rocks was being exerted, not by the massive machine, but by its driver, so the authority being exerted in grace is always the authority of the God whose grace it is.

The glory of God
When a sinner comes under the influence and power of grace he is being conducted along a pathway prepared and planned, set out and approved by, the infinite wisdom of God. For this reason, Paul, having spoken of his former persecuting zeal, can speak of his conversion as the fruit of an earlier action of grace: 'It pleased God who separated me from my mother's womb, and called me by his grace, to reveal his Son in me ....' (Gal. 1:15, 16). Where guilty sinners are rescued and retrieved from eternal destruction, their rescue and retrieval not only harmonise with all the perfections of a divine majesty, but also honour and glorify that majesty. Not only the mercy of God but his justice, not only his grace but his holiness are acknowledged and upheld in the salvation of every sinner saved.

This is an aspect of gospel truth and gospel grace that should thrill the soul of every true Christian believer. God has not had to abdicate his throne or lay aside any of the perfections of his nature in order to save sinners. Yes, the Son became man in order to be a Saviour, but in becoming man he did not cease to be 'God of

very God', and infinite wisdom has re-arranged things so that
now sinners are saved by 'being justified freely by his grace
through the redemption that is in Christ Jesus' (Rom. 3:24) and
God can be 'just and the justifier of him which believeth in Jesus'
(Rom. 3:26).

There is no doubt at all that this is one of the great glories of
the grace that lies at the heart of our salvation. In its saving activity it aims not only at the rescue of sinners, but at the glory of
God. It is a marvel and a wonder that God can save sinners and
yet the full truth of the matter is much more marvellous and wonderful than that. Yes, God can save sinners but he saves them in a
way that sheds lustre and praise and glory on his name, and on his
Son, for all eternity. The fact is that no person in whom grace has
done a real saving work would have been content with a salvation
which did not honour God; a salvation which left rational, intelligent creatures to question the moral integrity of God would not
be salvation at all. A salvation which carried any kind of doubt or
left a tinge of suspicion about his righteousness would not only
fail to measure up to the standards of the God of the Bible, it
would fail to measure up even to the standard of the sinner himself.

Grace, when it comes into the human heart, comes with an
authority and ability that honours all the perfections of the divine
character and it comes in a way and by a route that satisfies all the
needs of the human heart. It speaks peace to the troubled conscience and it satisfies the sense of justice. It replaces enmity to
God with love and it gives new desires for righteousness. It instils
hatred for sin. It does all that is required to bring its subjects safely
home to the Father's house.

Perseverance and preservation

Another feature that belongs to the free sovereign authority of
grace is its ability to carry its objectives through to a complete
conclusion. Grace is as free to complete the work of salvation as
it was to start it. What it so freely begins, it carries on and com-
pletes with an equally perfect freedom. Conversion is only the
starting point in the way of salvation. There is a life to live which
will require grace in all its authority and power – a life that needs
grace just as surely as it was needed in conversion.

This is one of the truths about salvation which Paul was always ready to use for the encouragement of his fellow believers. It was to encourage Christians facing trials at Philippi that he said he was 'confident of this, that he who began a good work in you will carry it on to completion until the day of Christ Jesus' (Phil. 1:6). To the church at Corinth, a church in which party strife, immorality and abuse of the Lord's Supper were causing great trouble, the apostle was also to write words of reassurance. In this connection it is interesting to notice how graciously Paul writes, and how wisely. He has to say things that are heavy with correction and which will be difficult for them to take. But before he corrects, he encourages. He assures these believers that God 'shall keep you strong to the end, so that you will be blameless on the day of our Lord Jesus Christ' (1 Cor. 1:8). Paul is sure of this, not because of anything in the Corinthian believers, but because of something in God. He continues: 'God, who has called you into fellowship with his Son Jesus Christ our Lord, is faithful' (1 Cor. 1:9). On the Day of Judgement their blamelessness depends, not first of all on their own faithfulness to God but upon his faithfulness to them. Just as it is his grace that initiates the entire scheme of salvation and inaugurates the work, so it is grace which will bring it all to a triumphant conclusion.

When we look at grace from a biblical perspective we are greatly reassured in our hearts. We live in times when every Christian needs all the reassurance that is available in the Word of God. There are great, strong, abiding truths which we should search out and make part of our own experience and allow them to undergird our faith and inform our hope. When God has come to us in salvation, he will never let us go. Grace, acting with divine authority, does not rescue the sinner from destruction, and give him a new heart and new powerful impulses only to leave him to continue on his own as best he can. One lesson that thirty years of following Jesus has taught me is this: the sinner who trusts Jesus is never abandoned by him, is never left completely to his own resources. Once grace takes hold of us, it does not let go. This is implicit in many places in the Bible and is quite explicit and unmistakable in such texts as 'God has said, "Never will I leave you, never will I forsake you" ' (Heb. 13:5).

Conversion to Christ initiates a conflict and a warfare in the human heart. The new convert is called on to resist the tempter (Jas. 4:7) to deny and mortify his lusts (Rom. 6:12; Col. 3:5), to live in separation from the evil of the world (Jas. 4:4; 2 Cor. 6:15-18), to be holy in his whole life (1 Pet. 1:15,16), to achieve that obedience which characterises God's children (Acts 5:29), and, in short, to lead a life fortified by power and love. We are taught that the life of every true believer is 'hid (treasured-up, stored, reserved) with Christ in God' (Col. 3:3). Where is the Lord Jesus Christ? He is on the throne of Heaven, the central person of the Divine Trinity. Hidden with him the life of the believer is hidden in the heart of the Godhead. No wonder the believer has to live a very special kind of life.

If the presence and power of grace did not cover and cater for all eventualities and circumstances which could occur between conversion and the close of the earthly life of every believer, and did not have authority and control within these circumstances, then great areas of uncertainty would exist. There would be uncertainty, not only regarding the salvation of every believer but regarding the glory of God in the salvation of every believer. In the redemption spoken of in the Bible it is not only the safety of the Christian which is at stake, but the 'good name' of Jesus Christ as Saviour.

The 'good name', the reputation of a shepherd, or a stockman, depends upon the health and the well-being and the security of his sheep or his cattle. In the same way, the glory that is Christ's, not as the Eternal Son but as the Mediator and Saviour and Redeemer, the glory which attaches to him peculiarly as the 'Lamb of God who takes away the sins of the world' (John 1:29) or as 'the Lamb which is in the midst of the throne' (Rev. 7:17), is involved with the salvation of his people.

Much of the preaching we hear nowadays lays a strong stress and emphasis on what men must do for their salvation. If the drift of our studies in the biblical doctrine of grace is taking us in the right direction then we are learning that the emphasis of preaching should centre strongly on what God must do and on what God has done. Preaching which glosses over this truth of the powerful, sovereign, authoritative nature of the grace of God, is in danger of distorting or even denying the gospel, of ignoring the core element of the gospel of God's grace.

Let us keep before our minds that grace is 'God acting graciously'. That will help us and keep us from denying a freedom and sovereignty which, in the final analysis, is the freedom and sovereignty of God himself – his right as God to act like God.

Let us remember also that when grace comes into a sinner's life then Christ comes in as well. In the Gaelic language, which once predominated in the Highlands of Scotland, there is a little phrase which is used of one who was newly converted to Christ. Translated literally it said, 'he got grace'. Now, in saying that, the godly people of the Highlands were not implying that some strange, unattached, impersonal power had come into that person's life. They meant, of course, that Christ had come to indwell that person, and that it was all part of a mighty work of regeneration and renewal which could be expressed briefly in that phrase. We must never, in our thinking or speaking or teaching, divorce grace from Christ, or from God who in Christ is acting graciously in our salvation. One of the things that has divided Christians on this whole question of the authority and sovereignty of grace is the fact that it has all too often been thought of, or discussed, as though it were some thing, or quality, or power which could operate in complete abstraction from God.

We can sum all this up in a very simple way. Where Christ is, grace is. When Christ comes, grace comes. The two cannot and must not be separated. There is no such thing as saving grace where Christ is absent. What real, humble, trusting, instructed Christian believer would wish to deny that in Jesus the Saviour there is invested 'all authority in heaven and in earth' or that this Jesus, as well as being Saviour, is sovereign Lord of all?

SERMONS

1

Psalm 84:11

The LORD will give grace and glory.

Two factors are stamped very strongly throughout this psalm –
the factors of grace and glory. One only has to read this psalm
once to realise that it is the upsurging and outflowing of a great
work of grace in the heart of the psalmist. This is a man who
loves God.

We know from the Scriptures that the natural heart is at enmity against God. We know that this man loves God's house and
that he loves God's house because he loves the God of the house.
It is always a good test of the reality of grace to discover the
attitude of an individual to the house and to the worship of the
Lord God almighty. Throughout the psalm the evidence is there
that the psalmist knows from personal experience what he is talking about when he says, 'The Lord will give grace.'

By grace this man is being fitted for eternal glory. He knows
that a day in the house of Jehovah is better than a thousand other
days. He so loves the house of God that he wants to be in God's
presence all the time. He would rather be a doorkeeper, do the
humblest task in God's house, than dwell with the wicked. It seems
that when he is talking like that, his mind is being taken towards
the glory that God promises to his people.

As he thinks of the God who gives grace and glory he describes the character and nature of God in these words, 'The LORD
God is a sun and shield.'

He speaks of God as a sun. All the brightness and the glory of
the world that the psalmist knew traced back to the source of the
sun in the heavens and he said, 'That is what my God is like.' He
knew that the sun could be fiercely consuming and burning and
he is saying here that the wonderful thing about his God is that
although he is so bright and so glorious and powerful he has veiled

Preached 1 July, 1979

himself in human nature and has drawn near. God is not only a sun, he is a shield. He is the God who is the defender of his people.

I would like to take the word 'give' from the text and expound it further.

The Giver

The Lord Jehovah is the name of the covenant God. He is the God who takes people into covenant with himself in order to bless them. This is the giver that the psalmist has in mind. Who but Jehovah could give either grace or glory? You won't get them anywhere else. Do you want grace? Do you need grace? Do you long for grace? There is only one in all the wide universe who can give grace and who can give glory. That one is our Lord God Jehovah. Who else could give grace? He is the only one who is totally gracious. Who else could give glory? There is none glorious but the Lord God. To him belongs the totality of glory. He is the only one who is totally gracious and totally glorious in himself. It is absolutely fitting that he be the one who gives these gifts to his people.

Grace and glory sum up what God is in himself, his nature and his character. Take grace, for example. God has published his name in the Scriptures, published his name to his people. What is his name? Love – God is love. That is spoken of the Father who is the very font of Deity and who is the representative of the Godhead in the economy of redemption. God is love and he has proved his love to us: 'Herein is love, not that we loved God, but that he loved us, and sent his Son to be the propitiation for our sins' (1 John 4:10).

What grace there is in that sending of his Son! But God is not only love, although that love is a very special love, a gracious love. God's very nature is to give but he must give in a way that is consonant with all his other attributes. We remember some of these: he is not only love, mercy, wisdom, goodness, truth but also holy and just and righteous. Nehemiah, in his lovely prayer, addresses him as 'the great and terrible God' (Neh. 1:5).

God himself holds in existence and in reality all grace and all glory. In a sense, what the psalmist is saying is that God will give himself. That is what God has done. He gave his own Son for your redemption and for mine: 'He that spared not his own Son, but who delivered him up for us all, how shall he not with him also freely give us all things?' (Rom. 8:32).

Paul, in these words, is talking of the conscious, daily need of the believer. This God who spared not his own Son, who delivered him up for us all, also gives us all things. The proof that God is willing to give us all things is found in that he has given us Christ, the crowning gift. Paul's words echo those of the psalmist: 'The LORD will give grace and glory: no good thing will he withhold from them that walk uprightly.'

God gives himself. He gives grace and glory. God not only has grace and glory in fullness but he gifts them to us. If he were to keep all his grace and glory to himself he would be none the richer because he is perfect and you cannot add to perfection. He is perfect in grace. He is perfect in glory. His grace, like himself, is infinite. His glory, like himself, is infinite. You cannot add to or detract from either. Infinity is like a full well that is overflowing. When you take away all the outflow, the well is still flowing as fully and as freely as ever. God cannot enrich himself by keeping his grace and glory to himself. He cannot impoverish himself by giving them away. The giving to us of these gifts through his Son, the Lord Jesus Christ, does add a different kind of glory. It adds not an essential glory, but a material glory. The mediatorial glory of Christ is a special glory. It is the glory that is the special light of heaven: 'and the Lamb is the light thereof' (Rev. 21:23).

God does not sell grace or glory. There are multitudes of people who are trying to work themselves into the favour of God, into his grace, into his eternal kingdom. The moment you expect to receive grace from God on the basis of work or good deeds it is no longer grace.

Grace is not put up for auction to the highest bidder in moral terms. 'Who is the best-living Christian today?' This is the thought of many and the thought of many preachers – 'Who is the highest bidder in the realm of moral obedience to God? God will do great things for you. He will add grace.' If grace is given on those terms then it is no longer grace. If you think that by better obedience you can win God's favour, then you need his grace.

God freely gifts us his grace and glory. If we try to pay for a gift we hurt the giver in our lack of recognition of their love and goodwill towards us. God will give us his gifts freely or not at all.

Eternal life is one of the pictures that sums up what God is. He is eternal life. It sums up what God gives to his people – eternal life. Whoever believes and trusts has eternal life. The gift of grace comes through believing in the Lord Jesus Christ, a believing that opens up a channel for God's grace to pour in freely. Eternal life is not just something for the future, something that the Christian is going to get in the faraway and the beyond. Eternal life is ours here and now if we accept God's gift. It is not just a quantity of life. All will live in eternal life in the sense of ongoing existence. The souls of unbelievers live on. It is a quality of life, a newness of life and it is for the present as well as for the future.

It is the special glory of God that he gives grace and it is the special grace of God that he gives glory. The two are linked inseparably. Grace and glory cannot be divided or divorced from each other. God never gave glory to anyone without first giving grace. He never gave grace but he followed it up by giving glory. He cannot, he will not, give the one without the other. As one of the Puritans expressed it, 'Grace is glory in the bud and glory is grace in full flower.' There is continuity and identity between the two. Grace develops into glory.

Grace experienced

Grace is God coming into human experience. You cannot separate grace from Christ and you cannot separate Christ from the Father. If you have grace you have it because God in the Trinity of his persons has come into your life. He has come in through the Son: 'Christ shall dwell in your hearts by faith' (Eph. 3:17). That is what makes a Christian. It is not merely what a person believes intellectually. It is not what is done morally. What makes a Christian is Christ coming to dwell in his or her heart.

The Holy Spirit is involved as well. It is the Spirit who regenerates the sinner. He is grace in its aspect of power. We speak of irresistible grace, of a working of God in our lives that cannot be effectually stamped out.

Who does God come to? To whom does he give grace? He gives grace to those who feel the need of grace and come and ask for it. The paradox is that by the time you come to ask God for grace, it is yours already. It is grace, and only grace that will ask God for his grace. A sinful unrenewed heart, a conscience that has never been brought to some sense of conviction of sin, will never ask for grace. By the time you are crying out for grace, grace has already been at work in your life.

When God gives grace, he gives himself. He gives the sinner a Saviour and that Saviour brings his peace with him – peace of mind and of heart between the soul and God.

Grace is just the Lord Jesus Christ coming alongside us and taking our hand and saying, 'Come on, walk with me.' Grace is the Lord Jesus showing us that he loves us and that he wants to be with us. Glory is our being with the Lord Jesus in his heaven – and he wants us to be with him there.

The Lord gives grace and he gives glory. What is it to give glory? What will it be from our point of view? Spurgeon, when speaking on this subject, said that he would love to be able to tell his hearers what glory is and what heaven is like; 'But I cannot,' he said, 'because I have never been there. If I reached there and came back five minutes later to talk about it I couldn't because I would have seen things that it is not lawful for any man to utter.'

When I was thinking of these words over the past few days I tried to sum up the idea of glory in three ideas – to capture what it will mean for us.

First of all it will mean *full recognition*. 'Then shall I know even as also I am known' (1 Cor. 13:12). When God gives glory he is still giving himself. He is giving himself in this special way. We know that we have been recognised and blessed and bought by Christ and we will know it then in a very full measure. Christ will then be giving the final stamp and seal of his recognition and of his love and acceptance of his people. Do you remember how he prayed for his people at the end of the prayer recorded for us in John 17? 'Father, I will that they also, whom thou hast given me, be with me where I am; that they may behold my glory, which thou hast given me: for thou lovedst me before the foundation of the world.' He wants his people to look on his mediatorial glory. And he wants that because he wants to share it with us.

The second idea is that of *position*. Christ wants us to be with him where he is. Sometimes I'm sure, you must feel as I do that if we ever get to heaven we will find it an awesome place. We imagine that we'll feel a little bit shy and slightly afraid when we're ushered into glory. There will, however, be one thing which will make us feel perfectly at home – Jesus will be there, the same Jesus that we have known in this life. To be with Jesus – what peace, what blessing, what a sense of love. Throughout the Gospels, wherever we see Jesus dealing personally with people, their shyness and their fear all disappear. To be with Jesus in glory is to enjoy the fullness of what Jesus the God-man is.

The third idea is *fruition*, the coming to full flower and perfection of all that God has been doing in us through this life. 'Beloved, now are we the sons of God, and it doth not yet appear what we shall be: but we know that, when he shall appear, we shall be like him; for we shall see him as he is' (1 John 3:2).

The fruition of glory for God's people is the fruition of God's great redemptive purpose for the world, the undoing of what Satan and all the fallen host of angels have done. In Revelation 22:3-4 we are shown a glimpse of this glory: 'There shall be no more curse: but the throne of God and of the Lamb shall be in it; and his servants shall serve him: And they shall see his face; and his name shall be in their foreheads.'

God will then be sovereignly reigning in *grace* and in *glory* and he will have given you and me all that these two words mean. What a God is our God! He is the Lord who will give grace and glory.

2

Grace Abounding

'But where sin abounded, grace did much more abound'
(Romans 5:20).

Paul introduces these words to us by making a strange statement about sin and the moral law of God. The law entered in the giving of the ten commandments at Sinai. The word 'entered' can be translated as 'came in quietly'. There was sin before the giving of the law in the ten commandments. You would have thought that the law was given to curb sin, but what Paul is saying is that the law was given so that the guilt of sin might be seen to be very real and to be very terrible: 'By the law is the knowledge of sin' (Rom. 3:20).

The moral law came in two sections. The first dealt with our relationship with God and the second with our relationship towards other people. The moment the commandments were spelled out and God forbade certain behaviour the consciousness of sin was deepened and the reality and the offensiveness of sin to God became clearer. For example, how do you plan to spend this afternoon? God has said to remember his day and to keep it holy. He has said it to us and because he has said it our transgression of what is a clearly spelled-out command will be very offensive to God and it will deepen our sin.

Think of the word 'abound'. Something that abounds is very plentiful, almost beyond measure and will be noticeable, remarkable. When we consider how the holy law of God is transgressed in our own day we see how the offence abounds.

The terrible picture of abounding evil that is in the mind of Paul as he writes makes him think of another mighty abounding – the abundance of God's grace. Here Paul brings together two great biblical themes and he sets them over against each other in contrast. The Bible deals with sin and the offensiveness of sin to a holy God and then, blessed be our God's name, it deals with God's undeserved love and mercy towards sinners – his grace. And Paul says that although sin was so evident and although its destructive movement towards death so sure, we have a surer hope in the abounding grace of God. That is the comfort and consolation of every believer here today as they battle with the prevalence of sin around and within them. Surely it is the hope of every unconverted person here this morning that where sin abounds grace does much more abound.

Let me illustrate that truth *historically*. Go back to the very first sin mentioned in the book of Genesis. That sin caused separation, not only between Adam and his God, but between God and all humanity. Adam was our representative, the one with whom God had made a covenant for all his posterity, and so sin abounded down through all the generations. Adam cut himself off from God and his action brought guilt into his experience, and fear and darkness into his mind. It wreaked havoc in his personal relationship with God. That was bad enough, but it also brought all these things into the race that was to descend from him. How sin abounded historically.

Follow down through the story and it was the son of Adam that shed his own brother's blood. How quickly sin revealed its ugly, vicious and death-dealing nature. Sin reigned unto death – the death of one son at the hand of another.

Adam had a freedom of the will that none of his descendants have and Adam's will freely led him into sin against God. God would have been perfectly just in cutting Adam off without mercy. Instead God came down and walked in the garden in the cool of the day. God in his grace was patient and in the evening his voice was heard in the garden. Was it the voice of judgement? No – it was the voice of grace, in the very place where Adam had sinned and brought destruction and death, there came God's grace. 'Adam, where are you?' What a wonderful call that was. It was the call of mercy, not of judgement. As we follow the story we read of God sparing the very first murderer and even marking his forehead so that no man or animal should take his life.

When you follow the course of history it is only by the grace of God that this world has not been destroyed. Man in every age has done his very best to destroy it. Do you wonder at the sophistication and the power of the minds that achieve so many wonderful things in the world today? Do you wonder that, with all the gain and achievement and intellectual power and all the capability in the field of technology, the human mind has also reached the place where it can destroy civilisation, where it can destroy the human race? How sin, working in the mind and in the gifts that it has darkened, has abounded! But in what greater measure the grace of God has abounded. He has kept man thus far from total destruction. Only God's grace can restrain evil.

At Calvary men crucified the Son of God, our Lord Jesus Christ, the one who was meek and calm, the one who radiated holiness and brought the consciousness of God's presence wherever he went, the one who had declared that he had come to save. Every time he touched a life he touched it for blessing and for good.

How sin abounded and how clearly we can see it abounding when it took the Lord Christ himself and nailed him to the Cross. But God's Word makes us stand and look at Calvary again. We see not merely the wicked hands of men, the height of man's sin, but in the most sinful act that men ever committed we see the most gracious deed that God ever accomplished.

We can look at this theme not only historically but also *personally*. We can understand it in our experience when God deals savingly with us. Have you come to know in your own experience that in your heart, in your mind, in your life, sin abounds? You may have been agreeing with everything that was said when I was talking historically. Are you agreeing with me now when I'm talking experimentally? Every one here who has come under the hand of God's saving power certainly agrees with me. When the law comes home to the sinner's mind and when God's claims are forced upon the sinner's notice then, Paul says, the law is doing a wonderful work. It is revealing one's own sin to oneself. It is the law revealing sin in its sharpness that prepares for grace to abound. Grace would not abound, indeed grace would not even be grace, if it were not for the reality of sin. It would be an insult to offer mercy to innocence. Innocence needs no mercy. It is sin that requires mercy and in the case of sinful men before a holy God the mercy required is an absolutely gratuitous mercy. There is nothing in the individual to call forth the mercy of God. It is not even our need and our lostness that make God move to save us. It is not anything in our nature. It is the nature of God that gives grace.

The very nature of sin is enmity towards God. That God should move in love towards people who would tear him from his throne – that is grace and it is abounding grace. When that grace touched your life and showed you your sin, then it was abounding. Perhaps you didn't think so then, yet it was grace that was lighting up the reality and the eternity and the power of God's holy law. It was grace showing you that God is God and that he is holy. It wasn't the law alone that showed you your sin: it was grace shining on the law and showing you the demands in God's character that must be met before you could be saved. It was showing you something else. It was also showing you the darkness that had to be dispelled from your own soul. To know yourself as an unworthy and miserable sinner who deserves to be lost is deeply disturbing. As Paul says later in this passage, 'In me dwells no good thing.'

In the experience of the convicted sinner's heart where sin is seen to abound, grace is at work. The giving of the law at Mount Sinai was in itself a gracious act of God. It was bringing the reality of sin into our experience in a very simple, straightforward way. We are aware of what constitutes sin. We know it although we may not feel it. Knowing we are sinners and feeling we are sinners are two different things. What is sin? It is the transgression of the law and it is sin whether or not we feel its guilt and its heinousness. The moment we transgress the law we are guilty. It is when sin and the offensiveness of sin abounds in the heart that we are under conviction of sin. The law is doing a work.

If we are Christ's then God took us to the place where we knew we could do nothing for ourselves and there we saw that God had moved in wonderful love and had done all that was necessary for our salvation. All we had to do was to rest on the sinner's Saviour. I can remember still the night that God by his Spirit enlightened my mind to the fact that grace was abounding. The most amazing thing to me was this – that I didn't have to do anything in order to be saved. God had done it all for me already in Christ. There at the Cross, full free salvation for sinners was being provided. Christ was offering himself a sacrifice for our sins, for those who are eternally unworthy of his love. He was bearing our sins in his own body on the tree.

How close Christ came to being made a sinner. He was without sin. He was holy, harmless, undefiled, but how close he came to sin when he took our sin in its guilt and in its offence into his own human body. I once heard John Murray say, 'When our sins were laid upon Christ he came so close to being made a sinner that it is a razor edge between his being made sin and his being made sinful.'

Dr. John Kennedy, minister of the Dingwall Free Church of Scotland last century, in a sermon on the words of Christ on the Cross – 'It is finished' – and speaking of the sufferings of Christ, said that perhaps the deepest part of his suffering was his being brought into conjunction with the sin of his people. In that conjunction he was regarded as sin itself. He stood in the place of the curse. How offensive it must have been to every fibre of his holy soul.

And yet he did it. Why? Think of the abounding grace of the Father as you see it at Calvary when God spared not his own Son but delivered him up for us all. He was delivered up to that conjunction with sin. He was delivered up to the Father's penalising and punishing. He was delivered up to bearing an infinite pain in his soul, for he was removing sin – infinite sin against an infinite God.

When God draws all the threads of the pattern of time together, then all the Universe will see clearly that where sin abounds grace will much more abound. For when sin will be put into the eternal darkness of hell for ever, there will be then a reconstituting of the Universe, a new heavens and a new earth in which righteousness will abide for eternity.

Do you become depressed and despairing when you look around and see sin abounding? Do you wonder how the Christian or the church of Christ will survive in the midst of so much evil? Remember that grace is at work and that the eternal purposes of grace can never be frustrated. God is on his throne. Grace is abounding. Because there is abounding grace at work, all God's purposes for the least of his people will not only be amply and sufficiently fulfilled – they will be gloriously and wondrously fulfilled for he is God and our salvation is of him. It is all of grace. Grace is nothing else and nothing less than God acting graciously. Because God is acting graciously we can have strong abounding hope.

If you are without Christ then you are without hope. If you don't see your sin you don't see your need of grace. I would ask you to use two very simple prayers. Ask God to show you the offensiveness of your sin in his eyes and then ask God to show you the sufficiency of his grace in the Lord Jesus. When he shows you all that, then your soul will be safe for time and for eternity.

The Lie of Satan – The Grace of God

> And the serpent said unto the woman. 'Ye shall not
> surely die: For God doth know that in the day ye eat
> thereof, then your eyes shall be opened, and ye shall
> be as gods, knowing good and evil (Genesis 3:4-5).

This is a key chapter to an understanding of the whole of revelation. Our understanding of the world in which we live and certainly our understanding of redemption and the gospel of salvation will be specifically conditioned by the events recorded for us in this part of the book of Genesis. Satan has tempted into disobedience the man God has made and from there we have the principle of iniquity at work in the world. However, it is not merely a principle, not just something that took place long ago and doesn't touch your life or my life. It is something that is still at work and which each one of us knows in our own personal experience to a greater or lesser extent.

We have seen man fail and fall under the influence of sin, accepting that which was spoken by Satan as the truth. In accepting the word of Satan as truth we put a question mark over what God has said. We take reality and turn it round until the lie is accepted as truth and truth is accepted as the lie. That is not only the mystery of sin, that is the evil of sin. It makes God a liar and accepts the lie of Satan as truth. This evil is still at work in us all. You must ask yourself why men are so blind to the truth of God. Why is it that the vast multitude in our own day do not believe the gospel, do not pray, do not enter a church and do not esteem God? Why is it that man is so unwilling to believe the truth?

When we bring our questions back to this passage of Genesis we begin to understand that the minds of men and women have been conditioned by sin. The Bible tells us that there is a veil over their faces even until today and that the only hope is that God will

take the preaching of the gospel and bless it and enlighten the
mind and renew the heart. In face of all these facts that under-
write the great principles and the teaching of Scripture we perse-
vere because we see the pattern of God's Word being proved to
be true. We should not be surprised when we see people continuing in unbelief. When we see minds enlightened and when we see
the truth believed and the Lord Jesus trusted, that is when we
should marvel, for there we see God at work.

Having seen the activity of Satan and the success of that activity
– man brought into the place where he is more ready to believe
the lie than to believe the truth – let us go on to look at the coming
of God and the action of grace. God comes into the scene where
man has disobeyed him and where his enemy who has threatened
already his throne has been at work. The blasting, devastating
effect of evil has shown itself. This is the coming of the holy
God, of the just and holy God, the God who said: 'But of the tree
of knowledge of good and evil, thou shalt not eat of it: for in the
day that thou eatest thereof thou shalt surely die' (Gen. 2:17). He
comes into the darkness of the place of disobedience. Look at
these words in Genesis 3:8: 'And they heard the voice of the LORD
God walking in the garden in the cool of the day.'

Down through the ages men and women have been made aware,
in the same way, of the coming and the reality of God and they
have heard his voice. In Hebrew the word here translated as 'voice'
is literally 'speaking'. Adam and Eve heard this speaking of the
Lord God as he walked in the garden in the evening hour, at the
time when everything was becoming quiet and preparing for rest.
It was the evening of the day when they had sinned and believed
the Tempter. We can believe that this was a habit of the Lord God
– as it is stated in so calm and so matter-of-fact a manner. We
have no way of knowing, from the Genesis narrative, how long
there was between the creation of man and the Temptation and
the Fall. We have no way of fixing a time but it would seem from
this verse that God had been in the habit of coming in the cool of
the day and conversing with those he had made in his own image.
They were used to the talking of the Lord God in the garden, his
coming and his walking with them. We can picture in our own
minds what scenes of happy fellowship there were between the
Lord and his creatures. What worship and what delight there must

have been in their hearts as they talked with their Creator. What love he had poured out upon them and now it was all changed.

So God comes as was his habit and when he comes 'Adam and his wife hid themselves'. Perhaps on previous occasions, as soon as they heard his footsteps and his voice calling them, they had run with delight to meet him, thrilled that the Lord was there again. Now they are running from him. Sin has already come between God and man. They run and hide themselves. How foolish. How can anyone possibly hide from an all-seeing God? Some tree it would take to hide the sinner from the eye of God.

What are you hiding behind today? Your own good works? Pride in your Bible study and prayer? Your churchgoing? Fine preaching? Listening regularly to the most blessed of ministers will not save your soul. It will not do as a tree to hide from God. Today, multitudes are hiding from God although it is such a foolish, futile thing to do.

The call of divine justice
God, walking in the garden in the cool of the day, called and the call was this, 'Adam, where are you?'

There was no word of God to consign them to everlasting chains of darkness as were the angels when they sinned. It is not the voice of vengeance. It is not only the voice of judgement. If God had thrust them down into hell at that moment they would only have been treated justly because they had broken the commandment of their Creator. But God comes with mercy and grace and he deals with them, not on the basis merely of justice, but on the basis of a full free love that we call grace. Instead of casting them down he calls them with words that will bring them out from their hiding place.

How I hope and pray that if you don't have Christ, God's voice will come and call you out from wherever you are attempting to hide. I hope he will call you out into the light of his grace and into his free, redeeming love in the Lord Jesus. *There's* the gospel. It is not hiding behind trees of your own righteousness, of your own goodness. God calls in the garden in order to bring Adam and Eve out to himself. That is what the gospel is designed to accomplish – to bring us to the place where we will meet with God.

Yet this is the call of divine justice because it is the call of the

God who cannot overlook sin. Justice is calling them out and this call will bring every man and every woman who has ever lived to appear before God. It will come to you and it will come with a power that you cannot refuse. It stands written, 'We must all appear before the judgement seat of Christ' (2. Cor. 5:10), and 'It is appointed unto man once to die but after this the judgement' (Heb. 9:27).

Almost everything around your life and mine, reason as well as Scripture, tells us that in this evil world the balances will have to be adjusted and the wrongs righted. The Judge of all the earth will do right.

The call of divine sorrow
Here we have the call of our God whose heart is broken because of sin. You may feel that such language is too strong. I don't think so. The cross of Christ justifies such a description. There we see the broken heart of God because of sin. The handing over of his Son to justice was a costly act within the divine being. We talk of God all the time in human terminology because we ourselves are human creatures. He has revealed himself and accommodated himself to our human language.

The call of divine grace
It is the call of a God who has a purpose of mercy. The call of justice will go out to every son and daughter of Adam. The call of divine grief and sorrow comes to everyone also, 'What have you done?' And the call of divine grace comes because this God comes, not to swiftly cast down into hell, but to redeem with a tender touch. 'Adam where are you? Come to me.' That is the essence of the gospel. Before the call of justice reaches your heart and ushers you into the presence of a judgement throne, there is the call of grace. If you listen to that call and obey it with your whole heart and with your whole mind, you will be ushered, not before a throne of judgement, but before a throne of mercy. You will be clothed in the righteousness of Christ and when you come to judgement you will stand there, not in your own disobedience, but in his full and perfect obedience. His righteousness will be accounted to you as righteousness. This is the whole basis of the biblical doctrine of justification through faith in Christ Jesus. This is how sinners

are saved. They are covered with the righteousness of Jesus.

When Adam was tested in the garden, God had seen evil triumph there. Man believed the liar rather than the truth. The wonder of it was that where the first Adam failed in the testing, God looked forward to another day where the conditions were different but the same things were at stake. He looked forward, not to a garden where man would be supported and undergirded by every blessing he could possess, but to a wilderness where there is thunder, where God's face seems to be hidden and where the second Adam doesn't even have the bare necessities of life. There every thought must come under testing, every thought of the goodness of God must be stamped with a question. At the end of it all Christ is tested and the same forces are engaged. Human nature is coming under the same trial again and Satan uses the same approach. Read the account of the temptation of Christ. But where the first Adam failed and fell, the second Adam stands strong. When he faces the Tempter he uses the Word of God – 'It is written'; 'God has said it'; 'I will not believe the lie. I will hold to the truth because truth has the shape of things as they really are.' The Christ, the Son of God in human nature, held on to the truth and uses the truth to show up and to rebut the lie. Where the first Adam failed, the last Adam is strong and he conquers.

When God came walking in the garden in the cool of the day, he was seeing that future field of conflict and seeing the One who would conquer. God was saying to Adam, 'I can be God and just and still justify the ungodly because of what I have purposed to do in my Son.' There is a promise here of a coming Saviour. God's plan of redemption transcends all the wicked purposes of sin. The purpose of God is to overturn the purpose of evil. God's master plan included Satan's evil devices – a plan that would show forth God's love and mercy as nothing else in Creation could do.

The events taking place here have a far more than local significance. We are dealing here with factors and principles and realities that stretch out into the whole of history. They touch and affect every life and reach out beyond into eternity. They are factors that deal with man's destiny and ultimately with more than man's destiny. They deal with the righteousness and holiness of God himself. Will God live and allow iniquity to overturn his

throne? Will he be God or will he not? God's plan of redemption
tells us that God almighty will be God. He will be vindicated in
every facet of his character. His mercy will be gloriously and
wonderfully revealed in the redemption of sinners like us.

These are great truths. I believe them with all my heart and I
would urge you to believe them and relate your life to them. If
you fail to do so, to take these things into consideration and to
link your life to God's great redemptive purpose by faith in the
Lord Jesus, you will be under the sway and the power of what the
Bible describes as 'darkness' – a darkness that is everlasting. These
events are immense and they are real. Don't live as if they didn't
exist.

There are basic principles in this chapter that explain your life
and the world in which you live as no other truth that you will
ever find can explain it. But it does more than explain. It relates it
to a God who is almighty and of great wisdom and of great power.
But more – he is the God of all grace. Even if there are things we
cannot fathom, questions we cannot answer, implications of the
principles that we cannot understand, let us cast ourselves upon
the God whose principles they are. Let us cast ourselves on the
love that walked in the garden in the cool of the day and called so
graciously and said, 'Adam, where are you?'

In the gospel we meet the same God, with the same voice,
with the same grace, with the same mercy and tenderness. When
he says, 'Where are you?', he looks at you and at your sin and
asks, 'What have you done?' He does that in order to bring healing and peace and blessing to your heart. And he does it in Christ.

4

The Conversion of Lydia

And a certain woman named Lydia, a seller of purple,
of the city of Thyatira, which worshipped God, heard us:
whose heart the Lord opened, that she attended unto the
things which were spoken of Paul (Acts 16:14).

If you are unconverted don't be without hope. There are many
promises scattered all through the Word of God that should encourage the unconverted to seek God with all their heart. I want
to attempt to encourage hope in you, to encourage a hope that
will make you look away from yourself towards Christ and towards God.

Every single believer was once as you are, and if God can do it
for them surely God can do it for you too. Take hope from the life
of every converted person you know, because they were once just
as lost as you are. Take hope from the story of Lydia, for Lydia
once had a heart closed against God – but he opened her heart.
Let's look at some of the things which this story teaches us that
should encourage us to seek salvation and to persist until we know
that we are in Christ and safe.

Four important things can be traced in the conversion of Lydia
which have a bearing upon every single conversion.

The importance of God's working in providence

God's working in providence is the ordering and arranging of our
circumstances. You may be here this evening for various reasons
but one thing is certain, God meant you to be here. Look at how
providence worked for Lydia's conversion. God's providence
brought Paul to Philippi, the chief city of Macedonia. Paul was
not in Philippi just because he wanted to be there, nor even because he had planned to be there – in fact he had planned to be
elsewhere. He left on a journey in order to go and preach in Asia

but the Holy Spirit did not allow him to do so. Then Paul changed
his plans and tried to go to Bithynia instead. Again God put out
his hand and 'suffered him not'. God did not allow him to preach
in Asia and did not allow him to go to Bithynia.

God directs his providences and overcomes the plans and aspirations of men. I'm sure Paul must have wondered at being
hindered twice by the Holy Spirit, but then God gave the apostle
a vision where he saw a man of Macedonia who cried, 'Come
over into Macedonia and help us.' There were souls in Macedonia crying for light in their darkness. God was listening and was
going to answer those cries. He began to work the wheels of his
providence and in doing so changed the mind of his apostle. God
sent Paul in a different direction in answer to a cry.

God directs providence. It is of the directing of God's providence that you are here. God must have some reason for it. He
had a reason for bringing Paul all the way to Philippi: Lydia was
one of the first Christian believers in what we call Europe.

In addition to it being an amazing providence that Paul should
be sent to Philippi at just the right time, so it is equally amazing
that Lydia should also be at Philippi at the same time. She didn't
belong to Philippi; actually she came from the very place where
Paul had been prevented from preaching the gospel. Why didn't
God keep Lydia in Thyatira and send Paul there? We don't know.
God's purpose was that Lydia should be converted at Philippi.

Lydia is in Philippi on business and probably living in a rented
house. She's there to sell one of the special wares of Thyatira,
beautiful purple cloth which sold very well to the Romans who
were fond of the royal colour. I'm sure she went to Philippi, a
Roman colony, just in order to further her business. She didn't go
there looking for Christ. I'm sure when she set out from Thyatira
the last thing she expected was to be converted. When you read
down through the history of the church, how often that has been
the case when God has touched a life.

Perhaps there are people here and they had to move into
Glasgow because of their business commitments. Wouldn't it be
wonderful if God used your move to Glasgow to transform your
life and your home!

The importance of Lydia herself

We can see that Lydia was important to the Lord because she was converted. She was in the election of his grace, she was one pre-destined to be brought to Christ. But God's predestination never cancels out human responsibility. There's a great deal about pre-destination and election that even the converted human mind can't understand. But one thing the Bible teaches about election is that it does not cancel out human responsibility. You cannot be in the position where you will say, 'If I am going to be saved I will be saved anyway', because you will not be saved against your will. Lydia wasn't saved against her will. God makes his people will-ing 'in a day of his power'. And a day of power came into Lydia's life.

Although Lydia's heart was closed to the truth as it is in Christ, she obeyed the light that she had. That's a point I want to make especially to the unconverted who are troubled by predestination and election: are you living up to the light that God has given you? Lydia was a proselyte to the Jewish faith and her new faith demanded that she keep the Sabbath day. And on the Sabbath Lydia was at the prayer meeting where she attended to the things that were spoken by Paul. Do you really listen to the Word preached or do you lull yourself into a lost eternity?

My friend, you are important to your own conversion and un-til you realise that you will not make one step of progress towards conversion. Ask God to make you willing in a day of his power.

The importance of Paul

God will work through means. The Westminster Confession of Faith says that although God is able to work above means or with-out means, he ordinarily uses means in the conversion of souls. The means that he ordinarily uses is the preaching of the Word. How Paul works! Paul works as if everything depended on him. He doesn't say, 'Oh well, if God's going to save these people over in Macedonia he will do it without me. If they're going to be saved they'll be saved.' If the preacher twisted his theology the way some of his unconverted hearers twist their theology, they wouldn't have a hope. Just as it is untrue for the sinner that 'if they're going to be saved they'll be saved no matter what they do', so it's untrue for the preacher to say that.

So Paul goes and there he adapts himself to the circumstances. He goes on the Sabbath day to the one place where there's a prayer meeting. He doesn't preach to the people as he did in Athens where they were used to philosophical argument and long discourses. When he arrived at this prayer meeting in Philippi he sat down by the riverside and began to chat with them. He didn't preach at them, he talked to them. And I'm sure that he spoke to them about the one thing that was necessary – salvation through Christ alone.

The importance of the Lord himself
It is the Holy Ghost who shows us the way of salvation and makes us rest upon Christ alone. He opens sinful minds to understand, he opens sinful hearts to believe, he opens sinful lives so that they become obedient to the Word of God, he loosens sinful wills in order that Christ freely offered in the gospel is accepted as Saviour.

Has the Spirit done that for you? There is something required of you: you are asked to obey, to believe and to repent. The Spirit cannot do these things for you, but he can enable you to do these things yourself. When you have done your best, my friend, you are helpless: it requires God to open your heart as he opened the heart of Lydia to the truth as it is in Jesus Christ. That very fact throws every one of us on to God's mercy and grace. Don't think that you'll be able to convert yourself when and how and as you please, it will take a miracle of God's saving grace to do it. So you must seek God with all your heart and mind and strength. When should you seek him? I can only say what God's Word says: you must do it now. 'Today, if you will hear his voice, harden not your heart', but ask the Lord to open it and to fill it with the love of Christ and the joy of salvation.

5

Confession and Forgiveness

If we confess our sins, he is faithful and just to forgive us
our sins, and to cleanse us from all unrighteousness
(1 John 1:9).

Nothing, absolutely nothing, should be more highly valued by us
than the forgiveness of sin. That God has equipped himself to
forgive is from our point of view, as sinners, the most marvellous
truth that God has revealed to us. A famous Highland preacher of
last century, Archie Cook, one of two brothers from the island of
Arran who became ministers in the North, said of this text: 'These
words leave their every hearer without excuse for every sin that
they allow to go unconfessed, uncleansed and unforgiven.'

Let us look at some of the facets of the truth found in this text.
The truths expressed here touch our lives at the place where we
really are. It is the gospel as it comes to us and makes its claim
upon us and makes its demands on our lives.

Confession of sin

If we confess, he forgives. Behind the reality of this seemingly
simple truth is the movement of God in grace. Behind this statement is the marvel of the Cross, the glorious person of our Lord
Jesus Christ and his atoning death. He had to ascend and be glorified at the pleasure of the Father before this text could ever be
written. How humbled we should be this morning that God touches
the greatest problem that the Christian has in such a beautiful
way.

What do we do with our sin? We speak of it sometimes as our
failure, sometimes as our weakness, sometimes as our infirmities. These all come under the heading of sin.

Why does God ask his people to confess their sin? John has
hedged his statement around with two others. The first is this: 'If
we say that we have no sin, we deceive ourselves, and the truth is

not in us.' And he follows the text with another statement: 'If we say that we have not sinned, we make him a liar, and his word is not in us.'

Through these two statements God has safeguarded the marvellous grace of forgiveness. They emphasise strongly just what confession is. John knew how ready men and women are to deny or to excuse sin. We will call sin, in our hearts and in our thoughts and in our lives, by any name but that which will denominate it as trespass against our holy God. That is why John safeguards confession of sin.

Before there can be confession of sin there has to be a *consciousness* of sin. An awareness of sin is the first step in confession. This means a sensitivity to God and to his holiness, and enlightenment as to the requirements of God. One of the sad things about our present society is that there is very little consciousness of sin, along with a very low concept of God, in the minds of most people. There is scarcely any concept of God as the holy One.

There is, however, no-one who should be more sensitive to sin in its evil than the Christian believer. If the consciousness of sin produces no sense of pain or disquiet or guilt, we can be almost certain that we are in a poor spiritual state. A conscience that feels no pain in the presence of sin is a seared conscience. A conscience that draws no pleasure and finds no peace in the mercy of God in Christ is equally at fault. It is a hardened conscience. The love and mercy of God are ultimately greater realities than the reality of sin: 'Where sin abounded, grace did much more abound.' Therefore we do not despair. We are not grappling with something with which God himself has not grappled. He has grappled with sin in Christ. Praise his name for it!

The conscience is not a perfect monitor of right and wrong. It needs to be instructed and often to be readjusted by the living Word of God. There is such a thing as a conscience 'void of offence before God and man'. It is very closely connected with the awareness of sin and the confession of sin.

John lays great stress on how Christians can deceive themselves in order to allow the continuance of a particular course of action. We deny the Word of God if we say we are not sinners. '*All* have sinned, and come short of the glory of God' (Rom. 3:23).

We must not go against what our enlightened conscience tells us, what our experience tells us, and what the Word of God tells us. There are few Christians who are not very conscious of sin in their lives, and one of the major battles raging in their Christian lives is their battle with sin day by day. That is why there must be confession of sin as a first step to the forgiveness of sin – and we are all in constant need of forgiveness.

The link between pardon and confession

In a sense we have been seeing our way into this linkage already. Why does John link pardon and confession together? Sin unconfessed is sin retained. Sin unconfessed and unacknowledged is sin condoned. If you as a Christian believer have today not confessed your sin to God there is a very real sense in which you are condoning that sin. Sin covered over is sin allowed and, to some extent, sin loved. At that point sin is loved more than God himself is loved.

Sin confessed is something very different. In the words of Psalm 32:5: 'I acknowledged my sin unto thee, and mine iniquity have I not hid. I said, I will confess my transgressions unto the LORD; and thou forgavest the iniquity of my sin.'

Why are we so ready to deny our sin, even to ourselves? God is 'ready to pardon' – he has equipped himself to pardon through the death of our Lord Jesus Christ. God is ready to pardon both in that sense and also in the sense that he is *swift* to pardon. The word that is translated as 'ready' means 'always on the move'. There is no halting or hesitation. God is ready to pardon immediately and instantaneously. How it should thrill our hearts to think of a God who is ready to pardon the moment we confess our sins. That is the good news, the root and heart of salvation.

It is this same God who also *refuses* to pardon. He refuses to pander to sin and he refuses to pardon sin that is unconfessed. Unless there is confession there is no pardon. So many say, even on their deathbeds, 'Surely I'll be alright. God is a God of love and look at what he has done for the world in giving his Son.' They have no idea of what is the costly love of God. Yes, God is the God of love. But he is also the God of perfect righteousness and holiness and he says that he will by no means clear the guilty – unless the guilty come to the only means of atonement and forgiveness that there is under heaven.

Why do we think of the God who refuses to pardon as a terrible God? Do you know what God is doing when he refuses to pardon someone whose sin is unconfessed? God is taking that person at their own evaluation and dealing with their sin at their own evaluation of it. If it is not worth confessing, then it is not worth forgiving. The God who refuses to pardon acts in perfect harmony with the man who refuses to confess. The God who is ready to pardon acts in perfect harmony with the one who is ready to confess.

Confession is a revelation of inward attitude

God regards the heart. The Greek word that underlies the word 'confess' here is not the usual word in the New Testament for confession. It is a word that is used very frequently in other connections. It means, 'If we admit our sins, if we acknowledge our sins' then there is pardon. This is not about Christians confessing our sins to others. We must admit to ourselves first that we have sinned.

If I had to confess to one of you, there are two ways in which I could do it. If I come to you and say, 'I lied to you yesterday,' I would be stating a truth but I would not be confessing sin. But if I said, 'Yesterday I sinned by telling you a lie,' I would not only be stating a truth but I would also be confessing a sin. I am evaluating the lie at its worth before God. This would be true of any sin. I could come and say, 'I lost my temper with you but that is because I am very emotional after my recent illness.' It is very easy to state a truth and not confess a sin. I have no business to lose my temper with my Christian brethren.

How ready we are to make statements that are not confessions. I'll never forget a conversation with a man who had been attending church for many years. I asked him if he ever thought of himself as a sinner. 'My goodness, no, Mr. MacMillan, I'm not that kind of a person.' 'Man,' I said, 'you're unique in all of Aberdeen.' That illustrates the way we tend to feel about ourselves.

True confession is *realistic* in its base. The fact that God has tied pardon and forgiveness together shows us his marvellous knowledge of us. This is great spiritual psychology. Psychologists tell us that the only way to deal with deep and hidden things

that trouble us is to bring them out into the open and talk about
them and face them. I believe that that is based on the nature of
man. It is also based on gospel truth. God will not allow sin to
fester and be a sore in the heart and life of his people whom he
loves very dearly. He will have them, by his grace, look at it honestly and deal with it biblically.

You don't have to wait. He does it immediately. All you have
to do when you have looked at it yourself is to hold it out to God's
eye and say, 'I'm sorry.' In repenting you are already enjoying
the forgiveness of our gracious God. Forgiveness brings peace
with it and joy unspeakable. That is the source of the Christian's
happiness.

6

The Dying Thief

And Jesus said unto him, Verily I say unto thee, Today shalt thou be with me in paradise (Luke 23:43).

Here we have a man against whom all the odds seem stacked. It seems that he had trifled with the things of God and the things of his soul until the hour of mercy had come and gone for him. Although the odds were stacked against him and although we would think that surely this man was going to be lost, the grace of God is such that he was saved.

Very often when we think of the story of the dying thief we think of a man who was plucked by the God of grace from the very brink of a lost eternity. Too often we dwell on that fact alone. Other factors have to come into our consideration. From this event we learn that when Jesus Christ was at his very weakest, when he was suffering agony and undergoing the pains of hell in his soul, even then he still had compassion on a terrible sinner. Even then Jesus still had the power and the authority and the might to reach out to covenant with him that on that very day he would be with the Saviour in paradise.

That is not all that we learn from this event. We learn that we should not use it as an encouragement to presumption. Someone once said to Bishop Ryle when he was reasoning with them about the urgency of salvation, 'Ah, Bishop, remember the dying thief.' To which he replied, 'Yes, but which one?' We cannot presume. There were two thieves and only one was saved. We cannot presume on God's mercy, love and grace. To say that because the dying thief was saved at the twelfth hour then you will be saved on your deathbed is to abuse the story. You might as well say, 'That thief was saved so I will be a thief.' That is the same kind of reasoning.

I have seen very few, if any, deathbed repentances. You cannot say that when you begin to feel you might be approaching the end of your life then you will come to trust in Christ. You are not even promised tomorrow. Very few people meet death with all their faculties sound and clear.

What did this man see and hear to bring him to repentance? What did he see in Jesus to make him trust?

The means God used for this man's conversion

The man himself was in an extreme condition. It is hard to imagine how he could think and talk about the things of his soul. He was undergoing the same kind of bodily agony as the Saviour himself – he was enduring crucifixion. Yet God was at work with him. How? God brings a soul to Jesus through knowledge – he had to know about Jesus before he could trust him. The gospel must be heard before it can be believed. This man heard and saw enough to bring him to the feet of Christ in spirit and in heart. The other thief heard and saw enough to condemn him because of his unbelief.

This man heard no sermons. There was no revival going on. Some of us like to say that if we heard a really powerful sermon or if revival came then we would be saved. He had none of the privileges that we enjoy but he could see Christ physically. He saw a man like himself, condemned by the law to death. Here was a man who had been scourged and beaten and who had been made to carry his own cross out to Calvary. He saw many people weeping. There were women crying as this man was crucified.

He heard Jesus himself. He heard him pray for the soldiers who nailed him to the tree. What a prayer he heard! As he himself was being nailed to the tree his heart must have been bursting with hatred and with terror. And then he heard the prayer of Christ, 'Father, forgive them; for they know not what they do.' How that must have moved his heart. In that prayer he heard the mercy of God.

He saw the inscription over the Cross: 'Jesus of Nazareth, the King of the Jews.' Pilate had chosen these words and would not change them to please the people. That must have made the thief think. Maybe he remembered what he had learned as a child from Psalm 22 – 'they pierced his hands and feet.' As he heard the shouts and jeers of the crowd did he remember the words that were written, 'All they that see me laugh me to scorn', and did he recall that these words were written of the promised Messiah? Did he suddenly begin to throb with the feeling that prophetic Scripture was being fulfilled at that very moment?

As the events of the day continued and as the time passed, did his interpretation of what was happening become clearer in his mind by the enlightenment of the Holy Spirit? He heard the very words that Psalm 22 prophesied would be said. He would begin to understand who this man was who was suffering beside him and he would begin to hope. The light of God's Word penetrated this man's mind.

The means that were used for this man's conversion were very unlikely means. There was the awful scene that was taking place and the blasphemous, mocking taunts of the crowd. The means may have seemed unlikely but they were perfectly adequate. Many Christians will testify that a few words was all that was used to bring them to Christ.

The strong faith given to this man

When the whole thing started it would have been hard to differentiate between the two men who were crucified beside Jesus. It would have seemed very unlikely that either of them would be saved. Now here was one of them coming to trust in Christ. He came to the point where he looked for help and strength from one who was in the very same condition as himself – being crucified. In doing so he displayed great faith. This was faith against all the factors that human nature would calculate. Faith is often like that – a leaping over all the difficulties that our minds and our circumstances put in front of us. It is an acceptance of the Word of God. He was totally committing himself to one who was being deserted by his own followers. He had no-one else to whom he could commit himself.

Ultimately, for any of us, there is no-one else. Our situation is just as desperate as this man's and he was trusting in Christ and committing himself to him at a time when nearly everyone else seemed to have forsaken him. If God can stir hope and faith in the heart of a man in such a desperate situation, he is able to stir faith any time that he pleases. This gives me great hope for you today. You may have been refusing to believe for years and years. You may have been resisting sermon after sermon and the witness of family and friends. Still I would not give up hope for you. The Holy Spirit who stirred faith in the heart of this man at such a time can do it for you as well.

The prayer of this man carries in it the essence of all prayer. It was very simple. It was very short: 'Lord, remember me when thou comest into thy kingdom.'

If only you would pray like that. You may feel you can't pray and that you don't know what to say. You can pray as this man prayed. His faith was going out to Jesus. It is likely that his faith couldn't answer all the questions he was already asking. He would not have been able to explain the whole theology of atonement by substitution, nor describe the incarnation nor the resurrection that was yet to come. His faith went through every searing question and rested on the Saviour.

You have questions and perhaps you have been telling yourself for years that if you knew the answers then you could trust in Jesus. You will never in this life find all the answers about life and about eternity and about God and the way of salvation. If you trust Christ your questions will all be answered in eternity. 'For now we see through a glass, darkly; but then face to face: now I know in part; but then shall I know even as also I am known' (1 Cor. 13:12).

This man's faith laid all the questions aside and went straight to Jesus. He is worthy of all our trust. What strong faith this man was given. How often we read of people who trusted God in spite of themselves and their circumstances. God often comes and stirs faith in people who were not even looking for him. They are given a faith that leaps over all the barriers and rests in Jesus alone. To have Jesus is to have everything. This man had none of the opportunities that we have but as he hung there on his cross he must have become aware of the love and compassion and power that were in Jesus and he must have been affected by the power of the darkness that came down for three hours. He had no church or sermons or sacraments or Bible, but he had seen Jesus.

The results of this man's faith
The answer to his prayer came immediately – 'Today shalt thou be with me in paradise.' If you would pray as this man prayed, your prayer could be answered almost before you finish speak-

ing. 'Tonight you will be part of my kingdom.' Wouldn't that be
a glorious answer to your prayer?

See how this man witnessed to his faith. He didn't have very
long to live his Christian life, but how he lived it. He was never
baptised, he was never able to confess his love for Christ by sitting at the Lord's table. But he confessed Jesus.

The first thing he did was to witness to the faith that God had
given him. He witnessed by rebuking his fellow: 'Do you not fear
God, seeing thou art in the same condemnation?'

He spoke to him of Jesus as the just one, as the one who had
done nothing wrong and he acknowledged the justice of their punishment for wrongdoing. He was aware of his own sin and of the
goodness of Christ and he pointed this out to his companion. He
defended Jesus the righteous one and he learned to pray the prayer
of faith. How quickly his faith bore fruit. May each of you come
to like faith.

7

Loving the Lord

I love the LORD because he has heard my voice
(Psalm 116:1)

Real Christian faith lies, not in outward Christian observances,
but in the reality of inward religious experience. Where there is
such experience there will be, of course, the outward religious
observance. The very heart of Christianity is the soul's experience of God.

The fact shines out of almost all of the psalms – the praise
book of the Church of God. You cannot read or sing the psalms
without being brought face to face with the fact that experience
of God in every phase of life, in the dark, trying places of life and
in the bright exalted places of life, is the very core of what religion really is. To know and to enter somewhat into the experiences of which these psalms speak is the greatest deterrent to one
of our greatest dangers – the danger that our religion becomes
merely an outward observance of religious ceremonies.

To love the Lord is the core, the very foundation of Christian
living. Everyone who has known God's love at work has that
experience interpreted and explained in these psalms. Every one
of them catches the note of the melody of redemption.

What has prompted this love in the Psalmist? The Lord heard
him as he underwent terrible experiences – experiences that made
him cry out on God's name. His cry was heard and he was
delivered.

This psalm was one of a group of psalms that were sung at the
Passover. It was, almost certainly, one of the psalms that the
Saviour and his disciples sang as they left the upper room and
journeyed to the place of shadows, to the Garden of Gethsemane.
In that place this became true in the experience of the man Christ
Jesus. There is a very real sense in which it is peculiarly his psalm
and yet because it is his, it is ours as well.

There are many and varied ways in which the Christian believer
can profess faith. There is no higher confession of faith than this
– 'I love the Lord.' That confession touches the very core of our
concern. It touches on the reality of what our profession is. To
love the Lord rises higher than anything else that Christian
experience can aspire to. To believe in the Lord is salvation, for
none perish that trust him. To believe in the Lord is a miracle of
God's grace in the human heart. But how much higher can this
confession go! It is not 'I believe in the Lord,' but '*I love the
Lord.*'

To know the Lord is to fear him with a reverent trusting heart.
They that know his name put their trust in God but, high as that is,
to love him is even more than to know him. It is the fruit of knowing him as the God of love and the God of grace.

He draws near to us testing with a severe test the reality of our
experience, our confession, our living. Out of all your experience
of life and out of all your experience of God, can you this morning lift up your heart and say, 'Whatever else may be true of me,
this is true – I love the Lord'? If you can say that, you have everything compressed within it that God looks for in any of his people. Why do I say that? There are one or two things in the Gospels
that make this very clear. To love the Lord is absolutely contrary
to the heart of unregenerate man. It is impossible for the unregenerate heart to use these words in reality. The heart of man is enmity against God. As we are born into this world, we don't love
God. We cannot love God. Therefore before we are able to declare our love for the Lord there must be a marvellous miracle of
God's grace. Our natures have been changed and transformed.
We have been born again of the Holy Ghost. This confession of
love to God is the surest token of God's work within us.

Remember how Peter denied the Lord with oaths and curses.
Peter must have wondered about the reality of his experience and
whether he could possibly be a disciple of Jesus Christ. His friends
must have asked the same questions about him. His Lord took
him and dealt with him in a particularly personal way. He knew
that Peter needed special dealings. Christ didn't ask Peter, 'Do
you know me? Do you trust me? Are you repentant and sorry?'
He asked one question that pierced like an arrow to the real heart
of the issue. Three times he said, 'Peter, do you love me?' The

repetition of the question grieved Peter and at last he burst out with a loud confession of his love, 'You know that I love you.'

That is the surest mark that any one of us can have that our Christian faith and our Christian confession is authentic and real, the genuine article – the product of God's grace at work in us. You may fail, and be conscious of your failure in almost every avenue of live. There may be times when, because of denial of your Lord, you have walked in darkness. Maybe even at this moment you are following the Lord afar off but yet it is true that you love the Lord. This is the very heart of our concern to be right with God. To love the Lord is the product of saving grace alone.

Love to God is the highest thing that God looks for in any one of his people

He looks for many responses from us, but above all he looks for the love of the heart. What is the highest requirement of God's law? Remember how Jesus replied to one of those smart theological fellows that approached him one day in order to test him by asking which was the most important of the commandments. Jesus told him that the first and great commandment was 'To love the Lord your God with all your heart and mind and soul' (Matt. 22:37).

This is the priority that God's law in all its demands presses home to us. The whole summary of the first table of the law (or the first five of the ten commandments) is to 'love God'. That is the first and greatest requirement of God's law. Isn't it wonderful how God's grace, his love, his pity to lost sinners who cannot meet his law, produces that in them which meets his own legal demand and requirement? Grace works in the human heart that which satisfies the law of God. The law is the revelation of God's own character. Grace works in the lives of God's people that which is pleasing to every attribute of God himself.

The next commandment is like that one. It is a mirror image of the first: 'You shall love your neighbour as yourself' (Matt. 22:39). Or again, 'A new commandment I give you, That ye love one another' (John 13:34). We can only do that when we have first of all met with the demands of the first – to love God.

This love is the point of great reality for the psalmist. Is it the point of great reality for you today?

His present state of love to God roots in a past deliverance
Why does he love the Lord? He is able to tell us the reason for
that love. God has heard his voice, his prayer. On the face of it,
does that seem a rather mercenary reason? He loves God because
God has been good to him. He loves God because of God's goodness and condescension and grace encapsulated in the words: 'He
inclined his ear to me.'

Literally we have here a picture of a mother bending down
over her child, or of someone bending down over a person who is
too weak or ill to do more than whisper. They bend down to catch
the cry. Do you ever picture God like that?

God heard his voice. He doesn't say his prayer was heard –
that is implied. Perhaps he was in such a state of desperation that
it was only a cry and not an articulate prayer. Maybe it was only
a cry of the soul – every real Christian knows what that means.
Although not a sound may pass our lips, God bends down to hear
this cry from our inmost being.

One of the ultimate tests of the reality of our personal faith
and of the reality of our whole Christian faith and religion is
whether God hears and answers the prayers of his people. God
himself would make it a test:

> '... prove me now herewith,' saith the LORD of hosts, 'if I will not
> open you the windows of heaven, and pour you out a blessing,
> that there shall not be room enough to receive it' (Mal. 3:10).

What does it mean to 'prove God'? It means to ask in order to
receive. Are you asking God to bless you? Are you praying for
the good of God's church on earth? Are you asking for the good
of mankind? Are you proving God daily?

Do you remember the day that you cried for mercy? Do you
remember the day when you sought God and longed for his peace?
Do you remember how God gave you mercy and peace? God has
not changed. He is still the same prayer-hearing, prayer-answer-
ing God – and he will never change.

The psalmist knew the sorrows of death – the reality of the
wages of sin. The reality and the power and the fact of sin in all
its ugliness brings the sorrows of death bearing in on the human
heart.

He knew the pains of hell. He found trouble and sorrow in his body, but to a greater measure in his soul. Most of us will have known what it is to have physical pain that made us cry out to God for deliverance. Have you experienced something far stronger – the fact of the pain caused by sin in your inner being?

Jesus went through this experience because of our sin. He went through it in order to be our deliverer. The highest thing that is said about love is: 'We love him, because he first loved us' (1 John 4:19). That is how we know that God hears us. That is how we know that God loves us. The gospel of our Lord Jesus Christ which was manifested supremely at Calvary bore out the reality of the words of Jesus: 'Greater love has no man than this, that a man lays down his life for his friends' (John 15:13).

At Calvary, Jesus laid down his life for his enemies, for those who were in revolt against him. That is love. That is what draws our love to him. If we can say today that we love the Lord, surely we trace it back to the place where that love is rooted, to his love for us and to our past deliverance because of his love.

If we love people, we love to call on them. We go and visit them. We want to talk with them, to show our love to them and to see their love for us communicated in their expression. To know the love of God in Christ, and to know that love as a power that delivers us from bondage and darkness and sadness and sorrow, makes us long for fellowship with God. What keeps the Christian believer living a life of prayer? This one fact – that God has heard in the past and has answered. 'Hitherto the Lord has helped me.'

Where there is real Christian faith that knows love to the Saviour, and knows love to the Saviour because of past deliverance, that faith looks out into the future and makes this resolution, 'I will call on God every day of all my days.'

Sometimes we are afraid of the future. If the future brings the certitude of fellowship with God, of converse with God, and the certainty that our gracious, loving, compassionate, loving God will bend down to hear us, then surely we go out into the future with faith and confidence and gladness.

8

The God Who Waits

And therefore will the LORD wait, that he may be gracious
unto you, and therefore will he be exalted, that he may
have mercy upon you: for the LORD is a God of judgement:
blessed are all they that wait for him (Isaiah 30:18).

This chapter describes to us the actions of the people of Judah
when they were under threat of invasion from the Assyrians. Israel
had already been invaded and devastated by a huge army from
Assyria. It is clear that Assyria was being used by God to bring
judgement and affliction on a disobedient nation.

Despite their disobedience and rebellion, God was continuing
to ask the people of Judah to repent and to trust in him. He promised that if they repented and turned to him, he would take away
his judgement and there would be new days of power and blessing. God is ever the same. His attitude to Judah has been his attitude to his people in every age. When they sin and turn away
from him, he doesn't always visit them with judgement. Instead
he visits them again and again with mercy. He holds out many
great promises to them. He is the God of all grace.

Judah, instead of turning to God for help in their trouble,
rebelled and after taking council together, they went to Egypt to
strengthen themselves in the strength of Pharaoh. They went to a
nation that was at enmity with them and with God, to trust in the
shadow of Egypt instead of remaining in the shadow of the
Almighty God. They behaved as the church has done in every
age. When crisis comes, far too often the church turns, not to her
only real source of help and strength, but to some worldly power
and seeks worldly protection. The same is true of ourselves as
individuals. When difficult times come, when faith is being tested
and when sin is being chastened, we will often turn to any source
we think may be a help to us and turn away from the sure help of
God.

How does God react? Does he write us off as we would tend to do if someone persistently and continually refused our help? We are very impatient. The ways of God are not our ways and his thoughts are not our thoughts. He is gracious and patient and long-suffering with every one of us.

God is waiting to be gracious. Isn't that wonderful? Isn't the word of God thrilling? We have a great gospel. We have a great God who is waiting to be gracious to us. In our text we see a waiting God, producing ultimately a waiting people. Blessed are they that wait upon him.

Why is God waiting? The word 'therefore' points us back to some ground that is a foundation, a reason for God's waiting. In every activity and in every movement of his divine power, God has a reason. He does all things according to the counsel of his own will. He never acts arbitrarily, without a purpose.

What is behind the 'therefore' in this case? The answer is not in this chapter. The people of Judah were rebellious, they were lying and they didn't want a message from God through his prophet. They wanted to do away with God and with all his influence on them. 'Therefore' is not pointing to anything in the people or in their attitudes. There is no explanation there as to why God is waiting to be gracious. The explanation lies in the great, free, sovereign grace of God that acts graciously even in the face of the most sinful rebellion and that comes with love and tenderness to a lying, disobedient nation. This is the nature of the God with whom this people is dealing. He is the God who spared not his own Son but delivered him up for us all. What more could he have done?

'Who is a God like unto thee, that pardoneth iniquity, and that passeth by the transgression of the remnant of his heritage?' (Mic. 7:18).

What is God's greatest glory in your eyes? If you are Christ's it is this: that he has pardoned your iniquity, that he has taken away your transgression, that he has not visited you with the judgement that you deserve. It wasn't because of anything we did or were but it was all of grace. It was his grace that made us pray, that made us turn, that made us repent. Without his grace no sinner will do any of these things. With some of us he waited a long time – even into old age. The sin of the people of Judah revealed their need of God's grace and his power and his salvation. But 'where sin abounded, grace does much more abound' (Rom. 5:20).

What does it mean when the text says that God is waiting to have mercy upon them? Although God is waiting to exercise mercy, his very waiting is an exercise of mercy. He is holding back the very justice which should have punished them for their disobedience. Before freeing, saving mercy comes to anyone, there has been a long period of sparing mercy. Whatever your age today, even if you are only a little boy or girl, if you are still unconverted, it means that God has spared you and that his sparing mercy is around you today because no matter how young you are you are not too young to sin, or to need a Saviour. With some of the older people God's sparing mercy has been around them for many years. Why is he sparing you? He is sparing you that he may be even more gracious to you. I hope that that will be true for each one of you, whatever your age. I hope that one day he will show the majesty of his grace and love to you.

If any of us are lost for eternity it will certainly not be God's fault. He has been waiting. Everything is ready, prepared for your salvation.

'He will be exalted that he may have mercy upon you.' What does this mean? The word 'exalt' literally means 'ascend the throne'. God in the person of his Son left his throne. He came down and humbled himself and took on him the form of a servant. He was found in fashion as a man and humbled himself and became obedient unto death, even the death of the cross. Wherefore God also has highly exalted him. Why? God did all this that he might have mercy on us.

Why is there a lamb slain in the midst of the Throne of God? It is in order that that throne might be a place of grace for sinners like us. In the gospel, God is gathering the reins of sovereign power. He is ascending his throne. He is going to manifest his great mercy and he is going to say from that throne: 'I will have mercy on whom I will have mercy' (Rom. 9:15), 'I will build my church and the gates of hell will not prevail against it' (Matt. 16:18).

These people were a rebellious and lying people but God had loved them with an everlasting love and drew them with loving-

kindness. He gave the Son of his love that they might not perish
and that they might be redeemed and become sons and daughters
of the living God.

'*Blessed are all they that wait for him.*' They are waiting for
him not in order to be blessed. They are waiting for him because
they have been blessed. That waiting on God is a sign that God's
waiting has already borne fruit. His graciousness has made a people blessed. Have you been blessed in that way? Have you learned
that when difficult times come there is really only one deliverer?
Have you learned that Jesus Christ is your strength and that in the
shadow of the Almighty there is great peace?

If you are not yet a Christian, be thankful for one thing. Be
thankful for the patience of the long-suffering grace of the God
who spares you still and who spares you, we hope, in order to be
gracious to you. We will know that God has been gracious to you
when we see you waiting on him. He shows his mercy to all who
seek him.

9

'The Word of the LORD is against you'
(Zephaniah 2:5).

This phrase was the message of God to the inhabitants of the land of Canaan long ago. This morning it is my desire by the help of God to use it to speak very plainly and directly to the unconverted in our midst. Your condition, if you are not born again, is of great concern to me and to every real believer. Your condition through life cannot be a happy one for no unconverted person knows the peace of God. No unconverted person can know any real peace of mind or any real purpose of life. Your unconverted condition disturbs and concerns me a great deal because your condition as unconverted is not only unhappy in this life, it is altogether too fearsome for words or for thought regarding the life that is to come.

If you are unconverted, then the main thing in life for you is wrong – your relationship with God. And God's Word comes to you this morning with a very solemn and a rather terrible message. It says this, 'The word of the LORD is against you.'

1. The Simple Statement of a Terrible Truth
If you are not a believer in Christ, God says that his word is against you. If you are unconverted almost every syllable of God's Holy Word is against you from the opening book of Genesis in the Old Testament to the closing book of Revelation in the New Testament. If you are unconverted there is not one word and not one promise in this Book from which you can take any real comfort. The word of the Lord – the only revelation of God to men – that revelation given from heaven and finalised and culminating in the revelation of God given in Christ his own Son – all that is against you if you are unconverted.

Let me illustrate some ways in which this simple but terrible truth is a fact. The word of the Lord is against you if you are unconverted because the Bible states very plainly that all men

Preached 26 February, 1978

must be converted in order to be saved. If you are unconverted you are an unsaved person. I know that as I speak many other thoughts are rushing into your mind. You know of other people who are much worse than you are. I grant you that. You know of hypocrites in the church of Christ. I grant you that too. I grant you many things, but, my friend, I point you back to this one truth: if you are unconverted, then every word of this Bible and every word of the Lord is against you, because the word of the Lord says that except people become converted they shall perish. I'm not asking you to measure yourself against others. I'm not asking you to measure yourself against any Christian. I'm asking you to face up to the fact that God's own word is against you if you are unconverted.

There's a doctrine spread all through the Scriptures called the doctrine of *regeneration*. Every syllable gathered to systematise that doctrine is against you and your condition if you are unconverted. The doctrine of regeneration is explained in many ways in the Bible. For example, the Lord Jesus taught the necessity of regeneration very strongly when he said: 'Except a man be born again, he cannot see the kingdom of God' (John 3:3). Are you born again? I'm not asking you what you think you believe or your record with regard to God or church attendance or anything else in the past. I'm asking you, What is the truth of the witness of God's Spirit to your mind and to your heart this morning?'

Then there is the Old Testament teaching on regeneration. The demand of God upon Israel was this: 'Make you a new heart and renew a right spirit within you' (Ezek. 18:31). Don't start getting right with God by putting right things on the outside of your life, but start where everything starts, at the centre and heart of your life. The demand God clearly laid on his Old Testament church was the same as the demand of Jesus, and that demand is impossible for humans. It is a work of God. Again I ask you, in terms of the Old Testament, do you know that God's Spirit has worked in your life and given you a new heart? The entire teaching of the Bible about regeneration is against you today if you are unconverted.

There is another doctrine which we find all through the Bible and it too is against you if you are unconverted –the great doctrine of the *atonement of Christ*. This doctrine tells us that Jesus

Christ, who is the Son of God, went as the God-man to the cross to be the substitute of sinners, that he shed his blood in order that our sins would be cleansed and pardoned and taken away. Why did all that happen? It happened in order that whosoever believed in Jesus would be saved.

The very fact that the Son of God should taste death, the very fact that God has said that without the shedding of blood there would be no remission, no revoking, of sins, that fact is against you. Every word that the Bible says about the death of Christ and the achievement of his atonement, every single syllable that God says in his Book about what the death of Christ was and means and is, all that is against you today if you are unconverted. If you are unconverted you have no part in this atonement. Go in your mind and heart to that place called Calvary. My friend, if you do so you'll find that what God has done there condemns your unconverted state.

The blood of Jesus Christ, says John, cleanses us from all sin (1 John 1:7). And there is nothing else spoken of in the whole Bible as being able to cleanse from sin, but this – the blood of Christ. In the epistle to the Hebrews the writer says that nothing else can cleanse the conscience and purge it from dead works (Heb. 9:13, 14). Nothing else can speak peace to the heart when the heart knows its own sin. The blood of bulls and of goats and the ashes of an heifer, they could cleanse ceremonially, but they could not cleanse the heart or remove the feeling and awareness of guilt. But the blood of Christ can. And my friend, if you don't need to be converted and cleansed by that blood, why was that blood ever shed?

Not only the doctrine of regeneration, but the whole doctrine of atonement is against you if you're not converted.

And there's another doctrine that is against you. Why did the Father give his Son? One very simple answer which the Bible gives us is this, that 'whosoever believeth on him should not perish but have everlasting life' (John 3:16). I know there are other factors involved, but here is a very clear statement. I know that matters such as predestination and election and the secret decree of God and the mystery of God's ordaining whatsoever comes to pass rise to your mind because the Bible faces you with them. But the Bible also faces you with this fact that God so loved the world that he gave his only begotten Son. What God has done is a testimony from him today against your unconverted state. The word of the Lord is against you.

Think of the doctrine of *salvation by faith in Christ alone* – salvation by no other way. Even the Christian has to keep returning to this basic doctrine. We are not justified by works of righteousness. Works of righteousness are demanded of us, but how far short we fall when we try to fulfil these demands. Our works of righteousness condemn those of us who are Christians. Every time we are on our knees before God our works of righteousness condemn us just as forcibly as do our sins. To find peace we must go back always to the fact that we are justified solely by faith in the Lord Jesus Christ. See how important faith is: 'He that believeth on the Son hath everlasting life' (John 3:36). If you believe on the Son you *have* everlasting life and all hell and all heaven won't take it from you. That is what faith is all about.

But in that same passage in John we read these words: 'He that believeth not the Son, shall not see life; the wrath of God abideth on him' (John 3:36). Do you understand the doctrine of *eternal punishment*. How deeply and how terribly that doctrine is against you today if you are unconverted. I know that we live in a day when men have attempted to take away the rough, cutting, blighting edge of this truth. Recently I visited two people who have not attended church since I came here as minister. They talked of sermons they heard from Free Church ministers in the past. One of them said how much she had liked to hear sermons about hell, but then commented that people know better than that today. Do they? If they know better, they know better than the truth of the word of God. The very thought of eternal punishment is hard for both the hearer and for the preacher, but it is God's truth and we dare not tone it down.

Jesus said one of the most terrible things in the entire Bible about what hell is: 'where their worm dieth not and the fire is not quenched' (Mark 9:44). Even if that is pictorial language – what a picture. Even if the worm is the worm of conscience and the fire is the fire of guilt, to have a conscience seared for all eternity – what a future. It was Jesus who spoke of hell as the place of weeping and wailing and gnashing of teeth (e.g., Matt. 8:12). The doctrine is not the invention of past preachers. It is the teaching of the

Lord Jesus Christ, the eternal Son of God. If you are unconverted
how terribly the word of God is against you. It was Jesus who
called a lost eternity 'the place of outer darkness' (Matt. 22:13).
The apostle Paul called it the place of everlasting destruction (2
Thess. 1:9) where a process of disintegration of personality that
will never stop is initiated and continues. The whole of the Bible's teaching on eternal punishment is against you today if your
faith is not in Christ.

A Fact Which Must Be Faced

If the word of the Lord is against you it is no use hiding from that
fact. Face it in your own experience. How can you can tell that
the word of God is against you? Because you are against the word
of the Lord. Take the teaching about eternal punishment that I
was speaking of? Did your heart rebel as you listened? The word
of the Lord is against you because you are against the word of the
Lord.

The word of the Lord is also against you because you spend so
little time with it. How much time do your spend reading your
Bible? This is the only book that is able to make you wise unto
salvation and you are neglecting to read it. Why? Is it because
there are things in it that you do not like and because it convicts
you of your sin? Is it against things that are going on in your heart
and in your life? Of course it is, and it is against these things
because these things are going to drag you down to hell.

What about prayer? How often have you prayed in the past
week? How often does God hear your voice? How often do you
pray to be made new in Christ and to be separated from sin to
holiness, to be made fit to meet with death and to be made fit for
heaven?

Christ came preaching repentance. Do you know anything
about that in your life? Are you turning from sin and walking in a
new direction?

What about good works? What have you done to show others
that you are a follower of Jesus?

If the word of the Lord is against you, it means that the Lord
himself is against you. The word is only the reflection of what the
Lord is. If we are not trusting in Christ then fundamentally we are
against God. If God is against us we cannot prosper.

I cannot leave you there. Even if the word of the Lord is against you, then let that very fact drive you to trust in nothing but in Christ and him crucified. If you trust in Christ and him crucified you shall be saved to the uttermost. Then, instead of being against you, God will be for you. If God be for you then who can be against you? None. If God be for us then we can say, 'All is well – all is well with my soul.' When we can say that, we have said it all.

10

Consider Christ

'For consider him that endured such contradiction
of sinners against himself, lest ye be wearied
and faint in your minds' (Hebrews 12:3).

The apostle here is writing to those who were to endure hardship
and trials of affliction. He is writing about endurance in the prospect of trial and testing. In the context of this teaching he is warning about the terrible danger of apostasy, of walking with Christ
no more. And there is only one way for anyone who has professed Christ to know that he or she is not an apostate. It is that he
or she is presently running with patience the race that is set before
them, looking unto Jesus.

How do we know that the faith we have is not a temporary
faith? We know because we are still stepping towards the mark
for the prize of the high calling of God in Christ Jesus. And that is
the only standard by which we can know that our faith is that
undying principle of life in the soul which is the result of the
work of God's Holy Spirit.

This passage is part of a whole exhortation that begins in 10:19.
The exhortation is aimed at warning the Hebrew believers about
the dangers of going back from Christ. We can grow cold and
hard for years at a time unless God by his Spirit breathes upon us
continually and keeps us alive. We have to look at ourselves and
confess that there seems to be a sad lack in the totality of our
commitment to Christ and to the gospel and to the things of God.

To encourage us in our obedience and in our living we are to
focus our eyes on Jesus. We have to look not just to the crucified
Jesus, but to the enthroned Jesus. We have to count all things but
loss that we may win him and be made like him. Paul asks us to
pause as we look at Jesus and to 'consider him'.

The original word behind the word 'consider' implies 'con-

sider him as set in comparison with yourselves, reflect upon him
and look at the contrast between him and you. Look at the contrast between what he was asked to do and what you are being
asked to do.' For a little while forget about yourself – and all the
anxieties and trials and tribulations that bother you and hold you
back like chains – and consider him.

There is a race set before us and Jesus himself is the end of
that race. The culminating point of all our Christian trusting and
striving is, as the apostle John says, 'that we may be like him
when we shall see him as he is' (1 John 3:2). The ultimate of
redemption is that God will have a people with whom he can live.
Are you the kind of person with whom God can live? You and I,
in Christ, are being prepared to dwell with 'everlasting burnings'
(Isa. 33:14), with the holiness that sears and the righteousness
that is as clear as a crystal. No wonder Paul asks us to consider
him who has made all this possible.

Consider him all through what have been called 'the years of
obscurity'. For almost thirty years Jesus was giving daily, moment by moment, obedience to the will of God, and he was doing
it in a hidden way, to all appearances an ordinary man. Consider
twenty eight or twenty nine years of absolute humble submis-
siveness to the will of the Father, and let that consideration encourage you to endure.

Consider him too through his public ministry. Yes, his ministry was full of clash and conflict and he had to endure, but with
what a wonderful loving spirit of obedience, grace and kindness.
And you and I have to be like him.

Consider the kind of person he was. You never read of him
saying an unkind word. With what love and goodness he speaks
to sinners like us.

Consider his life of commitment. He committed himself to
God and to man, and he did it fully and absolutely. That is what
he asks you and me to do too, to commit ourselves firstly to God.

Consider him who endured such contradiction of sinners
against himself. What was that contradiction of sinners? It was
total opposition moving against Jesus Christ. The totality of that
opposition ended in his death. If you are to be totally committed
to God and totally committed for men, it will lead to only one
thing – the crucifixion of yourself. Sin is a contradiction of all

that God is. And the very fact of Jesus being who he was meant that he was going to meet contradictions all the time. But he endured it – he was patiently running the race that was set before him, he was enduring and persevering.

Contrast yourself with him. He had to undergo and endure the penalty of our sin, which means he had to undergo something we can never undergo. It takes away a worry and a dread from my heart and life. He is my perfect substitute. The contradiction he endured is the contradiction I find in my own heart, the contradiction of all the forces of evil which are around me and in me. It is my contradiction he endured. Consider him against your failure and your sin and your insufficiency.

Consider him in contrast to your difficulties: he was left without a friend in the world and he ultimately came into the place of the curse where he knew God's wrath, something you will never know. God's wrath never comes out against the Christian believer. The apostle goes on to show that chastisement and affliction are ours because we are children, not because we're not (Heb. 12:5-8). No stroke comes from God but that which is for our profit. Why? Because Jesus bore our sin.

Consider his full-hearted consecration. There was absolutely nothing held back. God was in all his considerations and all his plans and all his doings.

11

Come and Drink

If any man thirst, let him come unto me, and drink
(John 7:37).

The officers of the High Priest were after Jesus. Jesus knew, even as he spoke these words, that there were men present who had been sent to capture him and take him to a place of death and punishment. But he did not allow their presence to stop him from telling the good news of the gospel. Nothing would prevent him from bringing the gospel message to needy people.

Not long ago I was reading about one of the Covenanting ministers of Scotland who while preaching out on the moors was apprehended by a trooper. The soldier said to him, 'Sir, if you don't stop preaching I'll shoot you where you stand.' The old minister turned to him and said, 'Soldier, just you do your duty, I'm doing mine.' The most precious thing in life to him was the gospel of salvation in Christ. And supremely this was true of Jesus himself. He loved not his life unto death, but he loved us and was willing to lay his life down for us.

Jesus knew that, until the time appointed him of the Father, death could not hold him. In the middle of Jerusalem, crowded by people who had come for the Feast of Tabernacles, Jesus was preaching and teaching. It was a memorial feast observed every year to remind Israel of how God led their forefathers through the wilderness, a feast that told them that as God's people they were sojourners and pilgrims and strangers travelling to the Promised Land.

On each day of the feast a very interesting ceremony took place, a ceremony that pointed back to the occasion when the people were dying of thirst and God had smitten the rock and provided water for them. Every day at a certain hour the priests came out of the temple and went down a rocky track to the Pool of Siloam. They went in a formal procession followed by crowds of people.

The priests dipped golden vessels into the pool and carried them back up the track, in through the courtyard of the temple and up to the altar where they ceremonially poured out the water. As they poured it the people sang, 'With joy we shall draw water out of the wells of salvation.' This ceremony spoke to the people of how God had provided for their need in the desert. It spoke of a thirst that had been quenched by God.

On the last day – the great day of the feast – at the moment when the priests were pouring the water, Jesus stood up and said, 'If any man thirst, let him come unto me, and drink.' Anyone who comes to Jesus will have his life transformed and will become like waters in a dry land – useful and fruitful and blessed.

Jesus took something which was already precious in a spiritual sense to the people and he used it in an illustrative, allegorical way to point to the deeper spiritual truth that he himself is. He is saying that *he* is the one who is represented in this ceremony, that *he* is the rock out of which spiritual water comes.

The sermon Jesus preached
Jesus makes us think of our need. Thirst is one of the most pressing physical needs of human beings, an intense physical need. Not many of us know what real thirst is. I have a cousin who was on a boat that was torpedoed in the Pacific in 1940. For many days they clung to upturned lifeboats, but they lost all the food and all the water that had been in the boats. One of the most terrible things about the whole experience for my cousin was watching his companions go out of their minds with thirst. Without food man can live for days but he cannot survive long without water. Not one of the men from the boat had to ask what was wrong, each knew that he was dying from the lack of water – and many did die before they were picked up. My cousin returned to Scotland emaciated because of the experience he had undergone.

In Scripture we read of Jesus pointing out in the story of the rich man and Lazarus what a lost eternity would be like. 'Father Abraham, have mercy on me, and send Lazarus, that he may dip the tip of his finger in water, and cool my tongue; for I am tormented in this flame' (Luke 16:24) – the flame of a spiritual thirst that would never be satisfied. It was a flame that consumed and yet did not destroy. One drop of water – Jesus picked up on the most pressing physical need and the intense physical sense of deprivation and pain to teach deep spiritual truth.

What is Jesus talking about? He is talking about a thirst of soul. If any one has been made conscious of a deep, pressing, spiritual need then he is to come to Jesus. Down through history multitudes have been made conscious of a spiritual thirst and have experienced it with every fibre of their being.

Augustine plunged into all that this world could offer him as a young man in order to satisfy a yearning of soul that he felt but could not define. All turned to ashes in his mouth as it always eventually does. It was out of that experience that Augustine eventually said, 'Lord, our hearts are restless until they find rest in thee.' It was out of that experience of deep-felt spiritual need that Augustine would say that each person has a heart which has the shape of God in it, a space which only God himself can meet. Augustine pressed on until he found peace through Christ.

What sort of things do you thirst for? Perhaps you are thirsting for peace between yourself and God – to be able to live your days quietly in the peace and in the stillness of his presence. If we come to Jesus, he will give us peace. He is our peace for he bore our sins in his own body on the tree.

Do you long to be converted? Do you long to have the assurance that you are a Christian? Do you long to know that God by the Holy Spirit has done a real work in your heart? That is a thirst that comes from the Holy Spirit himself. If you have ever longed for conversion that longing and desire is a work of God within you. Where can we find assurance? We can find it only from Jesus. He will make us new men and new women.

This sermon is directed to 'any man' to any person regardless of who they are. If you thirst, come. Only one qualification is necessary – a sense of need and a longing for Christ.

The supply offered

Jesus is saying to us that whatever our need he is able to supply it. What a claim! If we didn't know that this man who is talking is God, we would say this is nonsense. One man standing over against the need of all men.

There is a grand simplicity in his words and a wonderful audacity. He is the only preacher who has ever said, 'Come to me.'

All other preachers said, 'Go to God.' His words are a claim of full deity. It is the claim of one who was conscious of possessing divine riches with which he could enrich the lives of men and women. He was aware that he possessed divine power by which he could save us.

12

The Touch of Jesus

Jesus, moved with compassion, put forth
his hand, and touched him (Mark 1:41).

All the Gospels refer to the touch of Jesus. The fact that they all mention this simple but lovely gesture should bring home to us some wonderful truths about our Lord Jesus Christ. There is something beautiful in the touch of someone who loves you and can sympathise with you. There is something very human in such a touch and Jesus Christ, who is very God of very God, was very much a real man. One of the wonders of the gospel is that we are redeemed and saved by one who is like us in all things but one – he is without sin. He is man as man should be. He is very human.

A heresy which arose in the early church made Jesus only divine – and the church is not rid of it yet. We must believe in the humanity of Christ. Mark emphasises his humanity without in any way detracting from his deity. He also lays far more emphasis on the deeds of Jesus than he does on his words. The theme of the Gospel of Mark is, 'he went about doing good.'

Christ is not afraid to let himself be seen as a man – to show friendship and sympathy to people in trouble. We have as our Saviour one who can give us the sympathy of a human heart, who understands our sadnesses and our difficulties. The Lord Jesus Christ is not one who 'cannot be touched with a feeling of our infirmities'. He was at times moved to the point of tears. The One who was moved to touch an outcast leper is the same One who is now on Heaven's throne.

In Scripture, leprosy is often used as a symbol of sin. How we should thank God that Christ was not afraid to touch that leprosy either! He took that leprosy into his own body when he bore our sins. He took our diseases to himself for our healing.

How close Christ comes to us in his tenderness. He is nearer

Preached 2 July 1978

than our very breathing and yet because we are sinners how far
we are from God.

While we learn a great deal about the humanity of Christ from
this event we also learn a lot about his deity. We learn about the
God who became Jesus in order that we might be saved. God in
the person of his Son touches the leper. God in the person of his
Son is moved with compassion.

Sometimes Jesus speaks only a word and someone is healed at
a distance, sometimes he touches deaf ears, sometimes he calls
out – every one is treated as an individual, as a unique human
being. Underneath every miracle of healing is Jesus' own will to
heal, the divine will to overcome and to destroy the works of the
devil in disease and in illness.

As God he touches this man and brings healing. We have here
a wonderful illustration of a principle by which God normally
works. God uses means (and the means he uses here is the human
touch of Jesus). Similarly, God uses the preaching of the gospel
for the healing of sick souls – preaching that is the wisdom of
God.

Because of the incarnation and death of Christ, God who is
eternal and unchangeable can touch us and does touch us at the
level of our human need. And when God touches a life there is
hope.

What a change he wrought in this man, one who was ceremonially, religiously and spiritually unclean. To touch such a one
would be the last thing any Jew would want to do.

Here was a man who for years had never known the
understanding or the sympathy or the affection of another human
being. For years he had to ensure that no-one would touch him.
His cry, 'Unclean, unclean' would keep everyone away from him.
If he was married he would not be allowed to hold his wife's
hand. If he had children they would not be able to take his hand
and say, 'Let's go for a walk, Daddy.' If any touched him they
themselves would become ceremonially unclean and also might
contract the disease. How that man must have felt! Only one person
could touch him according to the law of the Old Testament – the
High Priest. And he could touch him only when he had been healed.
The touch of the priest would pronounce that he was clean.

Look at this event now from the point of view of the Lord

Jesus. He is the great High Priest of God's house. Here he is acting in his office as High Priest as he reaches out and touches the
leper before pronouncing him clean. Instead of Jesus suffering
defilement and corruption from the touch, he destroys the corruption in the leper. Jesus himself does not become impure but he
imparts purity and healing. Similarly, our guilt and pollution of
sin are taken away the moment we are touched by this High Priest.

Jesus took hold of this man in all his need and transformed
him. Now that he had been touched by Jesus he could reach out
and touch others. Only those who have been touched by Christ
can really touch others for God. Only when we ourselves have
been cleansed can we speak of the gospel to others. Only when
we know what it is to be born again can we talk to others of the
new birth.

A leper touched, changed, cleansed. This man had faith to
believe that Jesus could heal – that Jesus would heal. Before Jesus touched this man physically he had touched him with his divine power – from that touch sprang his faith. He learned that
Jesus could heal him. Jesus would have no glory if he was not
willing and able to save people like us. Therein lies his glory –
that he will save us to the very uttermost.

If you are still not a Christian, learn that Jesus can make you
clean. The moment you ask him, Jesus will cleanse you. He will
change and transform you by his touch on your life.

13

Seeing and Believing

'And immediately he received his sight,
and followed Jesus in the way' (Mark 10:52).

It is a law both in natural and spiritual things that every effect
must have a sufficient cause, and here Mark links these two things
together in precisely that relationship. The fact that Bartimaeus
followed Jesus in the way owed itself to one thing only – to the
miracle of his being able to see.

A blind man sitting outside Jericho heard the noise of the
passing people and asked what was happening. Evidently he had
heard of Jesus for when he was told that Jesus was passing by
nothing, absolutely nothing would stop him from making contact
with Jesus and seeking blessing from him. Although it was first
of all physical healing that the Saviour brought to Bartimaeus, we
believe there was also spiritual healing.

The great thing about Christianity is that it centres in the personal experience of the grace of God. Christianity is not first and
foremost a belief in a set of doctrines, though that is involved, but
it is a personal contact with and a personal experience of the grace
available to sinners in Jesus Christ, in the amazing mercy of God.

I want to make some preliminary remarks before I come to
look at the text more directly. It was because Bartimaeus believed
in Jesus as the Messiah promised in the Old Testament and because he confessed him as the Son of David that Jesus stopped
and spoke with Bartimaeus. Jesus laid a great stress on faith –
that's the immediate link into our text – 'Thy faith hath saved
thee.' How invariably Jesus, in his personal dealings with people
of all kinds, sought and drew out and honoured their faith. Again
and again, Jesus honours faith. The faith we must exercise in Jesus is a simple trust and committal of ourselves to him as our only
Saviour. It is not merely an intellectual acceptance of historical
truths about Jesus, although that is involved. The heart as well as
the head was involved in the cry of Bartimaeus.

Preached 12 May 1991

Admire the way Mark arranges his gospel – he picks out the significant details and gives them a living touch. The devout people of Israel knew that when the Messiah came he would fulfil the prophetic utterances that had been made about him. One of these is from Isaiah 35:5: 'Then shall the eyes of the blind be opened.'

Bartimaeus perhaps had that on his mind as he called out, 'Thou Son of David.' He uttered a particularly Messianic term which had been used for about a hundred years or more before this. What a remarkably fitting introduction this is to the entry of Jesus into Jerusalem, focusing on him entering as the Son of David. Mark's purpose is to highlight the truth that the Son of David is not merely David's offspring, but David's Lord, a truth that Jesus himself emphasised. It's a question that he put to the Pharisees, recorded in Matthew 22:43: 'How then does David by the inspiration of the Spirit call him Lord?' They couldn't answer it.

Mark introduces the triumphal entry into Jerusalem by this miracle. His emphasis is directed towards the truth that Jesus is the unique and eternal Son of God. There is none other like Jesus.

'He followed Jesus in the way' is a marvellously accurate and descriptive expression of what the Christian life is. We can define what a Christian is in a variety of ways. For example, Paul says they are 'saints', that is, those who have been separated by the work of God's Spirit to faith in Jesus and service of Jesus. Jesus himself repeatedly used the simple word 'follow' to indicate the demands of God upon us.

Why did he follow Jesus? Because of what had happened to him he wanted to walk with Jesus. He wanted to know Jesus better and the most natural thing in the world for him was to follow Jesus. That is what makes a Christian. The impulse, the constraint, the channelling of everything we are and everything we ever hope to be into the marvellous privilege of following the Lord Jesus Christ. In a sense, it's all summed up in the words of a hymn:

> O for a closer walk with God,
> A calm and heavenly frame;
> A light to shine upon the road
> That leads me to the Lamb.

Surely that's the desire that was burning in the heart of Bartimaeus.

I want to look at five things.

1. Devotion exhibited

For every life that has been touched, transformed and brought into the light of God, this is the expression that is natural to it – to follow Jesus. The very first face that Bartimaeus looked into was the face of Jesus. And there's a sense in which that is true spiritually, no matter how our conversion takes place. The soul comes to life and the life finds expression in looking away to Jesus, and Jesus becomes all-in-all for us. Paul puts it like this: 'For God, who commanded the light to shine out of darkness, hath shined *in* our hearts, to give the light of the knowledge of the glory of God in the face of Jesus Christ' (2 Cor. 4:6). And Bartimaeus could never be the same man again because he had been given eyes to look into the face of the Christ of God.

2. Inclination demonstrated

His whole mind and heart were inclined to follow Jesus. He demonstrated that inclination, he made his Christian faith visible. How? By the direction in which he walked – he followed Jesus.

Love is intangible and yet the love of will, mind, heart, intellect – the love of a person for Jesus Christ, can be shown in a real, living, historical experience. To show our love we don't have to be soppy or sloppy. To show our love we obey the commandments of God and we follow Jesus.

Bartimaeus made his love for Christ felt and visible. Do your friends, neighbours, colleagues, family know that you love the Lord Jesus Christ? If they don't, what is wrong? Are you showing your love and faith in Christ so that other people can see it? It's easy to say that you are a church member and therefore everyone must know that you are a Christian. They won't. Can you echo the words of the paraphrase:

> I'm not ashamed to own my Lord,
> or to defend his cause;
> Maintain the glory of his Cross
> and honour all his laws?

3. The guidance experienced

As soon as he began to put his footsteps into the footsteps of Jesus he came under the control of the mind of Jesus. He was no longer in complete control of himself as he followed Jesus for his

Saviour was directing his pathway. Jesus was on earth with a mission and he was marching to fulfil that mission – and Bartimaeus became part of that mission. The moment we begin to follow Jesus we put ourselves under the control of the One who has loved and healed us. To know the rule, the direction and the guidance of the Lord Jesus Christ through the infallible Word of God relieves our minds of a great deal of anxiety. Let Jesus mark out your way for you and all you have to do is to follow him.

4. The problems that Bartimaeus encountered

For the first time he could see and his difficulties naturally arose from this. He would now be able to see the person who guided him every day to the place where he begged for a living. He would be able to see friends that he had previously known only by the sounds of their voices. Then there was the sky and the sun and the world around him and the mountains rising steeply. Jerusalem could be seen from miles away – the city of God, high on a hill. There must have been a thousand and one things that he could look at and examine. Yet, he had eyes for Jesus alone.

For the Christian there are many things that would pressurise us and keep us from following Jesus. There are lawful, natural, understandable things that we want to do. Bartimaeus had never walked in a crowd before and there were many distractions but he kept following Jesus. For us, there is the blessing of fellowship with other Christians that can sometimes crowd out the blessing of fellowship with Jesus himself. We can become content with a second-hand type of communion with Christ through fellowship with others. Such fellowship should never take the place of personal prayer and communion with God. When does a Christian begin to go wrong? It starts when too many things or too many people hide the Lord Jesus from our view.

The closer Bartimaeus followed Jesus, the more firmly he fixed his eyes upon Jesus, the easier it would be.

5. The destination that Bartimaeus reached

The immediate destination was Jerusalem. This man had had his footsteps set in to the footsteps of Jesus by the amazing, saving grace of God. He began to walk a pathway that led him to wonderful experiences.

He was there when Zaccheus the tax-gatherer was converted. There are few joys so great as the news of the conversion of a fellow-sinner. Are you living in the place where God is likely to use you in the conversion of others? If not, why not?

He must have heard many wonderful things from Jesus, and his faith must have been severely tested when the singing and the praising turned to cursing and trial and the calling for crucifixion. At first it would be difficult for him to believe it was all happening. How would he have felt when they took Jesus and led him away? Until you are down there with all your sin and all your need – it is only then that the horror and the hellishness of the crucifixion begins to fit in with the mind and the purpose of a good God, of a saviour God. It is only then that the disharmony of the Cross and the suffering of a Saviour make any sense in a world that is ruled by a wise and a good God. From there we can see the guilt of our own sin against the greatness and the goodness and the holiness of God. The guilt is enormous. Only the enormity and the wickedness of our own personal sin can explain the enormity and the wickedness that crucified the Son of God. The love of God in Christ Jesus is something that can only be experienced by those who trust him.

> Jesus, my Lord, I know his name.
> His name is all my boast.
> Nor will he put my soul to shame,
> Nor let my hope be lost.
>
> I know that safe with him remains,
> Protected by his power
> What I've committed to his trust
> Till the decisive hour.
>
> Then will he own his servant's name
> Before his Father's face.
> And in the new Jerusalem
> Appoint my soul a place.

Bartimaeus reached Jerusalem. There he saw the one sacrifice for sin that ensured his place in the New Jerusalem. The moment that Jesus passed by was a moment of destiny.

14

A Crown of Thorns

'When they had platted a crown of thorns, they put it
upon his head, and a reed in his right hand: and they
bowed the knee before him, and mocked him, saying,
Hail, King of the Jews!' (Matthew 27: 29).

Calvary is a strangely attractive place. It is attractive to both the
Christian and to the non-Christian. I remember, in my own unconverted days, how a sermon on Calvary would hold my attention as no other sermon would do. I used to wonder what the
whole theme was about. Jesus, such a good man, and yet men,
men like ourselves, took this good man Jesus and they led him
outside the city of Jerusalem and there crucified him. What was it
all about? I pray that if you do not yet know Jesus as your Saviour
that as we come to Calvary again, Calvary will leave a question-
mark in your heart and you will have to ask, 'What is it all about?'

Calvary brings us near to the heart of what Jesus was doing –
dying for our sins, taking our place before the majesty of the God
who is righteous and holy and of purer eyes than to behold iniquity. Why did the Lord Jesus go through with the crowning insult
described in the text? He was already wounded and bruised from
scourging and almost the only place that had not known pain was
his head. Why was he made to suffer this final indignity? This
crown would have caused him physical suffering. It must also
have caused him terrible spiritual suffering considering who he
was. That the Jews and the Roman soldiers should mock his kingship in such a cruelly tangible way – a crown for the King of the
Jews – and should force it on his head must have caused him
great anguish of mind and body and soul.

A symbol of all his suffering
Jesus had already suffered greatly. He had been led from one great
man to another. He had been roughly and brutally handled all
through the night. He had been stripped and scourged and flayed

on his back on the orders of Pilate. Now the soldiers are ready to take him away and to fulfil the cry of all the people to crucify him. Before they do that, they weave this crown and place it on his head – a symbol of all his suffering and of the fact that his greatest suffering is not physical pain. His outward sufferings were terrible. But we believe that these outward sufferings were nothing compared to the suffering of his sinless soul. It was John Owen who expressed this so beautifully when he said, 'The sufferings of his soul were the soul of his suffering.'

Think for a moment of who was being subjected to the sort of treatment that this text summarises. He was the one of whom John the Apostle wrote: 'All things were made by him; and without him was not any thing made that was made. In him was life; and the life was the light of men' (John 1:3, 4).

He was the one who from all eternity was with God and was God and had fellowship with God, face to face. He was the one who was 'the upholder of all things by the word of his power' (Heb. 1:3). He was the one who was upholding the very people who were subjecting him to suffering and to indignity and mockery. If this is true, and we believe with all our minds that it is true, what a sharpness there must be in his suffering. The creatures he has made in his own image, that he had made to fellowship with, that strangely he had loved from all eternity, of whom he had said prophetically, 'My delights were with the sons of men' (Prov. 8:31) – they rejected him. The rejection comes fully to light here when they make him suffer the great indignity of the crown of thorns.

A symbol of his substitution

In Genesis 3:18 God said to Adam that because he had listened to his wife and had eaten of the tree which had been forbidden to them the ground would be cursed and thorns and thistles would grow – symbols of God's curse on disobedience. The same truth is set out in Hebrews 6:8: 'that which beareth thorns and briers is rejected, and is nigh unto cursing; whose end is to be burned.'

What is happening when men take Jesus and weave a crown of thorns and place it on his head? Something is happening of which they are not aware. Something of which these soldiers have never dreamed is taking place in this simple, cruel transaction –

something that will be spoken of as long as the gospel is preached. They are taking the symbol of man's sin and disobedience and they are weaving it into a crown. Who will they crown as the chief of sinners? Who will they crown as the one who will stand in the ultimate place of God's curse? They take the one who is holy and harmless and undefiled and they take this symbol of sin and they crown him. Why? Because this is why he came. This is why he is there at all.

He is taking delight in doing the will of his Father. He is coming into the place of the shadow. He is coming under the shadow that came into God's universe when created intelligence turned round and attempted to wrest God from his throne. He is coming under the shadow of that mystery of iniquity. He is coming into the place where evil is crowned and holds sway. He is coming in there as the one appointed so to do by God himself.

Who is he when he comes under the shadow? Who is he when he stands under the cross with a crown of thorns on his head? He is the man who takes your place before God. He is wearing the crown that you should have worn throughout eternity. That crown is a symbol of what happens when a holy God comes into contact with sin. When his curse comes out it bears thorns. What a crown there must be for those who go into eternity without Jesus.

What is the spiritual reality of which this speaks? What will it be like for the soul to stand in the place of the utmost curse upon sin – to bring forth, not fruit, but briars and thorns in its own living spiritual experience? We don't know, but Christ knew and went through the depths of pain for us. He knew it personally.

That was just the outward crown that men made. But there was another hand at work. There was the hand of God the Father, the representative of triune deity, the representative of a Godhead that is holy and just and who had said, 'The soul that sinneth, it must die.' That hand wove another crown that can't be seen and laid it on the man Christ Jesus. It is the crown of God's eternal curse on the sins of all his people. Jesus stood there and bore the wrath of God. I don't know what that is, nor do you. He bore the wrath of God although he did no sin. What sort of twisted, awful thing must sin be when it does such a thing in one who is a substitute for others. What an awful thing sin must be if it can do this to the man who is God's fellow, if it can bring him into the suffering and the darkness and the death of Calvary. The crown of thorns is a symbol of his substitution, of his standing there for us, crowned with the symbol of God's curse.

He was a king, God's king and the king of God's people – and as king he was bearing God's wrath for them. He was never more of a king than he was then. He is now on a throne – the throne of God and of the Lamb. Because he suffered on the Cross, crowned as our substitute and representative, there is a place in the universe of God where these beautiful words stand written, 'There shall be no more curse' (Rev. 22:3).

What was due to your sin? What was due to my sin? What was due to us became his, and he took the curse into his own infinite and eternal being and he bore it away.

A symbol of his salvation

He's crowned in mockery, as a taunt. In this action we can see the distortion that sin brings into the mind of man. It is described to the smallest detail so that we will be able to appreciate the wonder of his saving love to us. When Paul wrote, 'the Son of God, who loved me, and gave himself for me' (Gal. 2:20), he knew that Christ loved him because he had given himself for him. How do I know tonight that Jesus loves me? It is because I can go to the place called Calvary. There I see what he bore for me and what I see tells me of the reality and of the strength and of the power of his love. That love brought him to the place of suffering. He endured it because of his love for you and for me. Oh, the love of the Lord Jesus to people like us! How do we react to it?

> Oh, the love that drew salvation's plan,
> Oh, the grace that brought it down to man.
> Oh, the mighty gulf that God did span,
> At Calvary.

What do you see in his crown of thorns? You see one great sign of his kingly love to your soul. How Jesus loved you! Words can't express that love, only the heart can experience it. I hope that you know it for yourself. The love that went as far as that is a love you can trust. Through any shadow or any darkness, through the melting of the universe itself, you could trust the love that stood there.

As Christ felt the thorns pierce his head he, who had suffered so much already, was willing to suffer this further indignity. He was willing to have the kingship of his divine nature mocked for your sake and for mine.

We would never have asked him to stoop so low, would we? Would we have asked that the Son of God, whose glory is the same as the glory of the Father, whose Godship and Godhead is as real as that of God the Father, would bring his love as low as this? Would we have believed that he would have brought his love from heaven's throne to the place where he would allow the scum of the earth to crown him with thorns? We would never have asked him to go so far but his love had to go as far as that because that was as far as man's sin went – where they could take God and crown him with thorns. That is the essence of sin – to tear God from his throne. That same sin works in us in myriad ways. We refuse to give God his lordship over us. That essentially is the same sin. It is the sin that will shut God out from any corner of the heart and from any part of the life and which will look at Jesus and say, 'We will not have this man to rule over us.' In order that sin in our hearts should be unravelled and removed from its rule over us, Christ came all the way to Calvary – and he came in love.

When they had crowned him with thorns they bowed the knee and they mocked him. 'Hail, king!' They didn't know how truly they spoke even although they spoke in mockery. Christ indeed is king. Is he your king in truth and in love and in salvation? Or is he your king only in mockery and in refusal and in rejection of his claims? Only you can answer that question. May God help you to answer it honestly and may God open your heart to feel and to know the love that stooped so low, and to experience the great salvation that is symbolised in this event. What can you do with this Jesus who was crowned with thorns for you? You can take him as Christ and him crucified and make him king of your heart and of your life and of all your days.

15

'How can I...?'
(Acts 8:31).

This question was in response to another question. The eunuch from Ethiopia had been asked by Philip if he understood the passage he was reading from the prophecy of Isaiah.

Not one of us needs to go outside our own experience in order to know the obduracy, the stubbornness and the wilfulness of the heart that is sinful and deceitful. Whether we are Christians or not we should know that the conversion of a soul poses great problems and difficulties. There was a difficulty facing God in providing for man's salvation because of God's own nature, because he was holy. That difficulty had to be overcome by giving his own Son and delivering him up for us all.

There are also difficulties in the nature of men and women. Their minds are darkened and hid from the glory of God. It does not take very long for someone witnessing to others of God's love to discover how difficult it is to win them for Christ. Every force outside of them, except one, is directed against their ever being saved. Every force within their heart, with the exception of none, is also in the most determined fashion directed against their salvation. The people of God are aware of these forces. They know from their own experience and from the teaching of the Bible that salvation is not something of easy access to the unenlightened, darkened heart that is ours by nature.

Although that is so we are not without hope. In reading and believing the Bible we cannot be without hope for the conversion of many people. Indeed, we cannot be without hope concerning the conversion of any person. The Bible forbids it. It does not permit us to say that for any person in this life conversion is an impossibility, no matter how self-righteous, no matter how religious or no matter how sinful and ungodly they may be.

The cry of the Ethiopian eunuch is the cry of many hearts,

Preached 7 May 1978

'How can we be saved?' If you are asking that question then understand that the obstacles are great but hope is still possible. There is one force working for the salvation of sinners. That force, when it is exerted on an individual, is irresistible. It is the force of God's saving power. There is not one Christian who would have been converted if it had not been for the gracious, merciful, saving power of God. This power was operating in the story of this Ethiopian. The cry of his inability was answered by the mighty grace of God.

Look at the ministry of God to this man in his need for salvation. That ministry came, first of all, through another man. It is strange that God can use men and women in this way, yet many of us thank God for those whom he used to bring us to blessing. Can we ever forget them?

Philip was one of the seven deacons who was appointed to serve tables, to look after the poor of the church at Jerusalem. They had been appointed in order to free the apostles and give them time and opportunity to devote themselves to prayer and to the ministry of the Word. This deacon became an evangelist. Through persecution God drives him from Jerusalem into Samaria. Many of the Samaritans had earlier become believers through the witness of the woman that Christ met at the well of Sychar (John 4:39-41). Now God had sent an evangelist back in among them. The people listened to the message with great attention and many were blessed. God was at work and many were healed and released from bondage. In the very midst of this work of revival, God put out his hand again and Philip was once more sent on his way. He was taken away to a desert and there he met this man from Ethiopia.

God also used an angel to minister to this man. Angels are ministering spirits, ministering to the heirs of salvation. They serve you, watch over your needs, are ready to attend you. There is joy in the presence of the angels when any one comes to faith in Christ. They were ready to minister to this man in his time of need.

In verse 29 we read that the Holy Spirit was there as well. He prompted Philip to go and join the Ethiopian in his chariot. It is wonderful that God uses other people and angels, but how much more wonderful it is that he sends forth the third person of the holy and glorious Trinity to minister to our salvation. God sends forth the Spirit of promise, the Spirit of power. It is the Spirit who brings the power of the grace of God to bear on the soul. It is he who makes the ministry of men effective. It is the Spirit who convicts of sin and brings to repentance. Just as he ministered to Philip and the Ethiopian so he will minister to you and to me.

One night when Spurgeon was preaching in the Metropolitan Tabernacle all the lights went out. Spurgeon had previously been in a similar situation in the Surrey Music Hall. On that occasion there had been great confusion and some people had died. Naturally he was afraid that there would again be panic on this occasion. He stopped preaching and he asked them all to sit still in their seats until the men attended to the fault in the gas supply. To hold their attention he began to speak from a verse of Scripture that had been on his mind all week. When the lights came back on he resumed his original sermon. Later on, when new members were being examined by the elders and deacons, Spurgeon discovered that the Holy Spirit had been at work that night when the lights went out. Three people had been converted – one through the word preached when the place was in darkness and one before and one after the break in the sermon.

How can you come? You cannot come until God sends his Spirit and his messengers to you and then the only question you will have is, 'Why did I not see it all before?'

Philip found the man reading the Scriptures and when he asked him if he understood what he was reading the man invited him to come up beside him in his chariot and explain the passage he was reading in the fifty-third chapter of Isaiah: 'He was led as a lamb to the slaughter and as a sheep before her shearers is dumb, so he openeth not his mouth.'

The prophet was speaking of the One who was to come in the future. Philip was able to tell the eunuch that the Messiah had come in the person of Jesus of Nazareth. As he spoke the Spirit opened this man's heart and mind and he believed. His profession was that he believed Jesus to be the Christ, the Son of God.

'How can I?' The eunuch believed and went on his way rejoicing. If you believe and put your trust in Christ to bring you out of your darkness, you too will go on your way rejoicing in Christ as your Saviour.

16

Clothed by God

'Unto Adam also and to his wife did the LORD God make coats of skins, and clothed them' (Genesis 3:21).

It is often said that the God of the Old Testament is not the God of the New Testament, that the God of the Old Testament is a fearful and terrible God. Such a dichotomy is completely false. The very first sight that we have of God as he visits this scene of rebellion and sin is, yes, a God whose natural reaction to sin is to curse it, to devote it to destruction, but we also see a God full of grace and ready to forgive and pardon. I suggest that we see a God who is no different from and no other than the God and Father of our Lord Jesus Christ.

In verse 15 we have the first gospel message. In the previous verse God has been speaking to the serpent who was the vehicle through which Satan worked. The curse at its real issue is directed to Satan. God is now going to put enmity between the serpent and the woman to whom he had seemed to be so friendly. There is to be enmity established between the seed of the serpent and the seed of the woman from which the Redeemer was to come. We believe that intimation of the Saviour's coming is found here in essence.

Verse 21 speaks of the clothing of the sinner by the God of grace. God has spoken to them of the reality and the effect of his curse upon them because of sin. One of the first subjective signs of the awareness of sin is seen here, the coming in of a sense of human guilt. The forbidden act has taken place. The implication of Satan's words to Adam and Eve was that God was denying them special knowledge and they believed his lie and fell for it. Satan still tempts humans that it will all be worthwhile if they do as he says. He promises them an experience and a pleasure that they would not otherwise know. Sadly, people still fall for his

Preached 28 January 1979

lies, but instead of an increase of knowledge and pleasure they are left with feelings of shame and guilt.

Adam and Eve, feeling exposed before God, try to cover their nakedness – the nakedness of a moral and spiritual guilt. They begin to make their own clothes. Why? Because of their sense of having sinned and that sense brought shame. For the first time they have a guilty conscience. Before this, their conscience had been 'void of offence'. But their attempt to clothe themselves is not successful. God seeks them out and faces them with their sin. Then he brings them the promise of a coming Saviour before he clothes them.

The price that their covering exacted

Their covering was coats of skins. Their covering by God was covering at the cost of life. Death had to enter into the world before they could be covered. The mystery of what death is had to be seen by man before he could be covered. Something entered into the world that was alien to it. Here was death, but it was death that provided a covering for the guilt and shame of man. Even as it does that, even as it holds out a promise to man that his moral guilt and his spiritual shame can be covered and taken away, it speaks to him of the cost of having his sin forgiven.

Isn't it wonderful that the very first fruit of death should have been an easing of the shame that man felt because of sin? Does that not tell us that grim as death is, at the very heart of it God has set a light? Even in this very act of God's mercy towards man a very solemn lesson was being learnt. Man was learning for the first time that the wages of sin is death. Have you learned that? He was learning a terrible lesson about the mercy of God; he was learning that God's mercy could flow out only when his justice was satisfied. God's mercy could flow out only on the basis of death. God had said that the 'soul that sins shall die'. This is no cheap mercy. God's mercy is as terrible as is his justice. God's mercy is costly and it can touch the sinner only because death takes place.

Even as they were being clothed they were being given a glimpse of what was in store for their own physical life. Although they had died spiritually the moment they had sinned – communion with God was cut off – their physical life is to be spared until

God's appointed time comes. As they are clothed and as their shame is taken away they see something of what God meant when he said, 'Unto dust you shall return.' They saw that they would return to dust by the way of death. The life that they were to live until God's time came for their dissolution was to carry the price-tag of death on it. Their very clothes spoke to them of their being under the sentence of death. Life was lived at the cost of the life of another.

Christian believers are living a life that carries the price of the death at Calvary in its every breath. All are living a life at the cost of the death of Christ. If it were not for his death all would have been cast off without mercy long before now.

The principle that their covering explained

Here was a gospel sermon, preached by God himself. This was the initial declaration to man of a principle that runs right through Scripture: 'Without the shedding of blood their is no remission of sin.' Without death there cannot be life. Man's covering by God carried that basic fact. Here was another dying in their place; God's sentence is executed not on them but on an innocent substitute. This is what the New Testament declares the atoning death of Christ to be. This is how the apostle Paul expresses it: 'The Son of God who loved me, and gave himself for me.'

God will accept the death of the innocent in the place of the guilty. The guilty did not die here but the innocent. Because the innocent died, the guilty were spared and the guilty were covered. The word that is translated as 'atonement' in our Bible is literally a 'covering'. That is what redemption is – a covering.

This verse points forward to the sacrifice of Christ. It is no ordinary substitute that God accepts for the sin of the soul. It is the substitute of his own Son in human nature. That sacrifice is depicted and foreshadowed in the sacrifice that took place in the clothing of Adam and Eve. By one sacrifice Christ has done all that was necessary. By one sacrifice Christ has paid the price of the wages of sin. He paid for the sins of the Old Testament church including the sin of Adam and Eve. He paid for the sins of the New Testament church. The virtue, the power and the efficacy of his sacrifice reached back in time and it reached forward. It is one sacrifice for sins for ever.

We can be covered because Christ died. Isn't that a wonderful
gospel? It was for Adam and Eve – to those who had sinned against
God in the garden, to those who had earned God's curse, to them
came God's mercy.

Here is man in his shame and his guilt and in his rebellion
covered by the sacrifice of the life of an innocent one. Let me ask
you to ponder this, to question yourself as to how your sin can be
covered over. Ask yourself what the death of Jesus was if it was
not a covering for sin. When you have asked yourself that question, then ask yourself if you have really and truly availed yourself of the covering. Have you allowed God, the God of all grace,
to clothe you?

In the book of Revelation we read of God's people being
clothed in white raiment, in the robe of Christ's righteousness
that the shame of their nakedness, the shame of their moral guilt,
should not appear.

The promise that their covering extended
The fact that covering came as the result of God's own action we
see in God's warmth and tenderness and mercy. That must have
been a tremendous wonder to Adam and Eve. It was done for
them both as individuals. They must have been aware that God
was pointing ahead to something greater. He had already spoken
to the serpent and had talked of the seed of the woman whose heel
would be bruised and of the crushing of the head of the seed of
the serpent.

We don't know how clearly they would have seen but we
believe that see they did. They saw enough of the promise of
Christ in what God did in the sacrificial death of these animals
and their being clothed in their skins. They saw that blood was to
be shed that would cover not only their physical needs but their
shame and their moral guilt. If Abraham could rejoice in the future
day of Christ, can we not believe that God, as he comes to initiate
his saving work with those with whom he had had close and
intimate fellowship, would reveal to them what he was going to
do in Christ?

They must have become aware of enough to stir hope and to
call forth faith and trust in the God they had called a liar and in
the God whose name and justice and truth they had denied. Now

they see their plight and they see their need and they are cast over on his mercy. Their faith can rest on this, that mercy will be there for them. That is what the gospel demands of us today.

'Believe on the Lord Jesus Christ and you shall be saved.'

17

Divine Sovereignty, Human Responsibility

'All that the Father giveth me shall come to me; and him that cometh to me I will in no wise cast out' (John 6:37).

In these words, the Lord Jesus fuses two truths together that theologians for about two thousand years have been attempting to separate from one another. The fact that Christ fuses them together and sees no contradiction between them should have made all the theologians more careful. Some are quite happy to accept the first truth, divorce it from the second statement and on that first part build a whole system of theology. Some people mistakenly call these theologians Calvinists. I don't think any Calvinist would be guilty of so grave an error as to build a system of theology on a half-truth. Another type of theologian has been pleased to ignore the first part of the verse altogether, to isolate the second part and on it to build a theology.

Why have men done this with these words? It is because they contain two apparently irreconcilable statements that the human mind has difficulty in fusing together (and any attempt to do so generally meets with failure). One part reaches out into the mystery of God's eternal purpose of election and salvation. The other part touches the responsibility of man and the way in which the gospel of salvation is brought to men's attention. It contains the wonderfully free and uninhibited promise with which the gospel is to be presented to sinners of all kinds.

The first truth tells us that there is a God who is sovereign over all things, a God who from all eternity has set his electing love on sinners, who has redeemed them in Christ and who will infallibly present them before himself without spot or blemish. Here is a truth that is revealed in God's Word and which tells us that the God of eternity, the almighty, all-wise and all-gracious God, out of the freeness and the fullness of his love, has come with a purpose of salvation. There is much here that we cannot understand. What moved God to save any sinner at all? We can only say that it seemed good in his sight. Why should he save any? It is the wonder of his grace.

People rebel at the thought of this truth, at the thought of the eternal election of God and the predestinating of sinners to everlasting life, because it seems to them that God is being unfair to some. There is no doubt that this is a mystery. Some are passed by. That is the teaching of the Saviour in these words. But remember that not one sinner out of the whole of humanity deserved the love of God. The fact that he should save any should amaze us. If you find this truth makes your heart sore, move on to the second part of the text and see how open the invitation is. What could be freer? What could be more wonderful? What could be more promising to a sinner than that?

There is no real contradiction in the text. Both parts are concerned with the love of God and with the salvation of sinners. God is concerned not just to make salvation possible for us but he is concerned to make salvation a reality. He is concerned with men and women who cannot do anything to save themselves. He is concerned with people who are dead in trespasses and sins. He is concerned with those who must have a sacrifice made for them and yet who, supposing they were to sacrifice their own lives, would but sacrifice that which was already condemned by God. So God himself provides the sacrifice. He provides it in the person of his own Son and then there is enough in his purpose to ensure that all for whom the Son sacrifices himself shall come to the Son and benefit eternally from the sacrifice that was made.

When someone asked C.H. Spurgeon how he could reconcile the two truths in this text he replied, 'I never try to reconcile friends.' These two truths are in harmony for they both speak of the undeserved favour and blessing of the holy God who was sinned against. They view salvation from two different standpoints. They view salvation first of all from the God-ward side and then from the man-ward side. We are to be concerned, as Scripture says, not with the things that are hidden and dark, 'for the secret things belong unto the Lord our God'. There is no doubt that election and predestination are among the secret things. Far too many people probe these mysteries and try to discover what God is doing instead of repenting and believing the gospel. We are first of all to be concerned with the gospel as it comes to us and touches our lives and our responsibilities.

Spurgeon talks about one occasion when he went sailing round the West Coast of Scotland. One night they anchored off one of the Hebridean islands. As they approached this island all they could see were its great high towering mountains. It looked as if it was going to be a source of disaster to the vessel. The captain seemed to be steering directly towards the most dangerous-looking cliffs. At the last moment, just as they came very close to the cliffs they saw that, in fact, there was a small opening that opened up into a lovely bay. They sailed into a quiet harbour and a good anchorage. Then the very mountains and cliffs that had seemed to threaten the little ship became her safety and her security. The wind could blow and the waves could roll but the little ship was as safe as could be because she was under the lee of the great mountain. The two truths we have been thinking of are like that. God's eternal purposes are like a mountain rising up that threatens us but as we come near and when we seek and find this God we discover one of the most precious truths – that God has loved with an everlasting love, and with a love that can never change and a love that will never let go.

All that the Father giveth me shall come to me
First of all, these words mean that some must surely come to Christ. No matter how small the witness and the cause of Christ may seem, no matter how powerless the churches may seem, God's purpose will be unchanging and some will come to Christ. Jesus spoke these words immediately after he had been talking of unbelief. This whole chapter is about people who came to him, not for spiritual blessing, but for material gain. How encouraged he must have been to reflect on this truth after coming up against so much unbelief, to know that his ministry would not be in vain. He went to the suffering and the death of the Cross knowing that there he would redeem by his precious blood a multitude that would come under the shelter and the cleansing power of his blood. What an upholding truth this must have been to the man Christ Jesus. What an upholding truth it is to every Christian worker today. Our God has ordained that by the simple preaching of Jesus Christ and him crucified, sinners will be brought to Jesus and they will be transformed by the power of the gospel. There is no

other message that will bring people to repentance. Many will
refuse but many will accept. If some must come to Jesus, why
should you not be among them? Why?

This is not a truth that excludes men and women but one that
includes them and brings them in by salvation in Christ Jesus.
Nothing between heaven and hell should stop you from being one
of those who must come to Jesus by the grace of God. Christ is
going to have a church. Heaven is going to be full. There will not
be one empty place in God's heaven. Why then should there not
be a place for you?

This truth was a great reassuring truth to the Lord himself, and
is to every Christian worker, to every preacher, to every person
who witnesses to the truth and to every sinner who listens to the
gospel. Why are you living in this age? Why are you the person
you are? I'll tell you why. God brought you into the world at a
certain time and made you the person you are. You had no say in
the matter. You may not like the idea of a sovereign God but that
is what he is. You were not able to choose your parents, or which
century you would like to live in. Who chose all that for you? The
same Lord who has put gospel privileges and gospel opportunities in your way. The very fact that he has done so is an encouragement to you to believe that you are numbered among those
who will come to Christ.

Do you see why people come? They come, not because of
some activity that starts in their own mind, nor because of something that starts in their heart, some root of goodness that is left in
human nature, but because of an activity of God the Father. It was
a giving to the Son in the form of a covenant of which Christ was
the head, the covenant of grace. Because they do come they are
saved. No-one is ever saved apart from coming to Christ. There is
no salvation in any other. You must come to Christ for salvation.
All who do come are absolutely and totally saved.

If you think that circumstances and the workings of your own
mind and your own heart and the reading of God's Word can
converge to make you come to Christ – you will find on reading
your Bible that you come essentially because the Father gave you
to Jesus. Behind all your circumstances, the preaching, your need,
your searching, lies the movement of God for your salvation from
all eternity. It was nothing of good in us that made us Christians.

It was the fact that God gave us to Jesus. The conversion of a sinner to Christ is the seal, and the only seal, of election. I did not find out that I was elect and then because I knew I was elect came and trusted in Jesus. I came as a sinner to Jesus and was converted. After I came I realised that I had been wonderfully included in the election of God's grace.

The sure promise of Christ: 'him that cometh to me I will in no wise cast out.'

This is a very generous promise. There is no more generous text in the New Testament. I find this text a great comfort – do you? Perhaps you haven't understood, or perhaps you have understood all too well, what is implied in the first part of the text. Concentrate now on this part.

The promise is generous in its invitation. *All* that come – there is no special mark. It doesn't matter what sort of a person comes, how good they are or how bad. Perhaps you are not as generous as that with yourself. Perhaps you are saying that God would never have anything to do with so grave a sinner as yourself. Many people are deeply aware of their sin. Many feel that God would have nothing to do with them. This God would. He gave his Son for sinners and his Son says that he will turn away no-one who comes. There is one thing that has to be true about you in order for you to receive salvation: you have to come to Christ.

There is no limit of any kind put upon our coming or the way in which we come, as long as we come to Jesus. There is no limitation as to age, or place or means. In Sutherland I met an old man, James MacKay, who was converted in his eighties. He had listened to the gospel all his days and had hardened his heart against it. How patient God is. One night James was listening to his minister preaching on the text 'Jesus of Nazareth passeth by'. Suddenly just as the sermon was nearing its close old James heard him say, 'Are you going to let him go by you again without accepting him as your Saviour?' It struck him how often Jesus had passed him before. He bowed his head and prayed, 'O Lord, give me grace not to let him go by me this time.' In relating this his eyes would fill with tears as he would recall, 'And he didn't pass me by and I wish I had come eighty years ago.'

You may feel you are bringing him the fag-end of your life –

the earlier years having been lived for self and for sin. Yet still he will not cast you out.

Do you know the story of the man from Wester Ross who emigrated to the States? At the age of 105 the text of a sermon he heard when he was nine years of age came back to him: 'Multitudes, multitudes in the valley of decision.' It had been preached at an open-air service with a huge crowd attending for the Communion. The scene came back to him after a life of godlessness and sin, after almost a hundred years, and God blessed it to him to his eternal salvation. There is no limit to age – you are not too young or too old to come to Jesus.

The promise is personal. Jesus began what he was saying with a very wide sweep: 'All that the Father giveth me'. When people think of election they often think of a very small number, but in fact it is a great multitude which no man can number that will be saved. Then Christ narrows down what he is saying to the individual person. It is a promise to you and it is a promise to me that if we come to Jesus he will never cast us away.

Let me illustrate for you the fullness and the freeness of the grace of God. It is recorded of a sailing ship that the crew had a very hard voyage from Britain to America. They were many weeks behind schedule. As they sighted land they were all in very bad condition. The weather became very hot and they ran out of water. One day they sighted another ship, the first they had seen for months. They exchanged signals and the British ship signalled for help: 'We are dying for lack of water.' They got a signal back saying, 'Lower your buckets.' They didn't understand but they did as they were told and heaved them up full. They were sailing through the clear fresh water of the mouth of the Amazon. They were sailing through the very thing they needed to save their lives.

What does it mean to come to Christ? It means to trust him for 'none perish who trust him.'

18

The Lamb of God

Behold, the Lamb of God
(John 1:36).

Already John the Baptist has spoken on these words. On the previous day he had said, 'Behold, the Lamb of God who taketh away the sin of the world' (John 1:29).

John knew that he was expressing the same truth on both occasions although this is seemingly a shorter version. The very essence of his message is found in the fact that Jesus is the Lamb of God. Jesus Christ is inconceivable to John and to his hearers apart from the function and work that the Lamb is to fulfil by taking away the sin of the world.

You have probably heard many sermons on this text. Why did John call Jesus the Lamb of God? He knew Jesus to be the Son of God. Why did he not just call him by that name? John here touches the very heart of the gospel. The Son of God had to become incarnate, had to become man, God in human nature. He had to give himself at Calvary as a sacrifice for sin before the sin of the world could be taken away. In essence, that begins to show us why John called him the Lamb.

John must have looked at Jesus of Nazareth, whom he probably knew well, and seen ahead to the events that were to close the life of Jesus on the Cross. From the Old Testament he would have a very definite understanding of what these events meant. John the Baptist was a man steeped in the Word of God – a preacher of the Old Testament. He knew the Scriptures thoroughly and he knew that the people to whom he was speaking and preaching had similar knowledge; they knew the technical language of Old Testament theology, they knew very vividly the language of Old Testament sacrifice. When John talked of a lamb these people would immediately think of the daily sacrifice for sin.

Preached 2 July 1978

Where did John the Baptist get his message from? He knew it from the fact that Jesus had been revealed to him as Messiah on the occasion of his baptism at least 40 days before this. While Jesus had been in the wilderness after his baptism, John had thought of this fact. It must have been a startling revelation to John to learn that someone he had known since he was a little boy was the Messiah of God. He had had to think very deeply about it. As John thought of these events he saw, in the light of all that he knew of the Old Testament teaching, truth, not only about the person of Messiah, but about the work that the Messiah was to accomplish.

Let us now also look at Jesus, the Lamb of God, through the eyes and the teaching of the Old Testament scriptures. As we do we will see the light from the Old Testament and from the New Testament focusing together to highlight God's way of salvation for sinners.

How can a sinner be saved from the consequences of sin? The story of the trial of the faith of Abraham foreshadows Jesus the Lamb of God opening up the way of salvation for sinners. The story would have been familiar to John the Baptist but now he would think of it in a new light for he now knew who the Messiah was. What did that story have to tell him? It would reveal to him some of the things that were to happen to Jesus of Nazareth.

The first thing would be that here was a father who was asked to put the life of his son at stake. Abraham was asked to sacrifice the son he loved, the son through whom would be fulfilled many of the promises made by God to him. Abraham would have some understanding from this experience of the love of God who was going to sacrifice his only Son for sin. Our thoughts go to the Father in John 3:16 – to the Father who gave his only begotten Son because he so loved the world.

Abraham was told to take his son and with him he was to take all the paraphernalia for sacrifice. He chops the wood and takes the censer of fire and the knife, and father and son go together to the place of which God had spoken – to the mountain of God's appointing. Just as Isaac has to carry the wood for his sacrifice up to the mountain, so Jesus 'went forth bearing his cross'. God was in Christ reconciling the world unto himself. Father and Son moved together for your salvation and for mine.

For three days, as they climbed the mountain, Isaac was dead to Abraham in his intention of obedience to God. For three days Christ was under the power of death. Do you see how this story illumined the understanding of John the Baptist? Do you begin to see how he understood from the Old Testament what Jesus was to meet and what Jesus was to do?

Abraham built his altar. How must Abraham have felt as he made preparation for the sacrifice of his beloved son! God is bringing Abraham into a new place of obedience. But he is doing more than that. God is taking Abraham to a place where he will see the day of Christ very clearly and where he will see the way of salvation through faith in Christ. He's bringing Abraham to the place where he must trust the God who can raise the dead in order to fulfil the promise.

'By faith Abraham, when he was tried, offered up Isaac: and he that had received the promises offered up his only begotten son, of whom it was said, That in Isaac shall thy seed be called: accounting that God was able to raise him up, even from the dead; from whence also he received him in a figure' (Heb. 11:17-19).

The question came to Isaac's lips: where was the lamb for a burnt offering? Why a lamb? Why a burnt offering? Sacrifice was because of sin. Burnt offering was to appease a God who was offended. Isaac knew what it was like to be under the knife of God's judgement. Isaac made no sign of resistance and he allows his father to tie him to the altar. He is seeing in a terrible and personal way what God meant when he said, 'The soul that sinneth, it shall die.'

His life is to be forfeited because of sin: that is true for all of us. Isaac believes that Abraham is obeying God and he does not question the rightness of what is happening.

When Isaac asked his father about the lamb, Abraham assured him that God himself would provide a lamb. Did Abraham see already that as he trusted God with the life of Isaac so God would answer that trust? And God did. The voice from heaven spoke. The hand of Abraham was stayed and God provided a ram, caught in the thicket by its horns. Isaac was freed and God's substitute lamb was sacrificed. The knife was poised to make sacrifice for sin but the victim was replaced by another. The knife comes down, life is taken and God's demand is met. Isaac's life is spared because the life of the lamb is taken away instead.

Abraham must have understood more of what God was going to do through this whole incident. It must have been of this event that Christ said, 'Abraham rejoiced to see my day' (John 8:56).

Isaac is free. He is given back his life, a life that in the mind and heart of his father had for three days been forfeited. He is alive because of another death.

In Jesus, John the Baptist saw the answer to Isaac's question, 'Where is the lamb?' The lamb on Mount Moriah was a symbol of the Lamb that would be slain for sin. This is why Christ came. This is why there was a place called Calvary. This is why he bore his cross. God's sacrifice provided the way of salvation. The knife of God's justice poised over your life and mine falls not on us – it fell on Jesus the Lamb of God.

John saw that Jesus was to die in your place and in mine. Because death was visited on him for *our* guilt – he had none – death now has no claim on us if we trust in Christ.

Why does John say, 'Behold the lamb of God'? He says it because it is by looking to this Lamb and trusting in him that sinners are saved. John's words contain the very essence of the gospel. He was explaining as clearly as it can be explained how sinners may be saved. They are saved because God has provided a sacrificial substitute for them – his own Son. You are invited to behold Jesus as the Lamb of God and to trust in him as your Saviour. Isaac was untied and freed – you too can be made free by trusting in what God has done in Christ.

19

Who Touched Me?
(Luke 8:45)

The Christian gospel is essentially very simple. It does have many complexities, and theologically and doctrinally there are things in it which even the greatest minds are unable to plumb or understand fully. But essentially it is very simple, and it is simple because the one who is the gospel and the very heart of God's Word to us, the Lord Jesus Christ, has never changed. Although he is glorified and reigning in kingly splendour on the throne of God, he is essentially the same Jesus as we meet in the pages of the Gospels.

In the New International Version the entire story is headed 'A Dead Girl and a Sick Woman'. That tells us that this world is really one that needed a Saviour and a person like Jesus. Had I been responsible for giving a heading to this story, I would have wanted to add something else: 'A Dead Girl and a Sick Woman and a Marvellous Saviour', because he is the one that the gospel centres around.

I want to do two very straightforward things with the question. Firstly, I want us to look at

The scene out of which the question came

This is a scene which belongs not just to history, but in a sense is repeated in the lives and the circumstances and conditions of men everywhere. No matter where you travel, people are the same and they have the same needs as they had in the days of Jesus. The whole scene out of which the question comes is painted very vividly and very beautifully by the Spirit-inspired evangelist.

Jesus is as usual surrounded by crowds. That's one thing that meets us in the New Testament. Wherever Jesus went he attracted people. And really, there's something wrong with the Christianity or the gospel that doesn't attract people. Jesus himself did attract crowds of people and here they were pressing in on him and almost crushing him. People were always eager to hear Jesus. They were always eager to see a work of his power. I think that that is still true. People are still essentially eager to hear about Jesus himself and what he has to say. And whenever God begins to work through the gospel with great power, people are attracted and they come to see what's happening.

And then, two things happened. First of all, a man approaches. His name is Jairus, he's a religious man, one of the leaders of the religious life of the Jews. He probably was surrounded by people who were very critical of Jesus, because the Pharisees and the rulers of the Jews didn't like Jesus and what he was doing. It may well have been because of the criticism that he was hearing about Jesus that Jairus came looking for help at all. However that may be, he came to see if Jesus would help him. Perhaps you are a little critical of all these Christians and the fuss they make about the Lord Jesus and about salvation and about Calvary. Perhaps you've got friends who are critical of Jesus. Well, there were people critical of Jesus in his own day. But even criticism draws Jesus to our attention and it probably drew the attention of this man as in his moment of need he sought Jesus out.

Sometimes I like to think about the people who crowded around Jesus. When I try to picture how Jairus must have looked, I always think of him as being very burdened, shadowed and troubled. Why? For a very simple reason: it was his little girl that was sick and dying. To help a little girl of twelve a father will do anything. He'll even go to the despised prophet of Nazareth. Jairus is one of the men who would have said, 'Can any good thing come out of Nazareth?' So he goes and asks Jesus for help, and gets an immediate response. I have not come across anyone in the whole of the New Testament who went to ask Jesus for help and was refused. Now supposing you learn nothing else that's a marvellous thing.

Jesus immediately goes with Jairus. He probably changes direction to go to the house where Jairus' little daughter is ill. When I think of the progress they were making, I always picture Jairus being just a little bit ahead and urging Jesus on, 'Come on, hurry along now, because she's really very ill.' Then all of a sudden the whole thing stops. And I can always imagine Jairus saying to

himself, 'Oh dear, dear, dear. What's wrong now?' And Jesus
asks a question and it seems so utterly irrelevant, and it must
make Jairus feel at first a little bit hopeless. It's almost an absurd
question: 'Who touched me?' He's asking his disciples and they
feel that it's an impossible question to answer, because there are
so many people round about Jesus and they're actually crushing
in on him. What on earth does Jesus mean by asking, 'Who touched
me?'

Well, Peter picked up on the point of the question. I suppose
he spoke for everyone that was around when he said, 'What do
you mean, "Who touched me?" The crowd are thronging you and
pressing you, hundreds of people have been touching you!' Jesus
ignores the difficulty and says, 'Someone did touch me.'

The very fact that Jesus stopped and asked this question should
make us pause and think. Jesus never asked irrelevant or stupid
questions. Everything Jesus did was meaningful. Why did he ask
this question? He asked it because, although people can crush in
and be around him, there is a touch that goes beyond the touch of
the crush of the crowd. He felt that he had been touched deep in
his spirit and that 'virtue' (power) had gone out of him. He knew
that he had been touched not just physically but spiritually. It was
possible in the days when Jesus was alive on earth to be all around
him, crushing in on him, yet never really to touch him with the
real touch of the spirit and of faith and of trust. Augustine long
ago commenting on this incident said, 'The flesh presses; faith
touches.'

The woman was brought out to the front. It would seem the
question took the woman out from behind Jesus where she had
touched what would be the tassel of a blue cord around his cloak
– the word means that she had actually grasped it and held it.

She was brought round in front of him and there she went on
her knees. Jesus looked at this poor sick woman and said a very
tender word to her, 'daughter'. It's probably the most tender word
he ever uses to a woman recorded in the New Testament. 'Daughter, your faith has made you well. You've been healed because
you trusted.'

And where was Jairus through all this – the woman coming
out and nervously telling Jesus about her illness and how long
she had been ill, and what she had done and all the rest of it. I

think that Jairus must have been a little impatient and very anxious, worried about his little girl and saying, 'When on earth is all this going to be finished?' Because these were real people, they reacted the same way as you and I would react. And yet Jairus' anxiety began to be taken away when he heard the woman's story. Here was something to help him. He had come to Jesus for help and, lo and behold, this woman is saying, 'Lord, I touched you, I held on to the tassel of your robe and I've been healed of something that was draining the life out of me for twelve years.' Jairus must have been saying to himself, 'Well, I've come to the right person; if he can help this woman, he can help me.'

If you're not a Christian believer and have never come to know and trust the Lord Jesus Christ, and to know his peace and the healing of spirit that he can bring, there are people and their testimony is that when we do touch Jesus by faith he brings healing into our lives. That was one of the things that helped me before I was a Christian myself. The testimony of godly people who had been helped by Jesus.

Then, even as Jesus is speaking, the whole scene changes again. A messenger comes from Jairus' house and says, 'Don't bother the Rabbi any more, your little daughter is dead. It's too late.' I'm sure for a moment Jairus was absolutely stunned. It's a terrible thing suddenly to be told that someone you love is dead and beyond the reach of man. Into the dream world that had suddenly come upon Jairus, Jesus spoke, and again he uses almost the same words as he used to the woman who had been healed. He said, 'Don't be afraid.' How often Jesus gave needy people that advice. 'Don't be afraid. Only believe and she will be made whole too.' He used the same word about the little girl as he used about the woman. 'Trust. Look to me and she will be healed, made whole again.'

Why did Jesus ask this question?

Against the background of the stories, I want to suggest that the question was asked first of all because it *discriminated*. Jesus never saw crowds of people just as crowds. They were always individual persons to him. Individuals are important to God. The narratives of the New Testament and the dealing of Jesus with people are always the dealing of personal relationship. Jesus never

looked merely on a crowd; he looked on a person. He does that
with you. His question searched out one person out of all the hundreds who were around him. The woman had to confess and come
out in front of him. Someone had reached Christ in a way that
made him vividly conscious of it. Hundreds pressing around him
touched him, and yet out of the hundreds there is one who touches
him in a special way.

And you know, that happens and has happened all down
through history. Under the preaching of the gospel people listen
to the same sermon under the same circumstances, and then by
faith a soul reaches out and it touches the Saviour and a transformation takes place: a person is made whole inwardly. That's what
conversion to Christ is, and it is ours the moment we trust in Jesus.

The question not only discriminated, it *unveiled*. It brought
the woman out of anonymity, out to stand in front of Jesus the
Son of God. That's what the gospel does with us. Again and again
over years of preaching I have had people come to me and say,
'You know, Mr. MacMillan, when you were preaching, all of a
sudden it was as though you were just speaking to me.' That wasn't
my preaching, that was God bringing a person to stand right in
front of himself, as it were. And Jesus did that with this woman.
He brought her out of the crowd and he unveiled the marvellous
thing that had happened to her. He got her story in just a few
simple words. In bringing her out of the crowd in front of himself, he was bringing her nearer than she had been able to come
until then. In a sense, she had come very near when her faith, her
trust, her hope, had made her lay hold of him. But now she was
brought in front of him so that he would bring her nearer still. She
had made contact with the very person and the very power that
she needed.

She had tried all sorts of remedies before. Luke doesn't say
too much about it but the New International Version omits one
phrase which the Authorised Version has, that she had tried many
avenues of healing. Luke himself was a doctor and he often speaks
in terms of medicine and disease, but Mark is quite blunt – he
doesn't bother too much about safeguarding doctors. He says about
this woman that she had gone to many doctors and she was no
better, indeed she was a good deal worse than she had been. There

are things which doctors can't do, there are things which the marvels of medicine cannot heal. Jesus is God's great physician and where everyone else had failed with this woman, Jesus healed her.

Luke describes the illness she had very carefully, in terms which tell us that, because she was a Hebrew woman and because of their religious laws, she suffered all the more. For twelve years this woman would have been excommunicated from temple worship. For the last twelve years until this moment she would have been disallowed fellowship with the people of God whenever they went to worship. More than that, it's highly likely that because of her illness she had had to be divorced from her husband and separated from her family, because her illness involved ceremonial religious uncleanness. This woman was defiled because of her illness. You see the marvellous tenderness of the thing that Jesus did for someone who had been an outcast from society, who had been wasting away for twelve years, who had been cut off from the privileges of public worship and the public preaching of God's Word. He brings her out in front and he says, 'Daughter.' He brings her back into the family of God, healed and restored and strong, and the twelve years have vanished away in the face of his power.

Now that has a lesson for us also. Jesus not only gives all who trust in him new life and restores spiritual health and strength, he brings them into the family of God. To be a child of God is a marvellous privilege and Jesus uses the word very specifically, very significantly, 'Daughter, your faith has healed you.'

His question discriminated, unveiled and it also *determined* the whole relationship of this woman to God, for evermore. Her confession brought her into a deeper experience of the Lord Jesus Christ. She had been healed. Now she was brought out in front of him. Contact became confession as she told what had happened.

In a sense, she need never be far from Jesus again. She can rest in assurance of his love and his power. The faith that she has used and acted upon – perhaps it was a very desperate hope, perhaps it was hoping against hope, the very last thing she could try – had been honoured by Jesus. And when he took her out and she confessed what she had done, he had called her 'daughter' and honoured her faith. Sometimes I speak to people and they say,

'Oh, I wish I had a strong faith, my faith is so small.' And sometimes people say, 'I don't know whether my trust is a real saving
faith or not.' If it's the kind of faith that drives you to trust in
Jesus, it's the kind of faith that Jesus will honour and use.

Probably this woman would have very little idea theologically
about who Jesus really was. She may also have heard of Jesus
only through criticism. But she must have heard enough to make
her believe that he could help her and that was all that was necessary. I'm sure that she learned much more in the days after this.
You don't need to have all the theological and philosophical questions answered. If you have enough sense of need to bring you to
trust in Jesus, he will honour that faith and give himself to you.

Jairus must have been very anxious and yet he waits until this
woman had been dealt with completely. Patience, love, trust, everything was tested for Jairus. And yet everything was worthwhile.
I sometimes think of Jairus as he's listening to this woman and
suddenly the word 'twelve' strikes him. 'Twelve years! She has
been ill for twelve years. She has had this shadow in her life, this
darkness, this bleakness which had left her all alone and lonely.
And for twelve years I have had the sunlight of a little girl and her
love and the joy of watching her growing up.' He must have
thought it very strange. It's more than a marvellous coincidence;
there's a lesson to learn from it. Jairus must have said, 'If he can
heal a woman who has been twelve years ill with her life ebbing
away, surely he can help my little girl.' And, of course, Jesus did.

This Jesus never lacks resources for helping people. If this
Jesus can have virtue drained out of him to help one, he always
has more virtue. He has all the resources of Godhead in his own
person and he can draw on all these resources through the Holy
Spirit who is fully his. 'Jesus,' says one old commentator, 'is
never at a stand in face of need.' That means that Jesus is never
helpless before any individual's particular need. He is always able
to save to the uttermost all that come to him.

Jesus, I think, brought the woman out so that she would confess him openly and testify to the healing she had received from
him, for the benefit of some of the people that were in that crowd.
There were men around him there who were already plotting his
death and destruction. And so he brings this woman out, has her
confess her contact, her touch, her healing, in order first of all

that she can be brought closer to him and into the family circle and, then, so that Jairus' faith will be encouraged to look forward to what's going to happen in his home when they finally arrive there. In all of this Jesus himself will be glorified and will be known as the only one who can heal the deepest wounds in the human heart and the human soul.

Ultimately that is what is required of us as well. Jesus asks us and the gospel invites us not merely to believe in our hearts, but to confess with our mouths and to be unashamed of the Jesus that we are brought to trust. This is not merely history, it is a continually recurring reality. Again and again and again, down through the years, individuals have touched Jesus and been healed and changed and transformed. Perhaps it's true that even since the sermon began God's Spirit has worked and encouraged even one soul to reach out in faith, out of need, to touch Jesus and draw on his power. If that's so, be sure of this, you will never perish. Your faith makes you perfectly whole. Not very long ago I heard someone repeat verses of a hymn, which fits in here very nicely. It was something like this:

> The healing of his seamless dress
> is by our beds of pain
> We touch him in life's throng and press
> and we are home again.

It's as simple as that. None perish who trust him.

Pilate's Dilemma

'What shall I do then with Jesus which
is called Christ?' (Matthew 27:22).

Sometimes texts for sermons are long and involved. This text is short and simple – crystal clear. Not one person can evade the point of the question that is being asked. Evasion of this issue can be done only by a very deliberate act of your mind and your will.

Pilate, long ago, asked the people this question. Every one of us at some time in our life must face and answer the same question. Perhaps we could say that every one of us is answering that question in a practical way every day. You may not be answering it consciously, or thinking deeply about it, but your every act, your every thought, your every word is in and of itself an answer to the question as to what you are doing, or what you have done, with the Christ of the Gospels. You are either rejecting him – putting him out of your heart, out of your thoughts, out of your life – or you are crowning him Lord of your life.

There were two streams of influence converging on Pilate's decision. He could either free Jesus or he could condemn him and have him crucified. One influence was saying to Pilate to have nothing to do with the condemnation of this just man. The question Pilate asked showed that he understood the charge against Jesus. He called him the Christ – the Messiah. Pilate, and every Jew who stood in front of him, had the claims of the Son of God as the Anointed One put before them on the day that Jesus was crucified.

The other influence on his decision was that if he didn't do as the Jews wished there would be a rebellion and a revolution and he would be in trouble with Caesar. There was one voice telling him what was the right thing to do with Jesus. But there was the voice of this world and all the claims of this world that would

Preached 29 August 1978

have Jesus crucified. The same two strains of influence are still working. There is the power and mystery of iniquity and there is the power and the grace and the voice of God.

There are many issues involved in the acceptance of Christ. The gospel involves a whole system of truth as well as the acceptance of Jesus as Lord and Saviour and Redeemer. In essence it comes down to the fact that people can do only two things with Jesus: they can accept him as Lord and Saviour or they can reject him and leave him out of their lives altogether. Jesus himself made it very clear that there is no halfway position. You cannot sit on the fence. You cannot serve two masters. You cannot serve God and mammon.

What does Pilate do? He first of all tries to avoid making a decision. Perhaps you have been doing that for twenty years or longer. Perhaps if you hear a sermon that sears into your mind or knifes into your heart and makes you face the truth, you will do anything rather than come to a decision. Any triviality will do to cover up your conscience and your heart. You will do anything rather than face up to what really matters.

First Pilate sends him to Herod. In this action he tries to make out that Jesus is not his responsibility, that because Jesus came from Galilee, he didn't have to deal with him. But he was the Roman governor, the man with the real power and authority, and God was forcing Jesus upon his attention for his decision. Each one of us attempts to do the same as Pilate did. We try to evade the claims of Jesus. We try to turn the stream of God's Word and God's influence and the striving of the Holy Spirit away from ourselves. There is in human nature that which shrinks from making a clear-cut decision about Christ. We can excuse ourselves on the grounds of how busy we are, how much study we have to do, or that we are too old or too young.

Pilate then tries another strategy. He remembers a Jewish custom and uses it in the hope of shifting the responsibility from himself. At the Passover the Jews had a custom that they released a prisoner who was under condemnation. Pilate thought of the most notable prisoner that he had – Barrabas. He was sure that because Barrabas was such a wicked and infamous man, these self-righteous men would have nothing to do with him. If they were given the choice between the release of Barrabas or of Jesus,

Pilate was sure they would choose to release Jesus. He must have been stunned when the crowd shouted for the release, not of Jesus, but of Barrabas. Again the responsibility could not be shifted to someone else.

Just as surely as you will one day stand and answer to Jesus as your judge, your response to Christ, freely offered to you in the gospel, is your responsibility and no-one else's. No other person can refuse God's offer to you in the gospel but yourself. No other person can put you to hell but yourself. Not even God can send you to hell if you are willing to be saved.

You will not be able to stand before Christ on the day of Judgement and say that God never gave you a chance. God has given you many opportunities to commit your life to Christ as Saviour. It is not God's fault that you haven't used these opportunities. The responsibility is yours alone.

Pilate now tries to evade the voice of conscience. He knew that there was only one right thing to do. We all know what is right but still we trample the truth underfoot. There was the voice of Pilate's conscience and there was the voice of his wife telling him to have nothing to do with this just man. She had had a very strange dream about Jesus. We all have voices and memories telling us what the truth is. Maybe it is the memory of godly parents, praying friends or other influences of home and upbringing and environment that plead with us. All that will have to be trampled underfoot if you are going to reject Jesus again.

Supremely for Pilate there was Jesus himself. As he asked this question, there was Jesus standing in front of him. It must have been difficult for Pilate to condemn him, but he managed it. Jesus is drawing near to you in his love and his mercy. It is difficult to refuse him but it is possible. Is that what you are going to do? You can do one of two things. You can accept him as he is freely offered to you in the gospel or you can reject him again. If you reject him and refuse his claims, you have no guarantee that he will come and plead with you again. The Scripture says, 'Today if you will hear his voice, harden not your hearts ....'

What will you do with Jesus? What have you been doing with him throughout the past years? If you have been rejecting him, ask God for grace and for power to crown Jesus in your heart and in your life, to have him as your own Redeemer and Saviour.

21

The Believer's Experience of Sin

Thou forgavest the iniquity of my sin
(Psalm 32:5).

Here is a phrase that is weighted with the saving grace of the gospel of Christ. It is a phrase fashioned out of a living personal experience of the greatest gift that grace can give.

Forgiveness is at the dawning of every real experience of Christ. It is at the opening of every Christian life. The same free, abundant forgiveness of God is there at the sunset of every Christian life as well.

Listen to the text again not only with your ears but with your heart. What a marvellous exposition of the mercy of God we have here! If you know that forgiveness you have the best that God can bestow. If you lack that, you lack all that is worthwhile in life.

The text is part of a book that abounds in a rich experience of God. There is no psalm in the book of Psalms that is more evangelical than this one. As you read this psalm about pardon and forgiveness in personal experience, you could feel that it was written under the shadow of the cross of Christ. It is amazing that one who was living at the time this psalm was written should have such a powerful impression and such a clear understanding of what God was doing in his grace. The text concentrates the theme of the psalm, which centres on forgiveness and the blessings that come with it.

In a sense, it requires the whole of the psalm to expound and expand on the marvel this man found in the blessing God gave him. The psalm does this by the recall of devastating and wonderful spiritual experiences, leading the psalmist to exalt the blessings of God in the forgiveness of sin. He is thinking back to the conditions of mind and of heart which prevailed in his life before the blessings of forgiveness came to him. There may be some

Preached 28 May 1989

amongst us today whose experience of life is still in the circumstances the psalmist is recalling, men and women who know nothing about the forgiveness of God and the blessings which forgiveness alone can bring. If you are in that condition, remember that here is a godly man who once knew that situation as well; he came out of it, so don't give up and don't lose hope.

Throughout the psalm we find a threefold cord of profound and, in some ways, disturbing spiritual experiences. This threefold cord highlights the experience which underlies the text and the psalmist's marvel as he looks to God and says, '*Thou* forgavest the iniquity of my sin.'

The first strand of personal experience we could call *the experience of personal sin*: this man knows and speaks of sin in his own life. He is not merely talking theoretically, nor is he merely talking doctrinally. He is talking of something which had pervaded his whole experience of life. He had come to know the grip and the power which sin wields in human experience, and the accompanying inability to serve God acceptably. He had come under conviction of his guilt and had felt the burden and the bitterness of sin. Most of us know that sin is burdensome and that it pays bitter wages.

The second strand is *the experience of silence* that accompanied his personal sin. In verse 3 we read: 'When I kept silence my bones waxed old through my roaring all the day long.' How could he be silent at the same time as roaring? Because the silence was a God-ward silence, not the silence of assurance but the silence of guilt; sin closed this man's lips in the presence of God. Sin inevitably and invariably does that in the Christian's experience too. You fall into sin and you find that your prayer-chamber becomes a place where you can't speak to God honestly – your prayer life has gone. The psalmist didn't know what to say to God. He had no case to plead. He had no light, no peace, no prayer, no pathway back into the fellowship of the eternal God. The experience of sin led on to the experience of silence.

And the experience of silence issued in *the experience of sorrow*, the third strand through the psalm. The sorrow is described in figurative language and mainly by inference. In verse 6 we read of 'floods of great waters', in verse 7 of God as a hiding place, preserving from trouble, and compassing about with songs of deliverance. If you draw the inferences from these, you discover what this man was like before he found the blessings that God gave along with forgiveness. Floods of water, sweeping storms, torrid circumstances, chains of bondage, every one of them an occasion of sorrow. Sin inevitably brings sorrow with it. Man was not made to be a sinner nor to be offensive to God; man was made for fellowship with God.

We've looked at the threefold cord just in outline: the experience of sin, the experience of silence, and the experience of sorrow. All of these are intimately related, one issues from the other. But all are woven into this psalm so that over against them the psalmist can place the amazing grace of God that transformed and changed these circumstances. He is talking of his sin and his silence and his sorrow in order to demonstrate the truth that God forgives sin and that God blesses in forgiving. He is illustrating this marvellous truth, 'Thou forgavest the iniquity of my sin.' If this man knew *sin*, and he did, he had come to know the most important thing that a sinner can know – he had come to know the pardon of God. If this man knew *silence* and if his mouth had been closed in the presence of God, he also knew what it was to be instructed by God and given songs of deliverance. If this man knew *sorrow*, then the final verse tells us that he was given an experience of God that brought gladness and rejoicing. It is Christian experience highlighted by the convictions that led to it.

Let's follow these facts a little more closely. Come with me to the opening of the Psalm. In the Hebrew, what the Psalmist wrote in the first verse had no personal pronouns. Literally, he wrote, 'O, the blessings of transgression forgiven, of sin covered!'

He brings the marvellous exclamation 'O the blessings' into the sphere of personal experience, to the fact that God has equipped himself to forgive sin, to pardon sin, to cover sin. The word for atonement in Hebrew means 'to cover over sin so that the eye of the judging God sees it no longer'. The psalmist goes on to say in verse 2: 'Blessed is the man to whom the LORD imputes not iniquity', and these two blessings, transgression forgiven and sin covered, result in God not imputing iniquity to him. Now that's marvellous! God the Judge not actually counting the iniquity of sin and transgression against this man as he stands at the bar of judgement.

Let me comment on the words that the psalmist uses. The Hebrew word translated 'transgression' indicates an act of wilful, deliberate wrongdoing, a crossing over of the lines of God's law in an act which is personal, provocative disobedience to what God has said. The Hebrew word translated 'sin' indicates a 'missing of the mark', the failure to attain a standard that God has set (as does the Greek word for 'sin'). These two aspects of disobeying God's requirements, one of deliberately crossing them, the other of failing to meet them, are with us all, every day.

What is 'iniquity'? The word used means 'guilt'. The psalmist is dealing with sin in all its aspects. And he says 'O the blessings' of having your deliberate, wilful sin forgiven, 'O the blessings' of your failure to match up to what God requires being covered over. Somebody has spoken of these blessings and that which is behind them as 'the incredible mercy of God'. It is, and it becomes incredible to us only when a miracle of the Holy Spirit's work in our mind and heart shows us that it is there for us.

Now where does the psalm culminate? It goes from 'O the blessings' to the closing verse, 'Be glad in the LORD, and rejoice, ye righteous: and shout for joy, all ye that are upright in heart.' It goes from blessings which God commands with no personal pronoun pointing to man in it, to the place where man is rejoicing because God has blessed him. And all the way through between these two verses the psalm records the spiritual history of this man, the movement out of darkness into the marvellous light of the gospel. It is the history in broad outline of every true Christian believer.

Let's look at it quickly again. The personal experience of this psalmist doesn't stop with the word 'sin', but for him sin issued in a marvellous salvation. 'Blessed,' he says, 'is the man to whom the LORD imputes not iniquity.' God not imputing, but forgiving. One commentator on this psalm has said: 'In many ways sinners should be thankful that ultimately they have to please God and not man.'

Because of what he has done in the gospel, it is possible to please God. God knows all the details and circumstances of all our sins. And yet he imputes them not to us. If we sin against someone else, how difficult it is to get their forgiveness for this simple reason, that it is difficult for us to explain all the circumstances attaching to sin. God knows them completely.

But this is not all the story. In verse 2, we are told that 'Blessed is the man to whom the LORD imputes not his sin and in whose spirit there is no guile.' What is guile? Guile is deceit, the natural tendency of the heart to cover up, to deny, to excuse, to evade. And it would seem as though God has to take away that evil through his grace and bring us to the place where guile has gone, where our hearts are saying, 'I will confess unto the Lord my iniquity.' Have you been brought there? It is when we acknowledge our sins, when guile has been left behind us, when we're being honest with God and exposing ourselves to all the holiness and integrity of his nature, it is then, when we are saying, 'O God, look at me, I am what I am and I have no excuse for it', that God imputes not our iniquity to us.

Silence changed into the experience of confession, and guile has gone. What a danger there is in not taking our sin and confessing it daily to God, that we hide it and keep silent before him. If we look at 'Thou forgavest my iniquity' in verse 5 and work back from it, the first happening is the decision of the mind in the middle phrase, 'I said'. Who did he say it to? He said it to himself. The moment his heart decided to confess his transgressions unto the Lord, even before it came to the acknowledgement of the lips, God forgave his iniquity.

You don't need to wait. The moment your sin so appals you that you say in your heart, 'O God, I will confess it', he forgives and he pardons and he covers. That's the marvel of his mercy. One of the prophets has a beautiful expression, 'He is a God ready to pardon.' Far more ready to pardon than we are to confess or acknowledge. And it is not merely that he is ready to pardon volitionally, in his mind and in his purpose, it is that he is equipped to do it in his grace. As he looked down on the sacrifice of Calvary, and as the Eternal One sees it still, he is a God ready to pardon. He paid the price that enables him to forgive our sins.

And then sorrow was turned into singing. It is sin leading to sorrow that dispels the silence and makes a man open his mouth to God. And that safeguards the place of prayer. It is only when one is open before God, guileless, that God deals with our sin. Go back to the pictures of storms and floods in verses 6 and 7 and let me point out four things.

First, 'Surely in the floods of great waters they shall not come nigh unto him.' This occurs when the man has been forgiven. The same floods of evil and iniquity that were overwhelming him before are still there, but he is going to be safe in the midst of them. Why? Because he is in the hand of God. Man is kept safe. Christ, the godly of the godly, had to say, 'All thy billows and thy waves have swept over me.' Why? In order that you and I should be kept from them.

The second thing he says is, 'Thou art my hiding place.' Why do we need a hiding place? Because there are enemies around who would harm us. What a marvellous hiding place the Christian believer has. It is God himself. Ultimately, all fear traces back to our slavish fear of God because of sin. To escape that fear we can hide in God himself, in Christ.

Thirdly, he writes that 'Thou shalt preserve me from trouble' – not save me from going into it, but save me when *I am* in it.

And fourthly, 'You will compass me with songs of deliverance.' There's a New Testament illustration of this: 'At midnight Paul and Silas prayed, and sang praises to God: and the prisoners heard them' (Acts 16:25). Not songs when they get out of prison, but songs when their feet were in the stocks.

Sin, silence, sorrow. But over the whole psalm we have to write the word 'salvation'. From verse 8 onwards this man has become so conscious of the grace of God that it is now the voice of God we hear: 'I will instruct you and teach you in the way you will go.' That's the very thing he had been lacking, instruction from God and a pathway to follow.

However, he is not to be like a mule. He is not to make God correct him and put a bridle over his head and a bit in his mouth. That's not the kind of relationship God wants to have with his people. He wants them to have a relationship of fellowship where they will follow his guiding without these constraints.

And the psalmist finishes with praise: 'There are sorrows to the wicked'; he knows it out of his own personal experience. But he knows another reality: 'he that trusteth in the LORD, mercy shall compass him about.' So, 'Be glad in the LORD, and rejoice, ye righteous: and shout for joy, all ye that are upright in heart.'

If you are Christ's and you have trusted in Jesus and have been through something of the experience the psalmist talks about in this psalm, how blessed you are. God has blessings which will crown the blessing you know in this world, for one day you will be like Christ when you will be with Christ. If you haven't known the experience of forgiveness, what hope should this psalm extend to you? What became the psalmist's will become yours if you trust in the Lord Jesus.

22

The Presence of God

'The LORD of hosts is with us; the God of
Jacob is our refuge' (Psalm 46:7, 11).

Songs of faith given to us in the Psalter have nourished and
strengthened the faith of God's people in every age. Of all the
songs of faith this psalm is one of the most attractive. It is not just
a song of faith – it is a song of strong, confident and courageous
faith. As you go on walking with Christ, you will find what God's
people have found in every age – that faith requires courage and
that faith can have courage. The keynote of the psalm is found in
the expression of the text. It tells us who God is and where God
is. The LORD of hosts is with us; the God of Jacob is our refuge.
These words catch up the refrain that surges all the way through
this psalm. It encourages us to the same kind of faith. Is that the
sort of faith which you have?

There are many illustrations of how this psalm has been used
for the strengthening of the church and of individuals.

When Martin Luther was meeting furious opposition in his
reformation of the church and in his bringing the gospel back into
the church, he used to encourage his friend Philip Melancthon by
singing this psalm with him. After Luther died this same friend
was one day very downcast and was wondering how he would
manage now that the great leader of the Reformation had been
taken away. Then he heard a little girl singing this psalm in
Luther's translation. As he listened he said, 'Sing on, dear daughter. You'll never know what comfort you're bringing to my heart.'

Gustavus Adolphus, the Swedish king who turned back the
Counter-Reformation when he fought the Spanish armies through
the Netherlands, saved the Reformation for us and for our children with the help of many Scots (this was the beginning of the
Highland Light Infantry). Before he went into battle this general

Preached 28 July 1991

used to marshall his troops and make them sing this psalm.

Spurgeon commenting, from personal experience, on the first verse of this psalm said, 'We never know what strength is till our own weakness drives us to God's omnipotence.'

God is Jehovah of hosts and the God of Jacob – here is a two-fold truth about God that leads to a twofold statement that God is with us and is our refuge.

First, we will look at the declaration that the psalmist makes about God. He is the Lord, he is Jehovah. This is the name by which the deity, as self-existent and eternal and everlasting, was revealed to his people Israel. 'I am that I am.' For the Israelites this name meant the transcendence and the holiness and the awesomeness of God such that they would not even pronounce the name. The name Jehovah was so high and so holy to them that even today we are not sure how it should be pronounced. The believing people of God had such an appreciation of his grandeur and his splendour that they called him 'the beauty of holiness'. All this is compacted into the name Jehovah. It expressed the absoluteness, the otherness, the transcendence, the eternalness, the invariableness and the unchangeability of God; it speaks of God's total, inward, personal sufficiency for himself and for all that he has created.

What is in the psalmist's mind when he says 'the LORD of hosts'? The Bible speaks of the planets and stars of heaven as hosts (Gen. 2:1). The word is also used of angels. When Jesus was born the heavens were opened and the shepherds heard the sound of singing and praising from a multitude of the heavenly hosts – the angels of God (Luke 2:13). And God's own beloved people are spoken of as God's hosts.

The stars, the whole of creation, the angels of God's presence and the people God has loved with an everlasting love in Christ – he will so use them that *all* will work together for the good of those who love him.

'The God of Jacob' brings us suddenly to look at God from a very different and entirely unexpected perspective. The psalmist is bringing the picture of God in all the glory of his transcendent and his creative power alongside the picture of the God of Jacob. What a juxtaposition. Our thoughts are brought down from the glory and the light and the splendour and the beauty and the praises and the sound and the sights of heaven down to one little planet, to one little land, down to one lonely man.

There are two pictures in the psalmist's mind when he speaks of the God of Jacob. One is of a man who had gone out because of deceit and sin from all that he had ever known as home, and all he had for a pillow was a stone. There is something of the loneliness, the sadness, the inadequacy and the frailty of humanity in him. You might not be able to identify with the hosts of heaven or with the angels and the seraphim but you can identify with the loneliness, the desolation and the darkness of a man who lay down on the earth to sleep. Jacob met with God at Bethel.

Twenty years later God comes to him again at Penuel and he moulds and he breaks Jacob, not in order to destroy, but to re-make him. Afterwards Jacob could say, 'I have seen God face to face.' He was limping but he had seen God. Jacob – the supplanter, the twister – can you identify with that? Have you learned how near a brother you are to Jacob? Has God shown you your own heart? Then this God can still be your God. He is not just the LORD of hosts – he is also the God of Jacob. He is not just the Creator God but the Redeemer God – the God who draws near in mercy and in love.

The psalmist has shown us a picture of a God who is infinite in his majesty and also infinite in his mercy. The one who commands every intelligence that ever came into being and the one who loves with a passionate love men like Jacob.

Look at the declaration the psalmist builds on that truth. The LORD of hosts is with us. He is not so busy with all the hosts and beings he has created that he forgets us. He is with us. He will press all the hosts that are at his command into making us match his purposes for us. Let me remind you that God uses the angels, ministering spirits who are in the presence of God, to help us. God will use even the hosts of his enemies in such a way that where sin abounds grace will much more abound. The instruments that are sharpened against the people of God will be turned to their deliverance. The 'hosts of God' – do you ever think of yourself as one of the marching hosts of God? The church of Christ is made up of individuals and it is your privilege to minister to the needs of your fellow-believers.

God is our refuge – our high place. The idea is of one being lifted out of danger and being set in the place of ultimate safety and security. The God of Jacob is the one who came down, who touched and laid hold of Jacob – this God is our ultimate security. Perhaps you cannot believe that we are as safe and secure as that. Perhaps you cannot believe that angels and stars and even the enemies of God are being used under the hand of God for our deliverance or that God harnessed and brought into his redemptive purpose one who outshines all the angels, one who is greater than all the hosts of heaven.

All the hosts of heaven could not redeem one sinner. All the hosts of God on earth could not redeem one sinner. But there was one beside him on the throne, his fellow, his delight, and God spared him not. 'How shall he not with him also freely give us all things?' (Rom. 8:32).

Can I close by reminding you for your comfort how Paul, who knew these things so deeply, described the safety and the security of the people of God: 'Blessed be the God and Father of our Lord Jesus Christ, who has blessed us with all spiritual blessings in the heavenly places in Christ' (Eph. 1:3). And Paul also said this, and let this be true for you and for me: 'If ye then be risen with Christ, seek those things which are above, where Christ sitteth on the right hand of God. Set your affection on things above, not on things on the earth. For you are dead and your life is hid with Christ in God' (Col. 3:1-3).

There is the ultimate refuge – seated with Christ on the throne, in the very heart of the being who is God – Father, Son and Holy Spirit. When he placed you with Christ, God couched you in the very heart of his trinal power and his trinal glory. You cannot be lost.

Let me say to you if you are unconverted, unconvinced and therefore ungodly: 'None perish that trust him.'

23

The Holy God

Rejoice in the LORD, ye righteous; and give thanks
at the remembrance of his holiness (Psalm 97:12).

Deep-felt gratitude before the holiness of God is of the essence of
what the Psalmist is saying here in his exhortation.

We owe both the word and the thought of holiness to special
revelation. This is true even when we apply the concept of holiness not to man but to God.

You might think that wherever men have been aware of God
and where they have believed upon a god of some kind – even
where they have not been the recipients of special revelation such
as we have in the Scriptures – you would think they would have
some kind of conception of the holiness of God. The nearness of
God in creation and the impressions that all men have of his being and his power might lead us to believe that. I think it is not so.
I think that the Bible alone confronts men with a God who is
holy. When we look at pagan religions and at the religious conscience of people today, the thought of divine holiness, which we
might think would be paramount, is absent from their concept of
God. Therefore I say that holiness, the very thought as well as the
word, comes to us from the Bible.

We can think of many of the divine attributes – those aspects
of God's being and character which we can trace out in his Word.
We could think of many of them that would give cause for gratitude in our thinking of God and in our worship of him. For example, what a beautiful aspect of God's nature is goodness. Or what
a marvellous thing is the wisdom of God in the light of our own
folly and intellectual inadequacy. How thankful we should be that
there is a mind that encompasses all reality and that knows all
reality and that reaches out beyond knowing all reality into knowing all possibility.

Or what about his mercy? The more we grow into a knowledge

Preached 28 July 1991

of our sin and the very vileness that our sin can produce, the more we are aware of how wonderful is the mercy of God.

It's amazing that people like us should ever feel a flow of gratitude for the holiness of God. Perhaps that is because our ideas of holiness are not very scriptural or perhaps it is because the concept of holiness is so far beyond us that it is hard to grasp. Not many would say that they are thankful that God is a holy God. I believe that if we stop to think about the implications of God's holiness we would feel tremendous gratitude welling up in our hearts for this supreme and superb aspect of his being and nature.

What I want to do, if I can, is to stir that thought in your minds: 'How good it is that God is a holy God.'

1. The holiness of God should create gratitude within us because it is one of the fundamental principles of the divine revelation of God.

The Bible speaks of God as holy. He is frequently entitled 'the Holy One of Israel'. There is none holy as God is holy. There is none holy but God. 'Who shall not fear thee, O Lord, and glorify thy name? For thou only art holy' (Rev. 15:4).

The holiness of God should stir glory in your soul, should stir that which would glorify and adore and admire him. Is that the God that you worship and serve and delight in? He is an admirable God and all too often we distance ourselves from him. One of the reasons that we distance ourselves from him is our concept of his holiness. But that should not be a reason for putting God far away from us.

Every created being is excluded from the possession of essential holiness. God is in his character that which none other is and which none other can ever be. God's will is ever in absolute harmony with his perfect, divine nature. He is his own standard of holiness. God is in perfect conformity to his divine nature. All the attributes of God – his mercy and his goodness as well as his justice and his wrath – they are all qualified and imbued with the quality of holiness.

Is God angry with the wicked every day? His anger is righteous anger, holy anger, anger which if it was not there would mean an imperfection in the divine being in the face of evil and wickedness and transgression.

When the Bible talks about the holiness of God it does so simply. It doesn't embroil us in theological definitions although out of its teaching come all theological definitions. It sets God out as absolute in his holiness, as different from all others. There is an exclusiveness about God and an inclusiveness. He is holy by a necessity of his nature. No created being is holy in that way. The angels are not holy by a necessity of their nature or they would never have fallen without ceasing to be angels. Evidently holiness was not a necessity of human nature or men could never have fallen into sin without ceasing to be human. God is holy in such a way that it is unimaginable that he could be anything but holy. It is a necessity of his nature. He cannot be other and he never shall be other than holy in his nature. It sets God outside of all classification and it sets him apart from all categorisation. We do not have anyone or anything to whom or with whom we can make a comparison in our thinking about God.

He is apart but not alone, lofty but not lonely, because he is three. 'Holy, holy, holy.' In the Trinity there is the acme of perfect fellowship, cradled in and nourished by perfect holiness. What mars fellowship on earth? What mars fellowship between Christians? Unholiness and sinfulness mar our relationships – there is none of that in God. In Isaiah 40:25 we read these words: 'To whom then will you liken me, or shall I be equal?' saith the Holy One.

This is a rhetorical question. There is absolutely no basis of comparison within our human experience when we think of the holiness of God except the man Christ Jesus. That is why it is so important and so marvellous to get to know Jesus. This is why Jesus could say, 'I do always the things that please him' (John 8:29). He was as pleasing to the love of the Father as the man Christ Jesus as he had been through all eternity in his person as the eternal Son. His humanity and his servanthood, even his suffering, did not separate him from the holy love of his holy Father.

This question emphasises that God is incomparable. You cannot compare God with anyone or anything. He stands absolutely alone. Again and again Scripture uses the idea of holiness as a name for God. That only struck me when I was preparing this sermon. It has been before me all my life and I never really saw it.

The holiness of God is interwoven with all the history of God's gracious work among men.

Take the Bible, the biblical history of man fallen and man renewed, and the holiness of God is woven all through it. You can't remove the holiness of God from it. It is a fundamental theme of biblical revelation.

The holiness of God is the inspiration of all the poetry of Scripture, poetry that fires the mind and warms the heart and draws us to him. All the poetry in the Bible, where it flashes and shines and stirs is looking at the fact of the holiness of God.

The holiness of God is the foundation of all the biblical legislation. Take away the holiness of God and the ten commandments begin to make nonsense. That is why a church that has removed the absoluteness of God and replaced it with the relativity of man's ethics loses its way. The holiness of God is what undergirds and upholds the whole concept of law. His holiness is the only final measure we have of what is good and what is bad, of what is right and what is wrong, of what is worthwhile and what is only dust and ashes. Do you see how fundamental a principle is the holiness of God?

Take away the idea of the holiness of God from the Bible and the whole book falls into chaos. The Bible is so infused with the thought and the teaching and the breathing of the holiness of God that that alone is a good reason for setting the Bible off from every other book. It is one of the strengths of our belief in the inspired Word of God that it all hangs together so marvellously around the central, fundamental theme of the holiness of God.

What is redemption? It is a reaching out of the holiness of God in grace and love. What is the work of Christ? It is an undergirding of the holiness of God in salvation, enabling him to be just and the justifier of the ungodly who believe on Jesus.

2. There should be gratitude in our hearts because the holiness of God is a fundamental presupposition of the divine redemption held out to us in Christ.

God took a long time to teach men how sinful is the human heart. His work in preparing the world for the salvation that was to come took many centuries. The more we get to know of our own hearts and the more we get to know of the stiff rebellion of the human heart against the gospel of grace, the more we understand why God walked so slowly.

God gave even unfallen man a special day, his holy day, separate, different from all other days. When redemption was complete in Christ he made it the first of the week – beginning the week with the thought of redemption.

Did God give us a special word from himself to penetrate the darkness? He did. What did he call it? He called it 'My holy Word.'

Did God give a special house to Israel in the wilderness to teach them to come to a throne of grace, to teach them that there was a revelation? He did. What did he call it? He called it 'My holy Place.'

Did he give them a special name by which to worship him? He did:. 'Holy is my name.'

Did he make a spiritual people out of one little nation to teach the world through whom the Saviour would come? He did. What did he call them? 'My holy people.'

Did he give a Son to be a Redeemer? He did. What by the Spirit did he call the Son? How does he describe to us the Son in human nature? He is described as 'holy, harmless and undefiled, separate from sinners'. What a marvellous description of the One who had come to save. It staggers me, the older I get, to know that he was holy, harmless, undefiled, separate from sinners and I thank God that he was so. Do you? Do you thank God that Jesus never failed as you have failed? Do you thank God that Jesus has never sinned as you have sinned? Do you thank God that in his holy presence there is a holy man and that he is our Saviour?

Let me speak to the unconverted. How can you go on neglecting and walking past such a Saviour as Jesus is? In walking past him you are destroying yourself with an everlasting destruction. How can you do it?

There was a life and there was a death, and the life was holy and the death was undefiled. There was a grave and it was new; there was a resurrection – there couldn't but be a resurrection; and there was an ascension. There is a God-man at God's right hand who is the Saviour.

3. *We should be grateful for the holiness of God because it is the great prerequisite of Christian worship.*

What makes your heart bow before God? What makes him so attractive and so admirable in your eyes? If God were not holy, would he be worthy of the worship of your heart? If God – Father, Son and Holy Spirit – were not holy, then any rational creature worshipping him would be demeaning his own rationality. Any spiritual being worshipping an unholy God would be defiling his spirit. The God who calls you to obey him, the God who calls you to admire him, the God who calls you to love him with all your mind and heart and soul, he is perfect – morally, ethically, personally, spiritually. That is his holiness.

You and I can worship and love him by his grace with all our mind and heart and soul and we do not prostitute these God-given gifts of our personality. We lift them and we exalt them, and man is never, in the exercise of his personality and gifts, doing anything higher or more worthwhile than he is doing when he is bowing to and exalting and glorifying and admiring this God. If you are a Christian believer now, it will be your exercise one day to perfectly worship him in heaven and to join in the songs of the seraphim round the throne: 'Holy, holy, holy, Lord God almighty.'

And when you are there among them you will be holy too, and that will make the worship and the praise and the adoration and the admiration all the more beautiful because they will be tinged with that which in the character of God himself alone is perfect.

Give thanks at the remembrance of his holiness.

24

Earnest Prayer

'I have set watchmen upon thy walls, O Jerusalem,
which shall never hold their peace day nor night: ye
that make mention of the LORD, keep not silence, and
give him no rest, till he establish, and till he make
Jerusalem a praise in the earth' (Isaiah 62:6-7).

From our text we will isolate some words from verse 7: 'and give
him no rest'. There are places where marvellous truths are drawn
to our attention in a staggering way, with a boldness of language
from which any preacher would shrink and that would be unac-
ceptable if the language used were not the language inspired by
God himself. The very thought that God's people should bother
him and give him no rest and no peace until he hears and demon-
strably answers their prayers, until he comes forth and reveals the
glory of his name and his praise in the hearts of his people – that
is bold indeed.

One sphere of Christian life that is frequently set before us by
precept and by exhortation is prayer. If there is one place where
Christian life knows failure it is in the place of prayer. If there is
one place where in our day the church of God is weak in our land
it is, I believe with all my heart, the place of prayer. If there is one
place where the church of God requires to be strong in our land it
is there.

Relatively speaking, it is easy today to profess Christ and to
profess to be a spiritual man or woman. It was seldom easier to
attend a church where you will hear the Word of God faithfully
preached by sincere men and we thank God for that. It is com-
paratively easy to familiarise yourself to a great extent with the
Word of God. You can study the Bible in clear understandable
translations and if you go to Hell it won't be because you didn't
have a Bible in your hand. If you don't prosper as a Christian man

or woman, if you are not growing and if you don't have daily, hourly communion with God, it is not because you don't have the Word of God.

It is easy to say that we have a name to live, and yet to be as dead as a soul that has never come under the saving power of the Holy Spirit of God. Sadly, for young people growing up in Christian homes, it is all too easy to be content with a name to live. That is my greatest fear for young people growing up under praying, professing Christian parents. It is my greatest fear for my own soul – that I have a name to live and am dead. Why do I say these things? I say them because we have a need for the presence and for the power of God in a way in which we do not have them. There is only one way in which we can have them: 'Give him no rest till he establish and till he make Jerusalem a praise in the earth.'

Exhortations to prayer are rampant in Scripture. Alongside every exhortation to pray, almost without exception, there is an encouragement given. Sometimes the encouragement is very explicit and is by way of promise: 'If you seek me with all your heart, you shall find me.' When you seek God with all the energy of your being then you will find him.

We are also encouraged by example. Jacob is set before us as a man who was so laid hold of by God that at last he called on God and said, 'I will not let thee go except thou bless me.' Then there was Elijah – a man with the same failings and weaknesses and the same humanity as ourselves. He had the same unbelief plaguing his heart and his life, the same lowness of mind because of sin. He ran for his life one day and when he came to the end of his flight he said, 'Lord, let me die.' He knew what failure was, he knew what unbelief was, and yet the Bible tells us that when Elijah prayed, heaven heard. When God's people pray, heaven always hears.

In the prayer before us exhortation and encouragement are marvellously combined. They are linked and intertwined. The thought central to the text is that we give God no peace, that we bother him until he answers. We may be silent for days as far as prayer is concerned, but God's ear is ever open. If God is not hearing our prayers the fault is not God's – the fault lies with ourselves.

God has linked together prayer and spiritual prosperity
There will never be spiritual prosperity without prayer and there
will never be prayer without it resulting in spiritual prosperity.
    Spiritual prosperity on an *individual* level is linked with prayer.
If we do not pray we will not prosper. No man or woman will be
saved without prayer. I'm not saying that they will pray easily.
I'm not saying that they will pray regularly or as earnestly or as
spiritually as they should – but they will pray. Imagine a sinner
being dealt with kindly, graciously and savingly by God and who
has never asked God to deal with him or with her in that way.
Now don't make a mistake. I'm not saying that prayer saves a
sinner. You can be on your knees for years and that will not save
your soul. Prayer does not save a sinner but a sinner who does not
pray will not be saved. A sinner is saved by trusting in the Lord
Jesus and his finished work. A sinner is saved by calling upon
Jesus to become a personal Saviour and that call is the very heart
of prayer.
    On a *ministerial* level, prayer and spiritual prosperity are also
linked together and I'm speaking here of Christian service. Your
service will not prosper without prayer.
    Let me speak for a moment about ministry as the preaching of
the Good News of Jesus Christ and pastoring the people of God.
As we look back over history we know of men who were outstanding preachers and through whom many were brought into
fellowship with God – men who were used in the transformation
of their society. One thing has characterised all great and useful
preachers. Whatever their differences in appearance, in presentation and style – all were men of prayer. Prayer is paramount and
God will only give the blessing of the Holy Spirit if we ask in
prayer. Of the ministerial and of the individual levels of Christian
service, prayer is the most important element.
    What do we need to be effective Christians wherever God has
called us to live and serve? We need the power and indwelling of
the Holy Spirit: 'If ye who are evil, know how to give good gifts
to your children, how much more will your Father in heaven give
the Spirit to them that ask him' (Matt. 7:11). We need to pray the
prayer of Robert Murray McCheyne: 'Lord, give me as much of
the Holy Spirit as a saved sinner can have and can hold.'
    Then there is the *congregational* level. Here again is the very

heart and centre of a real family life within a congregation. Let me ask you a very simple question. Do you pray for your fellow believers in your congregation? Do you continually lift them up before God and pray that God will adorn them with grace and make them beautiful in your eyes, beautiful in the eyes of their fellow-believers and beautiful in the eyes of their Saviour? Do you pray that God will make them as bright shining lights in the darkness of this world? Do you pray for your fellow believers that they will be the salt of the earth? Do you pray that love, in all its power and intensity, would fill our hearts so that we really love one another and speak to one another and care for one another and bear one another's burdens? Do you pray that people will come under the power of God when they come in to your church? Without prayer there will be no prosperity on a congregational level. Do you expect your congregation to grow in grace and in the knowledge of Christ? Do you expect it to be a warm, caring Christian congregation? When unconverted men and women come in, will they be conscious that Christian people are in possession of something that they lack? Do you long to hear of old people and young coming to know Christ? Then *pray*.

The difficulty can be in putting theory into practice. One way to help that is to look at our text again: 'Give him no rest.'

God will not rest until he sees Jerusalem (the church on earth) a praise in the earth. The watchmen referred to at the beginning of verse 6 were there to warn of danger and may be representative of prophetic preachers. These watchmen are never to hold their peace. Those who make mention of the Lord, those who call on the Lord, are not to keep silence. They are not to take rest to themselves. Not only is it that God is to be given no rest but we also have to stir ourselves up.

The easiest thing to do in the Christian life is to rest from the urgency and the energy of true prayer. There is nothing easier to do than to fall out of the habit or to make prayer merely a habit. If there is one thing I have learned in thirty-six years of following Christ, it is that prayer is far from easy. I have also learned that to forsake prayer, to give up praying is the most fatal and deadly thing to our Christian profession. If you want to backslide, grow cold, distance yourself from God then stop praying regularly. I have never met a young Christian or an old Christian who has known the experience of backsliding and of falling into sin but they have confessed when they came back that they had stopped praying.

Prayer takes us to three places. It takes us to a place where we know *our continual dependence upon God*. It takes us to the only place where we'll ever come to *a just estimate of self*. We are apt to think more highly of ourselves than we ought. It will take us to the only place in the world where we'll find *God's perspective on what our lives should be*. The place where we will know continually and daily our dependence on God; the place where we will have a just estimate of what we are – dust of the earth; and a true perspective of what our life should be as we journey towards the judgement seat of a holy God.

'My voice shalt thou hear in the morning, O LORD; in the morning will I direct my prayer unto thee, and will look up' (Psalm 5:3).

25

The Forgiveness of a Holy God

'If thou, LORD, shouldest mark iniquities,
O LORD, who shall stand?' (Psalm 130:3).

This psalm is a cry out of the depths. It is not merely the cry from
the depths of a heart, but the cry of a heart in the depths. It is the
cry of a heart in the grip of a deeply disturbing and distressing
experience. That this distress was spiritual rather than temporal
is clear from the whole tenor of the psalm for it deals, not with
outward difficulties and dangers, but with inward and spiritual
ones. It deals, not with the merely passing and transient complexities of human life, but with the permanent and abiding realities of the divine-human relationship. That is its focus; that is its
framework; that is its burden. It deals with man in relation to
God. Its perspective is not temporal, but eternal; its values are not
material, but spiritual; and its concern is, supremely, the concern
of a God-conscious soul.

The concern of this man in his God-consciousness is not superficial; it is a deep awareness of God as *God*, of God as holy
and just and terrible. It is an awareness of God as the sin-marking
Jehovah. And that awareness of God as *God* has led to an awareness of self – of self as sinner. Out of this self-knowledge distress
has emerged – the distress of sinnership and estrangement – and
out of distress has come his cry: 'O LORD, hear my voice.'

That is the depths out of which this psalm has emerged, and its
very emergence is a message of hope to all who know distress
because of God and because of self. Such depths often silence
those they engulf, but this psalm tells us of one who, while yet in
the depths, laid hold of God as one in whom is 'plenteous redemption'.

The words of our text single out the attitude of God to sin and
the psalmist's sharp concern with it. To *mark* means to 'watch' or
to 'observe' – but to watch in such a way that what is observed is

noted and retained. In 'marking sin' God is taking cognisance of it, noting it and keeping his knowledge in retention for purposes of punishment.

The words of our text bring into perspective three factors that have a crucial bearing upon the divine-human relationship – three things that bear upon man's standing with God: (1) The Guilt of Sin; (2) The Holiness of God; (3) The Marvel of Forgiveness.

1. The Guilt of Sin: 'If thou shouldst mark iniquities ... who shall stand?'

It is easy to think of at least two ways in which God 'marks' sin, and indeed in which he *must* mark all the sins of all men. Firstly, he must mark it by seeing it, by observing its every occurrence, and secondly, he must mark it by being displeased with it. No sin of any man can go unobserved if God is truly the omniscient, all-seeing God the Bible declares him to be. 'All things,' says the writer to the Hebrews, 'are naked and opened unto the eyes of him with whom we have to do' (4:13). He is the one who is stated to be, not merely an observer of men's actions, but a discerner of the secret thoughts and intents of the heart.

No sin can be committed that does not arouse the great displeasure of God. If every sin is an offence against the character of God of which the Law is just a transcript, then the real guilt of sin lies, not only in its transgression of the Law, but also in its offence to the God who gave the Law.

These are two ways in which God marks sin, and marks it just because he is God. It inheres in his nature that all sin is observed by him, and that all sin is morally offensive to him.

As the word is used in the text, however, it goes further than that. The indication is that sin is being viewed in direct relation to its punishment. To 'mark iniquities' is linked to a supposition; it is '*If* thou shouldest mark iniquities', and supposition leads on, in turn, to an inference, and the inference is plain and strong: If God *should* mark iniquity, then none shall stand!

So the immediate context gives the word its fullest content. It means, not merely that sin is seen of God and that sin is offensive to God, but it means also that God has pronounced judgement upon sin. He regards sin as something which must be dealt with. He looks upon the sinner as guilty, and that guilt has incurred its

own penalty, as guilt always does. It means that there is further
action to be taken by God in relation to sin; there is yet to be the
imposition of its full penalty.

That is the supposition in the mind of the Psalmist. He is supposing the full infliction of punishment, so he asks, 'If that occurs, then, "Who shall stand?" ' If that occurs, then all must go
down; all must come to the experience of Cain who had to cry,
'My punishment is more than I can bear' (Gen. 4:13).

When we are being truly honest, we must re-echo what the
psalmist says. If God should deal justly with our sin, not one of us
could stand. If the wages of sin is death, then each one of us has
earned these wages for ourselves: for 'all have sinned' (Rom.
3:23).

This awareness is what conviction of sin really involves. We
become aware, not merely that we have sinned, but that our sin
has brought us to a place of guilt before God. True conviction of
sin carries with it the consciousness that our every sin deserves
the wrath and curse of God. The sinner under conviction sees sin
in a new light. He sees sin as something that has brought the soul
into real and abiding danger. He now sees that God's Law is righteous and just and holy, that God's Law is right, and that the law-
breaker is wrong. There is both the vindication of God and the
condemnation of self.

To think like this goes against the grain of the natural heart,
and it has always done so. No man likes to reflect upon his sin
and guilt and upon the punishment that his sin deserves from God.
Deuteronomy 29 speaks of some who, when they hear of God's
curse on sin, merely bless themselves and say they shall have
peace. Let the Law with its terrors be preached; many will despise it. It takes nothing less than a mighty work of the Holy Spirit
to convince the human heart of sin and of righteousness and of
judgement to come.

This fact tells us that the man in this psalm, the man who cried
out of the depths, and out of his distress, was one in whom God
had done a real work of *grace*. He had been brought to the place
where he saw the guilt and ill-desert of sin – perhaps that was one
of the factors in his distress – and he saw that if God should mark
his sin, things would go ill with him. That was one factor which
he saw as having a bearing upon his relationship to God. And it

has a bearing upon our standing with God also.

The guilt of sin is something God cannot ignore. It shuts sinners out from him in heaven, from peace. Therefore, seek peace while it is to be found.

That brings us to the second item in our text that bears upon our standing with God. This man clearly had a glimpse of:

2. The Holiness of God: If *thou* shouldst mark iniquities ...
The Psalmist sees God as the Lawgiver. He looks into the Law and there sees the reflection and transcript of a perfectly holy character. His awareness of God is the awareness of one who is just and righteous in all his ways and holy in all his doings. It is not just that God has the attribute of holiness. He *is* a holy God, and all his attributes – his love, his mercy, his justice, his truth, his wisdom, his anger – are holy attributes. He is the one of whom Scripture says that 'he is of purer eyes than to behold iniquity' (Hab. 1:13). 'He chargeth his angels with folly and the heavens are not clean in his sight' (Job 4:18).

For this man, there is nothing strange in a just God who will punish injustice and wickedness and evil. To hear from the lips of this God the words, 'Vengeance is mine, I will repay' (Rom. 12:19), or 'The wicked shall be turned into hell' (Ps. 9:17) does not sound strange to him. And that is because he accepts God as God and not, as one has put it, 'as an idiot of his own imagination, who turns a blind eye to evil and wrong and injustice'.

This is precisely what modern man needs to learn – that God is holy. Before this God Moses, one of the meekest of men, exceedingly feared and trembled. Sadly, we have to write over this generation, and even over the Evangelicalism of this age, 'The fear of God is not before its eyes.'

Let me direct attention to two places where the awful holiness of God shines out very clearly.

The first is the Garden of Eden. As soon as Adam had sinned he became conscious that God had 'marked' his sin. Adam was so aware of this awesome fact that all he could say was, 'I heard thy voice in the garden, and I was *afraid*' (Gen. 3:10). His fear was rooted in the simple fact that a holy God was coming to deal with his sinful and fallen creature. God was coming, and man no longer wanted to meet the God who had made him. Why? Be-

cause the meeting was unbearable for the one who was in the
wrong. It is never easy to meet even a friend that one may have
wronged. But what must it be to meet the holy God that we have
wronged? There was only one desire in Adam's heart at the
thought – it was to crawl away and hide. He tried it, but could not
achieve it. Where was the tree in the garden that could conceal
him from the all-seeing eye of omniscience?

The other place where the holiness of God is emphasised is
nearer to us in time than the garden of Eden. It is also a garden,
'the Garden of Gethsemane' – but the person is not the first, but
the last Adam. In and of himself the Lord Jesus never had cause
or occasion for any discouraging or uneasy thought. He was holy,
harmless, undefiled. He fulfilled all righteousness, performed his
Father's will in all things, and dwelt always in the favour and
love of God. This holy and righteous obedience could engender
nothing but the greatest peace in the heart of the man Christ Jesus.
The doing of God's will was his delight.

Yet when we see him in Gethsemane, when he was faced with
thoughts of God's marking iniquity and transgression upon him,
his soul was sorrowful unto death. He was amazed and heavy in
spirit. He agonised. He cried his most amazing prayer: 'Father, if
it be possible, let this cup pass from me...'. If there was to be
redemption it was *not* possible. There we see him with the sweat
running as blood. There is revealed to us what he reckoned it was
for God to mark iniquity.

And remember, the sin that he bore was not his own. There
were elements missing from his suffering that will be in the cup
of woe that the lost drink; there will be regret and remorse and
hatred of the hand that inflicts the penalty. There were none of
those in the sufferings of Christ.

The sufferings of Christ speak to men not only of the love of
God. They also speak of his great holiness, of his eternal justice
and of his spotless righteousness. Look at Jesus' sufferings and
remember what Scripture says, 'If they do these things in the green
tree, what shall be done in the dry?' (Luke 23:31). If that is God
marking iniquity, if the cry, 'My God, my God, why hast thou
forsaken me?' (Matt. 27:46) indicates the place where the sinless
Son bears the imposition of sin's penalty, where, oh where, will
the ungodly and the sinner appear?

Friend, have you had a glimpse of the holiness of God? This, remember, is the God before whom you must yet stand. But, the perspectives of our text are not only those of guilt and of holiness; there is the perspective of *forgiveness* as well.

3. The Marvel of Forgiveness: 'but yet with thee there is forgiveness.'

This man sees forgiveness as a reality. This is where the true work of the Holy Spirit leads. It makes the soul look away from itself for help and for hope, away to the everlasting love of God. The Psalmist sees that sin was not only against God's Law but against God's love. When awareness of one's own sin and God's love meet, it is then that the soul bows down in humble contrition and repentance. For it sees how divine love and mercy and grace and patience have all been exercised by the God of all mercies.

This love is revealed in only one place – the Cross. Love has come in partnership with justice and holiness. By way of the Cross the sinner sees that all the righteous demands of Law have been amply met and a fair basis for the forgiveness of sin has been laid.

Then the soul sees that it was as a sinner that God loved him from the very beginning, that God loved him while he was totally unworthy of that love. He sees that God's love is a gracious and free love, and that it flows out, not because of the beauty of its object, but because of the nature of the one who loves.

That is love indeed: gracious, free, eternal love. It is a glimpse of this love that leads to true repentance and that stirs and makes strong the faith that trusts unto salvation.

26

Jesus Satisfied With his People

'He shall see of the travail of his soul,
and shall be satisfied' (Isaiah 53:11).

No Old Testament prophet gives clearer testimony to Christ than Isaiah. Nowhere does Isaiah more clearly articulate the gospel than he does in this chapter. In it he describes, first, the sufferings of Christ, and then his triumph. In the first part of it, the Messiah is seen going forth weeping, and bearing precious seed; in the closing verses he is seen coming again with rejoicing, bringing his sheaves with him.

It is in the middle of the tenth verse that the descriptions of suffering close, and the unfoldings of victory and triumph begin: 'he shall see his seed, he shall prolong his days, and the pleasure of the LORD shall prosper in his hand.'

Our text contemplates Christ's completed work from a viewpoint quite different to that from which we normally have it presented to us. The precise subject to which our thought is invited is not what Christ is to believers, but what believers are to Christ. The satisfaction of which the prophet speaks is not the joy of a sinner in the Saviour who redeems him, but the joy of the Saviour over sinners whom he has redeemed. The *redemption* of the lost is still the grand object of contemplation; but here it is contemplated as seen, not from earth, but from heaven. Here we have, not a company of fallen men looking unto Jesus that they may be saved, but Jesus looking on a company of the *saved* that he may be *satisfied*.

1. The Reality of His Sufferings
All the sufferings which have earlier been enumerated are caught-up and brought to focus in the words, 'The travail of his soul'. This strong phrase points us beyond the outward to the inward. While the things done to him physically were very real and very terrible – wounding, bruising, scourging, stripes – every word

indicating increasing intensity of outward bodily pain – yet, the
inward sufferings of his spirit were by far the keenest and the
sharpest. They produced within him a terrible travail of soul.

The Hebrew word underlying 'travail' has not the distinctive
meaning which now attaches to the English word. The Hebrew
original has no reference to childbirth. It indicates, as 'travail'
did at the time our translators used it, severity of effort, painful
exertion, exhausting work, and refers to the whole work and sorrow of Christ as he engaged in the strenuous labour of atoning for
our sin.

That is the kind of work it was, a task which involved ex-
tremes of pain, both spiritual and physical. As Jesus engaged in
and carried through the work that could not be accomplished apart
from outward wounding and inward bruising, so he felt the full
agony of body and anguish of soul that the task inevitably ex-
acted of the one who would carry it through to completion.

The figure under which it is all described is not that of the
pangs of childbirth, but the toiling endurance of one who breaks
up the earth of a garden or field and, after much painful labour,
casts into it his seed. It is a labour in the sphere of death and
desolation in order to achieve the production of a living fruitful
harvest – a labour of the most exacting and anguishing kind.

What a picture this is of Christ and the task he came to accomplish! The sphere of his operation was this world, blasted and
desolated by sin, under the wrath and curse of God, a sphere where
death reigned. And Jesus came so that, through death, 'he might
destroy him that had the power of death, that is, the devil; and
deliver them who through fear of death were all their lifetime
subject to bondage' (Heb. 2:14).

From the glory of heaven he came – from its worship and
adoration, from its holy and happy environment, from its glorious throne – into a world where he was despised and rejected by
the very people he came to save. Instead of being worshipped, he
was mocked; in the place of gladly-given adoration, he was taunted
for his love and meekness; in the place of glory, he was humbled
and made to bear the lash of an unbelieving scorn. What a contrast!

And yet that is the outward contrast only. Inwardly, his holy
nature was pained by the laying on it of that which deserved the

Father's hatred and wrath – sin. He was made to feel the guilt which sin carries with it, and to bear the punishment which sin deserves. Yet, he did not shrink from the contact, and the pain of soul which that contact involved. Instead, he threw his whole heart into it and withheld not one iota of his energy and the toiling that the task demanded of him. His labour was soul-labour, and it was whole-souled labour.

So, his suffering was soul-suffering – a soul-suffering that was endured and carried through without any kind of withdrawal on the part of a nature that was hyper-sensitive to the touch of sin. That holy sensitivity exposed him to the sharpest thrusts of evil, as 'he was made sin for us, who knew no sin' – like laying a wound on flesh already opened to the quick. Those thrusts sank into a soul and conscience totally unarmed to meet them, as ours so sadly are, by the hardening processes that follow in the wake of personal sin which Scripture describes as the 'deceitfulness of sin'.

Not only his innocence, but his holiness of heart and soul contributed to the intensity of his sufferings. That comes out quite clearly in the words that fell from his lips as the shadows of the cross began to gather around him. As he prepared to minister at the altar of his terrible sacrifice, what do we hear from him? 'Now is my soul troubled; and what shall I say?' 'Father, if it be possible, let this cup pass from me.' The wounded spirit which 'none can bear' was never uttered but was signalled by the sweat, like 'great drops of blood falling down to the ground'. These were what the ancient church calls our Lord's 'unknown agonies'. His sufferings were real soul-sufferings for he was pouring out his soul 'unto death' as he met all the demands of inflexible justice and as he paid, with his life, the wages of sin.

2. The Result of His Sufferings

It is not to the realities of his sufferings that our Saviour looks, but to the results of them. 'Because of his sufferings, he sees and is satisfied.' His labour and the pain involved has not been in vain. Here the love of Christ to his people shines out very wonderfully. He looks beyond the travail of his soul and fixes his gaze on the results that it secures.

The soul-searching, wounding work which he has put into this

world of desolation – that field of sin and death in which he agonised and laboured – is bearing fruit, carrying a harvest which is
fast ripening into the golden sheaves which he will take home
rejoicing. Christ's sufferings were not in vain. Even in the midst
of them the end product was before his eye: 'Who for the joy that
was set before him, endured the cross' (Heb. 12:2).

What does he see?

A vast multitude saved. No man can number them – but he
did, and does.

A universe purged from sin – no rebellion or disobedience in
any corner of it – 'All things put under him'.

All ungodliness confined and devoted to everlasting destruction.

God glorified in the marvel of his redemptive love.

All this roots back to, and is because of, the 'travail of his
soul'.

3. The Reward of His Sufferings
He delights in the glory and completion of his work. Every redeemed soul is precious to him because he travailed for it. Christians take much satisfaction in such a Saviour – but not as much
as the satisfaction which the Saviour takes in them. He knows
what they have been redeemed from, as they never will. He knows
the cost of their salvation, as they never will.

This is what his soul-suffering has led to – his soul-satisfac-
tion. It meets all the requirements of his mighty mind; it gratifies
all the love that is in his large heart. What a view of that love is
opened up for us in the thought of satisfaction. He is completely
satisfied with what he has done and accomplished.

Bethlehem, Gethsemane, Calvary have left no regrets. There
is not the slightest grudge about the terrible price he paid – were
it still to be accomplished, he would do it over again. Looking
back on all that he has endured, and forward to all that it has
accomplished, he is totally content – he is fully and wonderfully
satisfied with the sight. Nothing more is required!

What peace for the Christian to know that his Saviour rejoices
in him.

Are there some who say, 'What must I do to be saved?' Is
hope restrained? Are you afraid to believe that the Holy One of

God would come so close and do so much for you? *Remember
this*. His work was not for the good, but for the bad people; his
travail and labour of soul was for sinners. He loves, not those
who cost him nothing, but those who cost him much, who cost
him in terms of tears and anguish and suffering and death. And
when an unworthy sinner believes, *then* that sight satisfies his
soul.

Are there those who cling, still, to sin? Such have no Saviour,
and the Saviour has no delight in them.

27

Brotherly Love

'To Titus, mine own son after the common faith:
Grace, mercy, and peace, from God the Father and
the Lord Jesus Christ our Saviour' (Titus 1:4).

Titus was one of the most useful and best loved of Paul's helpers
in the gospel. Along with Timothy, he seemed to hold a special
place in the affection of the great apostle, and that is not surprising for Titus and Timothy had in common an unwavering loyalty
to the cause of Christ. They both had a willingness to undertake
difficult missions, as well as a high regard for their spiritual father and superior, Paul.

Yet, in one respect the two differ. Titus is more of a leader,
Timothy more of a follower. Titus is the type of man who is able,
not only to take orders, but also to forge ahead of his own accord.
He seems more resourceful than Timothy – stronger, certainly, in
health, and having a strong will that can act on its own initiative.
One senses in him something of the aggressiveness of Paul himself when it comes to the work of the gospel.

Titus seems to have been a man of considerable initiative, of
sound common sense, of good business ability. He was a man
who could handle people. If Paul had any difficult matter to be
investigated, he usually sent Titus to do it. Although he is not
mentioned in the Book of Acts by name, he is mentioned thirteen
times in the other Pauline Epistles – and, in addition, there is this
Pastoral letter which Paul wrote to him.

Paul's estimate of him comes through clearly in these various
references. On one occasion in Macedonia, Paul tells the Corinthians that when he was 'troubled on every side, when there were
fightings without, and fears within', God comforted him by the
coming of Titus (2 Cor. 7:6). That says a lot!

From Galatians 2:3 we know that Paul made Titus a *test* case
in the question of the circumcision of Christian believers. Titus

was a Gentile believer, and Paul would not allow him to be circumcised for it was a ritual replaced with Christian baptism, and no longer necessary for the Christian.

It was Titus who was charged with the difficult task of solving the difficulties in the church at Corinth, and of imposing Christian discipline on the situation obtaining there. 'Thanks be to God,' says Paul, 'which put the same earnest care into the heart of Titus for you ... of his own accord went he unto you' (2 Cor. 8:16-17).

So it is easy to see that there was a strong bond between Paul and Titus. When Paul writes this epistle, Titus is in charge of the growing church in Crete. The letter was written to give Titus help and direction in the organisation of the young church there. By now Titus is a mature believer and a stalwart Christian leader (2:15).

Their relationship is an ideal and happy one, one that embodies the best of what Christian fellowship should hold: mutual trust, mutual respect, mutual love in the Lord. They are a picture of the growth and development of a fine spiritual relationship. This prayer of Paul's for Titus gathers up the substance of this great, loving relationship between them, and gives it lovely expression. It is a picture of the kind of fellowship that we want to build in our midst, and of the unity that we saw expressed at the Lord's Table this morning.

There are five things which indicate its bonds of unity.

1. The unity of the family bond: 'Titus, my genuine child ... in the Faith'.

This was a close relationship, closer even than the bond between father and child by which Paul so beautifully gives expression to it. For this relationship roots, not in the flesh, but in the Spirit. It is the creation of God's grace and flourishes as the result of his saving activity in the souls of men. It belongs, not to this world alone, but also to the world that is to come.

Many of us know something of the new relationships that grace has forged in our lives: warm bonds of fellowship and love, relationships that will outlast the ties of flesh and blood, relationships that will be stronger still in eternity for there the ties of blood and of natural love give second place to the ties of grace (there they neither marry nor are given in marriage).

How do such relationships come about? Through the preaching of the Word and the acceptance of the gospel that unites us to Christ and to one another in him. Paul was evidently the means used to bring Titus to Christ. He was Paul's child in the faith. On the human level he owed his soul to Paul. And, on the other hand he was a 'fruit' to Paul of the success of his labours in the gospel. A preacher can have no greater joy than to see his preaching blessed, to have children begotten to God. John says that he rejoiced to see his children walk in the truth (3 John 4). Paul's converts were 'his joy, and crown' (Phil. 4:1). Do we have any of whom we also can say, 'My genuine child'?

There is the family bond – and it is given expression by Paul.

2. Brethren in the faith: they shared something in common.
They believed the same great truths. They were united in the truth! When the truth unites, it overcomes every other barrier. That is the kind of unity we enjoy at the Lord's Table. What unites us there? The belief that Christ loved us, and gave himself for us.

They both had *a hearty confidence* in the Lord Jesus and the promises of God in him. They had found the same gateway to life – the cross of our Lord Jesus Christ.

3. A brotherly benediction: Grace, Mercy and Peace.
Here is how Paul prayed what he wished for Titus. It is a large prayer in small compass. It covers all that any Christian personally needs and it enfolds all that we would wish for our sisters and brothers in Christ.

Grace to save, to keep, to help in every time of need. No matter what kind of Christian you are, no matter what your task in the Lord, that is what you need.

Mercy is also what every Christian needs. It is the outflow of continuous pardon available in Christ.

Believers need *peace* for comfort, to soothe the heart and conscience, to help us fulfil our daily tasks in the assurance of God's love and favour. Peace garrisons the heart (Phil. 4:7).

4. They were debtors to the same God: All good comes from God the Father through the one Saviour.
The two are the one Source: notice that the preposition 'from'

is not repeated. All the grace, mercy and peace that come, come from the heart of the Father as it rests and rejoices in the work of the Son.

5. They had the same Saviour: The Lord Jesus Christ – our Saviour.

Jesus is *Lord* to all his people; this means obedience. But he is also the Saviour. Because of their common faith they had a common standing: *our* Saviour. Is it not lovely when two Christians can meet and share out of Christ not merely as *a* Saviour but as *our* Saviour?

These are the family bonds that forge this close relationship between Paul and his fellow worker Titus.

May they be the words which will forge us into a real, living Christian fellowship. And may they find frequent and real expression in all our work and witness together for our Lord Jesus Christ.

28

The Powerful Gospel

'I am not ashamed of the gospel of Christ, for it is the
power of God unto salvation to every one that believeth'
(Romans 1:16).

Condensation is a difficult art. There are few things more dangerous and more unsatisfactory than small books on great subjects,
abbreviated statements on large systems. Error lurks in
summations, and yet here the sweeping effects of God's redemptive revelation to lost men are gathered into the words of one
sentence. There is an old legend of a magic tent which could be
expanded to shelter an army and contracted to cover a single man.
That great gospel which fills the Bible and overflows on the shelves
of crowded libraries is here exhibited, without damage to its dynamic effect, in the compass of one saying which the simplest
can understand and which the most profound cannot exhaust.

Our text deals, not so much with the content, but with the effects of the gospel of Jesus Christ; and with these effects as they
centre on the apostle Paul and his conduct in the great metropolis
of Rome, the then mecca of modern civilisation and culture. His
desire is to 'preach the gospel to them that are at Rome also'. His
attitude and conduct there will be dictated by one thing: the effects previously produced and the effects that would still be accomplished by the gospel of Jesus Christ.

The words of the apostle display the effects of the gospel,
firstly, in:

1. An attitude of personal confidence in the gospel
It was wonderful, indeed, that Paul could speak with such absolute confidence about this gospel, anticipating the time when the
despised name of Jesus would be incomparably mightier than Caesar's, and when the truths which had their centre in the cross would
have prevailed over all the magnificent pomp and intellectual pride
of the ancient world.

The negative form of assertion with which he declares this confidence – 'I am not ashamed' – only serves to add to the positive nature of his statement. The sense it conveys is not that the apostle was unashamed to proclaim this gospel in Rome, but that he would proudly proclaim it. In effect, his statement means, 'I am ready to preach the gospel in Rome, for I am proud of the gospel.'

There were several reasons why this was true.

(1) *Paul had found in the gospel a satisfactory philosophy of life.* In the gospel he had found an adequate explanation of the great enigmas of the human situation – sin, suffering and death. Through the gospel he knew that sin, with all its diverse and destructive complexes, had been met and dealt with in the cross of Christ. From the gospel, he learned that suffering – the fruit and result of man's sinful disobedience – could be rightly understood and patiently borne only as it was viewed in the light of the sufferings of Jesus; for there the compassion, the care, the love and the justice of the triune God had been displayed. In the gospel Paul could trace the triumph of Jesus over the terror of death. There, in the resurrection of the God-man he could apprehend the eternal truth that 'God is life'.

So, in the gospel, Paul had a philosophy of life that he was not afraid to air in the circles of the city that had fused the philosophies of Greece and Rome into one culture. He had a philosophy that gave content and purpose and meaning to life in its totality – and he was willing to pit it against any philosophy that Rome could offer.

(2) *Paul was confident of the gospel he preached because it was good news.* The religions of Rome – and she had many – had no good news to bring men. The sum and substance of their message to the religious instinct of men was one of exacting trial and fear. The gods must be appeased; their favour was hard to earn, their blessing difficult to win. Men must stumble through life in darkness and despair and, more often than not, their affairs were dictated by the capricious whims of the unsympathetic and unfeeling gods. Then, too, Roman religion owned a fearful multiplicity of gods; so much so, that their devotees could only be baffled and frustrated in their endeavour to live the religious life.

Atheism, agnosticism and lawless immorality had found a
ready breeding ground as a result of all this, and if ever a place
needed the 'good news' that Paul's gospel carried, it was the great,
imperial city of Rome. Into such an environment Paul was proud
to bring his message, because he knew that it was a message which
would be effective. It was a message of a personal, living God: a
God who cared and loved, and who alone could bring hope and
peace and blessing into man's situation of dispeace and despair.

(3) *Further, Paul's confidence in this gospel lay in the fact that it
was centred on Jesus.* It was not Paul's gospel, but the gospel of
Christ. His message was not one that he had had to prepare himself, but it was one which had been revealed to him. His teaching
centred, not so much on a set of principles – although these did
follow – but upon a living Person. His message and its content
would be the same at Rome as it had been at Corinth: 'Jesus Christ
and him crucified' (1 Cor. 2:2).

The objective reality that lay at the centre of the gospel – the
person of Jesus Christ – lent authenticity and authority to what
Paul had to declare. His message was about a person. Take Jesus
out of Paul's gospel and he was left with no gospel. Remove the
incarnation, the crucifixion and the resurrection from the Christian message that Paul preached and there is no Christian message left. But Paul knew Christ, and because he did so he knew
that the message he preached about Christ was true. Because it
was truth he was not ashamed to proclaim it, even in Rome.

This personal confidence of the apostle has been the fortifica-
tion of every gospel preacher, and of every Christian, down through
the centuries. The fact that this is so, confronts you and me with
these questions: Do we, today, have the same, supreme, personal
confidence in the gospel? Is it the philosophy of our lives? Has it
proved to be 'good news' to us? Has it revealed to us personally
the Christ who is its theme?

Having now glanced at the effects that the first phrase of our
text displays within the context of the apostle's life – his attitude
of personal confidence in the gospel – we find that the following
phrase, 'for it is the power of God unto salvation', sets before us
the reason why the apostle's confidence was so unshakeable. This
reason we discuss under our second heading.

2. An attestation from his personal experience of the gospel
Here Paul delineates the dynamic that brings about the greatest
effect accruing to man from the gospel: salvation from eternal
death and eternal punishment.

How did Paul know that the gospel constituted this power? He
knew because he was a sharer in the gospel; because this gospel
was the power that had blinded and humbled and gripped him on
the Damascus road, and effected so radical a change in him that,
from being Saul the persecutor of Jesus, he became Paul the
preacher of Christ.

It was the power that had changed his view of himself from
being 'after the righteousness that is in the law, blameless' (Phil.
3:6), to that of his being not merely a sinner, but the chief of
sinners (1 Tim. 1:15). It was the power that had shattered his
religious self-reliance and thrown him into reliance upon the mercy
of God in Christ. That same power had been his greatest proof of
God's mercy.

Not only had Paul experienced this dynamic in his own life,
but as he preached the message he had seen the power of the
gospel become the dynamic of change in the lives of others. He
had seen it at work in the life of Lydia, whose heart it had 'opened'.
He had seen it at work in the experience of the Philippian jailer
and in the lives of countless others. He had proved this gospel to
be the power, the very dynamite of God, for the saving of sinners.

Here the question arises as to what the apostle meant by 'salvation'. What was the salvation which the gospel was so powerful to effect? The salvation it effected was a threefold one.

(1) *This salvation delivered from the guilt of sin.* His gospel taught
that Christ had made atonement for all the sins, past, present and
future, of all who would believe on his name. His death had effected a reconciliation between God and a lost, rebellious world,
and upon the basis of that atonement and that reconciliation, God
would forgive sin and could, with holy equity, justify the sinner.

(2) *This salvation meant deliverance from the power and dominion
of sin.* All who came under the power of this salvation, obeyed its
claims and rested in its promises, sin would not have dominion
over them. A new principle of life would be implanted in them

and it would outwork itself in creating desires after God and after
holiness, where formerly there had only been selfish and sinful
desires.

(3) *This salvation meant deliverance from future wrath.* Sin will
be punished, and unless personal sin has been dealt with in the
sufferings of the one who had taken the sinners' place, when he
died upon the cross of Calvary, the sinner must share in that punishment, and share it eternally. But the momentous thing that the
gospel had effected was the removal of the sentence of future
punishment, the curse of the Law. It had been removed because it
had been transferred – or accounted or imputed – to the Person of
Jesus. He had been made a curse when he became the curse-bearer;
he had been made sin when he became the sin-bearer. Thus he
had effected salvation and become the Saviour of sinners. In doing all this he had provided a full deliverance from the righteous
wrath of God.

At this point our text provides us with yet another set of important personal questions. Have we experienced the dynamic
power of the gospel? Are the saving effects of that power evi-
dencing themselves in our lives? Do we know the peace that results from a knowledge of sins forgiven? Has the dominating
power of sin in our lives been broken? Do we have the assurance
that the verdict passed upon us at the Final Judgement will be
'Enter into the joy of the Lord' and not 'Depart from me, ye cursed,
into everlasting fire'?

If our answer to these questions is not in the affirmative, let
our sole comfort from the text be that it speaks to us of a gospel
that is powerful; indeed, that it is the only power that can effect
the saving change that must take place in our lives. Our text makes
it very clear that salvation was a word and a fact that concerned
God, and over which God graciously moved in saving activity.
Let it not be true of us that salvation is a word and a fact that gives
us no concern and that leaves us completely inactive.

This may lead you to ask: 'What then shall I do?' The answer
is made abundantly clear in the last phrase of the text. The gospel
of Jesus Christ becomes powerful unto salvation and has its most
wonderful effect, within the context of the human situation, 'to
everyone that believeth'. This leads us to consider:

3. The appropriation through personal faith of the gospel benefits.

We have seen the effect of the gospel upon the apostle – his confidence in the preaching of it. We have seen, too, why he was so confident in the gospel he preached – because it was the saving power of God and produced dynamic effects. Thirdly, we have the manner in which these effects, or benefits, are to apply, in power, to the individual. It is through faith. By faith this power is to become effectual in the lives of men and women.

The only way in which we avail ourselves of this power, this saving dynamic, is by believing upon the Lord Jesus Christ. Jesus himself expounded this fact of power through faith when he said: 'he that believeth in me, though he were dead, yet shall he live' (John 11:25). The apostle, in answer to the question of the Philippian jailer (the same sort of question as you are, perhaps, asking in your mind at this very moment), 'What must I do to be saved?' gave this reply: 'Believe on the Lord Jesus Christ, and thou shalt be saved' (Acts 16:31). To believe, in this sense, is to stop working for our own salvation and to rest our souls – all that we are or ever will be – upon the finished, completed, perfect work of the Lord Jesus.

Notice, lastly, the extent of the warrant here given to faith: salvation is to *everyone* that believes. No-one is excluded. Every type of person, of every age, nation and tongue, is embraced in its scope. In the gospel no sort of qualification or limit is required or set; no restriction is laid down. It is everyone. The only limitation upon it is this: it is everyone that 'believes'. No matter who you are or what you are, no matter how good you are or how bad you are, the one thing required to make you a possessor of this powerful salvation is that you *believe*.

In conclusion, I must ask you this one final question, the question that the text demands: Have you yet believed in this manner? If you have not, will you believe *now*? A gospel of such power demands your verdict upon it. Let that verdict be one of wholehearted and believing acceptance of the message it brings. Seek the faith that strongly lays hold of Jesus as Saviour and brings within its orbit the power and dynamic of God unto eternal life.

If you have not yet believed – and will not believe – I ask you to think of the inevitable consequences. Where there is no faith there is no power; where there is no power there can be no salvation; and if you are in that category you are among those 'who shall be punished with everlasting destruction from the presence of the Lord, and from the glory of his power' (2 Thess. 1:9).

Believe on Jesus now and the effect will be the same as it was to Paul and to everyone who has so believed. You too will be able to make the words of the text your very own. You will be able to say, 'I am not ashamed of the gospel of Christ, for it is the power of God unto salvation to everyone that believeth.'

29

Faith

'Who is he that condemneth? It is Christ that died, yea rather, that is risen again, who is even at the right hand of God, who also maketh intercession for us (Romans 8:34).

These words are part of a triumphant challenge issued by the apostle in the name of God's believing people. 'Who,' he dares, 'shall lay anything to the charge of God's elect?' and the ringing confidence in the question is not ill-founded; it rests on the surest of all foundations, 'It is God that justifies.' Here is the real strength of his confidence. If God justifies, who can condemn? Then the apostle goes even further. Having shown that it is God who justifies, he shows in a few, chosen words of concentrated thought and brilliant, pointed exposition how he justifies: he justifies on the ground of Christ's redemptive work in its total compass of death, resurrection, ascension and intercession.

To gather the strength of what he is saying let us re-phrase it like this: 'It is God that justifies, therefore, who shall condemn? Who shall condemn, because it is Christ that has died – and is risen?' Do you see what he is saying? God the Father and God the Son have both been active to free us from *condemnation*.

The words are very strongly reminiscent of a parallel passage that was probably in Paul's mind as he penned them, a passage in Isaiah 50:8 where Christ prophetically views his redeeming work and cries, 'he is near that justifies me; who shall contend with me?'

There, in Isaiah, they were the words of Christ himself and referred to God's justifying him as he stood in relation to those he had come to redeem from their sin. Here, in Romans, they are the words of his redeemed and refer to God's justifying them.

Now the link of that double justification is a very strong and precious one. Why did Christ come into condemnation? He came into condemnation because 'he was made sin for us who knew no sin' (2 Cor. 5:21). His death was one of penalty; penalty for sin that was imputed to him. How did he come out from the condemnation involved in that penalty? By paying the price of the penalty in full.

Let us recall what that price was: 'The wages of sin is death' (Rom. 6:23). It was as the sin-bearer paying the wages of sin unto death that Christ cried, 'he is near that justifies me; who shall contend?' And it is to Christ as the justified sin-bearer that Paul looks when he cries, 'Who shall condemn? It is Christ that died.'

I want to look at our justification in relation to the death of Christ. We are very familiar with the dictum, 'We are justified by faith'. But faith has to have an object and here the object is clearly set before us: 'It is Christ that died'. As we proceed, let us bear in mind that justification is set out for us here as the reversal of condemnation: 'Who is he that condemns? It is Christ that died.'

Let us see where Christian faith puts its trust for justification.

1. Faith puts its trust in Christ

Faith has come to rest upon a Person. And that Person is set before us here under a very significant title, *Christ*. That very title leads to three remarks about faith in relation to this Person.

(1) *Faith rests upon one uniquely related to God.* This Person came as the Sent One, specially commissioned and anointed. The title 'Christ' conveys that he was anointed by God and sent by God. This speaks of God's free grace, his concern for our salvation and his activity for our salvation.

The first thing his grace did was to enter into special relationship with his own Son. That is indicated here for us: 'It is God that justifies. It is Christ that died.' There had been a very special relationship from all eternity between the Father and Son. But at the incarnation they began to sustain a new relationship to one another, and that new relationship is perhaps best expressed in the thought that the Son became the Mediator between God and man. That is what 'Christ' means – the anointed Mediator.

In that relationship both God the Father and God the Son had a specific office or function to perform and sustain. The Father became the representative of offended Godhead, the righteous defender of Deity sinned against, the upholder of eternal righteousness and universal rectitude. The Son became the representative of sinning, offending, unrighteous man.

In these offices both are active in our justification. God justifies – but he justifies only on the basis of what Christ did. Christ procured it, God proclaims it. This twofold aspect of justification is given in many places in Scripture, for example, Romans 3:24 puts it like this: 'Being justified freely by his grace, through the redemption that is in Christ Jesus.' There we see that God's free grace and Christ's active obedience meet in our justification.

One might ask where free grace comes in if such a price was paid as the death of Christ. Well, Christ did pay the price – although grace was involved, there was no mitigation of the punishment inflicted by violated justice. There 'God spared not his own Son but delivered him up for us all'. That is just where free grace was fully operative, and it did these two things: it gave the Son and it accepted his offering for us.

When faith rests upon Christ then, it rests upon one who sustains a unique relationship to God – it rests upon a Mediator.

(2) *When faith rests upon Christ, it forsakes all else.* As faith looks to Christ it looks away from self. There is something positive in faith when it rests on him – so positive that it forsakes all trusting in works or duties or even in graces. It does not trust in repentance or conviction of sin or knowledge, but only in the Person of the Mediator. It understands that to put anything alongside of Christ is to dishonour him and faith pleads this alone, 'It is Christ that died.' Faith is utterly content with Jesus because it sees him as the Christ, the One anointed and sent by God.

(3) *Faith rests upon Christ as revealed in the promise of Scripture.* Let me emphasise that true faith rests, not merely upon the promises of Scripture, but upon Christ in the promises. As Thomas Goodwin put it: 'The promise is but the casket, and Christ the jewel in it; the promise but the field, and Christ the pearl hid in it, and to be chiefly looked at.' This distinction is worth making because the promises are the means by which we believe, rather than the things upon which we rest; they are the pathways that lead to the Person. It is not that Christ is made yea and amen in the promises, but that the promises are made yea and amen in Christ.

Christ was revealed in the Scripture promises relating to his coming – yes, even in the very first one, for that was a promise of Christ's personal overcoming of Satan. Christ is also revealed in the absolute promises of the gospel as, for example, 'I am come that they might have life, and that they might have it more abundantly' or, 'The Son of Man is come to seek and to save that which was lost'. In the promises of gospel invitation also, it is Christ that is held out. In the promise, 'Come unto me all ye that are weary and heavy laden, and I will give you rest', note that the promise is not to weariness but to coming to Christ. Faith then lays hold, not just of the promise, but of the Christ that the promise reveals. Indeed, it is his person as Mediator that makes the promise take on an authentic and meaningful value for the trusting soul.

2. Faith puts its trust not merely in Christ, but in Christ crucified.

In seeking forgiveness or justification, faith is to look at the Person as revealed in his work. Our faith is to rest not just upon Christ as a unique Person but upon him made sin for us in death. This is how the Old Testament saints viewed him as set forth in the sacrifices. This is how John the Baptist declared him: 'Behold the Lamb of God that taketh away the sin of the world' (John 1:29).

So, when faith looks to Christ for justification, it finds it in his death. It is his death that makes Christ so suitable to the soul that truly sees its own sin and feels the weight of God's curse against its sin. Contemplating that death, faith looks for the main intention and purpose of it. Faith asks, What did God and Christ set out to achieve in this death on the Cross? It is in an acceptance and understanding of the purpose of the atonement that the heart is drawn to rest on Christ crucified. When a believer sees that Christ's aim and desire in suffering parallels exactly his own desire to have sin blotted out, then he feels that he can find rest in the work that brought the aim of Christ to fruition.

The whole story of the cross becomes, not just the tragic history of a good man suffering, but the activity of God by which one's sins can be fully pardoned. To this very fact Peter directs the faith of his countrymen when, having pointed out their sin in

murdering 'The Lord of Life', he adds that it was done according
to the pre-determinate counsel of God, and that it was 'even for
the remission of sins through his name'.

Let us remember what, in the final analysis, brought about
this death. It was not the malice of the Jews, nor the betrayal of
Judas, nor the cowardice of Pilate, nor the wickedness of the times
that brought Jesus to death. Rather it was his own perfect obedience
to the will of God and the purpose which that will had determined
upon. As Jesus went out of the Upper Room to go to Calvary, do
you remember what his cry was? 'As the Father hath given me
commandment, so do I. Arise, let us go hence.' And again, 'The
Son of man goeth as it was determined.' In Gethsemane he prayed:
'Father, if it be possible let this cup pass from me.' The Father
saw the necessity as so great that it was impossible that that cup
should pass. Christ also saw the necessity: 'Not my will, but thine
be done.' Why? Because he said, 'To do thy will I take delight.'

What was that will? The will of the eternal God in the death of
Christ was the 'taking away of sins'. As it is said in Hebrews
9:26: 'once in the end of the world hath he appeared to put away
sin by the sacrifice of himself.' He came to overthrow sin, to
cancel its power and silence its plea against us. He came so that
sin might not condemn us; indeed he came so that he might condemn sin. 'He died,' said Thomas Goodwin, 'in order to silence
the clamour of sin against us.'

Death was the righteous judgement against sin and in this death
its wages are visited by the righteous God upon his own Son, who
was so holy and innocent and so separate from sinners. We can
only believe that it was the utter destruction of what he hated –
sin – and the final establishment of what he loves – holiness –
that permitted a just and holy God to decree that death.

That was why Christ died. It is perfectly expressed in the plain-
est language by Paul himself: 'Christ died for our sins.' And we
cannot believe that he died in vain.

What shall we say then to these things?

Who shall condemn? Out of Christ, apart from him, you are
condemned already. The law condemns sin in you, but his death
satisfied God. God can demand no more. What more will you
demand? Let it satisfy you also.

30

Not Hearers Only

'But be ye doers of the word, and not hearers only,
deceiving your own selves' (James 1:22).

It is good to come to hear the preaching of God's Word. Hearing
has a great promise of reward attached to it by God, for, as the
Bible says, 'Faith cometh by hearing, and hearing by the word of
God' (Rom. 10:17). And when we recall that the Bible also says,
'without faith it is impossible to please God' (Heb. 11:6), that
makes the promise very precious indeed. We can even go further,
for it is widely and explicitly taught in scripture that faith is the
very first requisite for salvation – faith in the Lord Jesus Christ.
The Christ that we are to believe upon and rest in for salvation is
introduced to us only in the Word of God. 'These,' he said himself, speaking of the Scriptures, 'are they which testify of me'
(John 5:39).

But it is vitally important that we put what we hear and what
we believe into actual practice and that it influences the course of
our daily lives. When it comes to the real testing point, it is not
enough to have the theory of Christian living in our minds, we
must have the practice of it in our daily lives. We are all sharply
aware that these two can be divorced from one another in any
realm of life. It is possible to be a theoretician without ever becoming a practitioner in religion as well as other spheres, and this
is the thought uppermost in the words of our text. The manner in
which James has framed the thought attracts our attention and
deserves that we look at its truth very carefully.

1. The distinction which James draws
He draws a sharp line of demarcation between two things that are
very intimately connected – 'hearing' and 'doing' the Word of
God. They are so closely related that, apart from the first, the
second is not possible. No man will ever become a 'doer' of God's

Word until he has first become a 'hearer' of it. Nevertheless, although the two are wed together in this way, let us remember that they can be so widely divorced from one another that it is all too sadly possible to be a 'hearer' of the Word without ever becoming a 'doer' of it.

This distinction has always been present wherever the Word of God has been proclaimed. Scripture bears widespread testimony to it.

In the days of Jeremiah, God's Word came to his people urging them to repentance, and warning of coming judgement if they did not turn and make their ways and their doings good. What was the response? They said, 'There is no hope: but we will walk after our own devices, and we will every one do the imagination of his evil heart' (Jer. 18:12). They were hearers, but they refused to become doers of God's Word.

Ezekiel had to complain of this attitude; the distinction and divorce of these two things occurred in his day also. It was to him that God solemnly said, 'They come unto thee as the people – and sit before thee as my people, and they hear thy words, but they will not do them.' And God then goes on to point out what an abomination this attitude is in his own eyes: 'With their mouth they show much love, but their heart goeth after their covetousness. And, lo, thou art unto them as a very lovely song of one that hath a pleasant voice, and can play well on an instrument: for they hear thy words, but they do them not' (Ezek. 33:31-32).

Judas heard the word from the lips of Christ himself, but he was one of a vast multitude of people who, under the Redeemer's ministry, were hearers but not doers of the Word.

Let me plead with each one of you and ask you if this distinction, this divorcing of doing the Word of God from the hearing of it, holds true for you? Then, please pause, and reflect upon that fact.

There seems to be a widespread feeling amongst some today that if we come to hear the preaching of the gospel it will, somehow, and quite mysteriously, do us good – it will cleanse and take away our sin for another week – it will draw down the favour of God upon us – it will make us better people and entitle us to heaven at last. It will do all that irrespective of our response, or non-response, to it. Is that the set and current of your thinking?

Then, let me say to you – *not so*. Your hearing of the Word will do none of these things for you; only your *doing* of it will achieve them. Your thoughts of what mere hearing will accomplish are, in fact, closely allied to the very worst kind of religious superstition. God urges you not only to 'take heed *what* you hear', but to 'take heed *how* you hear'. Paul demands of those to whom he writes the great, redemptive truths of salvation that they must *think on these things*.

Let us remember what is at stake, here. When the gospel is being preached, and the Word of God expounded, eternal issues are laid in the balances. That Word under which you have brought yourself as a hearer proclaims nothing less than the eternal destiny of your immortal soul! James is sharply aware of this and so, quite bluntly and starkly, he divides hearers of the Word into two distinct classes – those who are *hearers only* and then, those who are also *doers of the Word*.

The difference he makes is absolutely valid. It is a difference that spans the enormous gulf of separation between the true Christian and the non-Christian: between those who are saved with an everlasting salvation and those who are lost in an everlasting destruction.

2. The development which James demands
James, and God through James, demands that we go further than being only hearers of the Word. No matter how good that is, it is just not good enough. We must progress to the place where we become 'doers' of it as well.

Obviously, the Word of which the apostle speaks is designed to have a practical effect upon its hearers. It is intended, and fitted, to act on the hearts and lives of real, living people. The Word, in fact, has a twofold revelation to bring to its hearers; it teaches, firstly, 'What man is to believe concerning God'; and then, secondly, it goes on to inform as to 'What duty God requires of man'.

In other words, what it teaches men about God is the kind of truth calculated, when truly believed, to prompt its hearers into obedience to all the commandments of God. Until, and unless, that believing obedience has been actively awakened into real, living, daily exercise, no man has any warrant to believe that his hearing of the Word has done him any lasting, saving good. He is still in the category of which Scripture warns when it says, 'the Word preached did not profit them, not being mixed with faith in them that heard it' (Heb. 4:2).

What a solemn warning is here. It is possible to have the mind furnished with the 'Word that makes wise unto salvation' – to have a mental grasp and intellectual appreciation of the great biblical doctrines of redemption – and yet to be utterly devoid of the saving effects of which they speak.

The Word is to be accepted, not only into the mind, but so accommodated and believed in the heart that the entire life will be radically affected by gratitude, reverence and love to the Saviour. There must be that repentance which turns one from sin to God, and that faith which actively rests upon Christ for salvation. Where these truly and genuinely are in exercise then there is a 'doing' of the Word that is nothing less than a holy, full-hearted obedience to the revealed will of God; an obedience brought about, not by slavish fear, but by a reverent, filial love. This was the spirit that marked the life of the Lord Jesus. He could say, 'I *do* always the things that please him' (John 8:29).

To 'be doers' has a force all of its own and conveys a thought quite distinct from that of the simple 'to do'. The expression carries the idea of *habitual occupation*; it points to constancy, endurance and perseverance in the pathway of active obedience to God. It sets before us as being real Christians those who make the 'doing of the Word of God' the main business of their lives; godly obedience has become so important that it affects, penetrates and pervades every sphere of life. Just as we say that a person is a doctor, or a teacher, or a joiner – thus denoting their life-work – so, speaking of character, the Christian is to be the kind of person of whom it will be natural to say, 'he is a doer of the Word of God'.

In every department of his life such a man will clearly demonstrate that he makes this his chief priority, and he will do it in secular as well as in sacred things. Indeed, that is a distinction that he will no longer make because he knows that nothing in life is really outwith the bounds of his religion or beyond the sphere illuminated by the teaching of the Holy Spirit in Scripture.

3. The danger which James designates

The apostle enforces his exhortation with a particularly solemn and powerfully strong consideration. Persons who are 'hearers only' and not 'doers of the word' have fallen into one of the most terrible traps that hell has devised to ensnare the seeker after godliness – the trap of self-deception. Such people have totally misconstrued the nature of saving religion and, all unwittingly, cheat themselves as to their true position before a holy God.

When a man hears, and accepts as true, that the study of divine truth, the reading of the Bible and the attendance on the preaching of the Word is the pathway leading to the entrance into eternal life he might allow himself, in his still unenlightened state, to be persuaded that in 'mere hearing' of the Word he has really entered in and that all is well with his soul. But, to rest satisfied with the means of grace is no sure indication that we have received the grace which the means puts within our reach. We must not stop until we know that we have actively closed-in with Christ as he is freely offered to us in the gospel. It is union to Christ that makes men doers of the Word, that makes them men of prayer, and of a godly walk and of a 'doing' life.

Self-deception is an awful thing, something to be feared and avoided with all the purpose and energy that the soul can command. It is sad to be deceived by others, but to be deceived by oneself is to be in the awful place where our blood is altogether upon our own heads. There is some likelihood that, if deception in religious things is more the fault of our teachers than our own, that one day the truth will be applied to us from some other direction. But if the deception lies with 'our own selves', as James puts it, then it indicates such a hardness and darkness of mind as will resist the truth no matter how faithfully it is proclaimed to us.

While being a hearer of the Word does carry the promise of reward, this word from the Lord enforces a truth that we neglect only at the eternal peril of our souls. It is simply this: any degree of religious profession, such as is involved, for example, in attending the public worship of God and the hearing of his Word faithfully proclaimed, is not to be equated with even the minimal requirements of our God upon us. No matter how religious we may suppose ourselves to be, the fact stands clear before us that if the heart is destitute of the love of God, that if the soul is untouched

by the regenerating power of the Holy Ghost, that if there is not
the sanctified walk of holy obedience, that if there is not the earnest
attempt to put the Word into actual practice, then our religion is
far more imagined than real and is no better in the sight of God
than utter mockery.

Let us remember that on no point of religion were the warn-
ings and appeals of the Lord Jesus more solemn and alarming
than on this one. It was he who said, 'Not every one that saith
unto me, "Lord, Lord," shall enter into the kingdom of heaven,
but he that *doeth* the will of my Father which is in heaven' (Matt.
7:21).

The real truth in this realm stands out with crystal clarity; it
could not be more strongly emphasised by God that to be a 'hearer
of the word' is to fall short of being saved; we must also 'be doers
of it'. If the word remains outside of us, it will have no power
over us. It may enter the mind, but if it does not penetrate the
heart and permanently regulate the life then we can be quite certain that we have not yet 'heard' to the saving of the soul.

ARTICLES

1

Evangelistic Preaching

This being 1988, and the opening lecture of our new College Session being the privilege of the Professor of Church History and Principles, it might have seemed inevitable that the theme would focus on one of the great events of 1588 or 1688 which have been engaging Christian interest through the year. The Spanish Armada, the life and labours of John Bunyan, or the political changes, still known amongst us, ecclesiastically, as the Late Happy Revolution, are among the topics susceptible to an interesting, and perhaps profitable, Anniversary lecture. The inevitable, however, is not always infallibly predictable and so, in actual fact, this lecture touches none of these subjects but concerns itself, instead, with Evangelistic Preaching.

Having violated your sense of the inevitable, let me reassure you that the choice of subject owes no more to perversity than it does to lack of historical awareness. It has been made, rather, in the light of the fact that the discipline of Church Principles now embraces Missiology and the teaching of biblical evangelism, a subject of perennial interest and paramount importance in training men for the ministry. But the chief reason in the choice of subject this evening could hardly be better expressed than it was by one whose brave, believing life – and death – paved the way for the political and ecclesiastical changes of 1688, the Covenanter, Donald Cargill. It was Cargill who constantly reminded preachers of his own day, as we continually need to remind ourselves in ours, that 'preachers must be most in the main things'. Our College exists to train preachers and so, rightly understood, the subject of evangelistic preaching lies at the very nerve-centre of all our activity.

An address delivered at the annual Opening of the Free Church College in 1988 by Professor J. Douglas MacMillan.

Descriptive categories of biblical preaching
There are distinctions in types and aims of preaching. There is,
for example, doctrinal, experimental, and expository preaching.
Each has its own aim and requires its own approach in preparation. Such categories represent types of sermon and styles of
preaching with which every preacher must constantly engage if
he is to preach the whole counsel of God. He does so over against
the differing needs and circumstances of his hearers. And the categories must make room for the evangelistic type of preaching
with which we are particularly concerned in this study. It is, argu-
ably, the most critical of all sermon types and fundamental not
only to the being, but to the well-being – the *esse*, and the *bene
esse* – of the church of Christ on earth. Without it the church is
not likely to flourish or grow.

Evangelistic preaching is, specifically, proclamation of the
good news of salvation through faith in Jesus Christ, with a view
to bringing about the reconciliation of sinners to God through the
Son, by the regenerating work of the Holy Spirit. The word derives from the Greek noun *euangelion*, good news, and verb
euangelizomai, to announce, proclaim or herald good news. Such
preaching is ordained of God as the chief means of winning souls,
and bringing hearers to saving faith. This means that if we are to
see people converted, we must preach evangelistic sermons, and
be constantly alert to the need for such proclamation. Before going further along this line of thought, however, let me give one
word of caution.

All preaching roots in exposition of the Word and will, naturally, be imbued with saving truth. Equally, evangelistic preaching, perhaps more than any other, demands and deserves careful
exegesis of the Word and instructive presentation of doctrine.
Preaching categories are descriptive rather than definitive and must
not become rigidly or mutually exclusive.

The biblical priority of evangelistic preaching
The Bible itself is full of evangelistic proclamation. It gives a
large place to explaining the need for, and the way of, salvation.
It does so by constant exhortation, gracious promise, earnest pleading and pointed personal application. That being so, it follows
that all biblical preaching must allow for evangelistic thrusts as

well. Only in this way will preaching reflect true biblical proportion in heralding the good news.

But not only so. The biblical polemic against man's innate bias to salvation by works, and its stress on grace and the nature of true faith, require the particular emphases inherent only in evangelistic preaching. If we fail to hold out Christ crucified to lost sinners with frequency, passion and urgency there is grave danger that the true conception of faith in Christ will be obscured. It is this danger John Murray has in mind when he writes, 'it is only when Christ is presented to lost men in the full and free overture of his grace that true faith can be elicited.'[1]

Church history demonstrates that evangelistic proclamation is a key factor in times of special awakening and spiritual revival. For example, the nature and aims of faithful preaching have seldom been epitomised more fully than in Thomas Boston, the well-known eighteenth century Scottish minister, and it has to be said that Boston's ministry moved consistently in the atmosphere of spiritual awakening. That is not altogether strange when one reflects on the way this particular man pursued his ministry. A prolific writer, an influential theologian, a master preacher, Boston gave himself to the conversion of people as few ministers have ever done. He had a gift for evangelistic preaching which, as one writer has put it, 'he sedulously cultivated, hiding it under no bushel, and which in the mercy of God did more to fan the flame of true piety in Scotland than [the preaching] of any other single minister in his generation'.[2]

That is no exaggeration. For almost 200 years Boston was by far the most widely read of the Scottish divines and influenced Scottish theology and spirituality more profoundly than any single man has done before or since. Speaking of the little church at Simprin where Boston entered on his powerful ministry MacDonald says: 'Here in this tiny edifice ... the young minister held forth with almost apostolic fervour, preaching, expounding, lecturing, and praying with and for these Simprin ploughmen and their families. He was intensely earnest – earnest with that fiery fervour, that lifts the poorest sermon above criticism.... he preached

1. John Murray, *Collected Writings* (Banner of Truth, Vol. 1), p. 147.
2. D.D.F. MacDonald, Introduction to *A Soliloquy on The Art of Man-Fishing*.

as if the angels were looking in on him and his little country congregation, and as if he actually expected to be carried home by them before another sermon day came round.'

Meditating on the words of Jesus, 'Follow me, and I will make you fishers of men', Boston sees the illustration as featuring, not the solitary angler patiently casting to hook a single fish, but a boat's crew setting their nets and hauling a harvest. The gospel is like a fishing net, he says, 'Because it is spread out to catch all that will come into it, Isaiah 55:1, "Ho, every one that thirsteth, come ye to the waters; and he that hath no money, come ye, buy and eat; yea, come, buy wine and milk, without money, and without price." God excludes none from the benefits of the gospel that will not exclude themselves; it is free to all'.[3] And it is worth noting the doctrine of the free offer held by this Scottish Calvinist twenty years before his discovery of the *Marrow of Modern Divinity* with its assertions of the freeness and genuineness of the gospel offer to all men and the debate to which they gave rise.

Now, of course, Boston is making a very important point here. It is an absolute necessity that the gospel net be spread out if the preacher is truly to fulfil his calling as a 'fisher of men', and recruit his people to pray, work and look for conversions in their congregation or community. That God brings in his elect by means of a gospel whose invitation is to sinners, as sinners, Boston was adamant. The setting of this net in ways and places where it implements the purposes of its designer was not, for him, just one among several options open to the preacher of the gospel; it was the chief task to which he had been called. For this cause it must have his highest and best endeavours. Only then would he be true to the balance and harmony of the doctrine, informing and undergirding his very call to preach. Boston's beliefs still deserve our attention. It is by hearing the Word that men are saved, as we know from Romans 10, and it was through preaching of the Word that the Lord added to the church daily, such as must be saved, in apostolic times. Without evangelistic preaching the gospel message will not be heard, and the church of Christ will not be vigorous, healthy and growing. Evangelistic preaching must retain its place of primacy among all the other categories of biblical preaching.

An interesting illustration of the practical effect of evangelistic

---

3. Thomas Boston, *The Art of Man-Fishing*, p. 29.

preaching upon the life of the church comes down to us from the middle years of the nineteenth century. It was the evangelistic preaching of such men as Dr. John Erskine of Edinburgh in the South and Lachlan MacKenzie of Lochcarron in the North which paved the way into the resurgence of evangelical life in the Scottish Church in the first twenty years of last century, and banished the cold Moderatism which had ruled supreme ever since the departure of the Erskines and others in 1733. Part of that evangelical resurgence was, of course, the conversion and powerful ministries of men like Dr. Andrew Thomson in Edinburgh and Dr. Thomas Chalmers in Glasgow. It was the evangelical teaching of such men that stirred the Church into awareness of the terrible social needs of the crowded cities thrown up by the new Industrial age. The fact is that wherever the gospel has come into the lives of men in real power, whether in Central Africa or Central Scotland, it has awakened Christian values and Christian concern for others. The names of men like Chalmers, Guthrie and Begg, with their enormous contribution to the welfare of the needy in their parishes and cities, is a lasting reminder that social concern and evangelistic preaching are not enemies, but friends. The evangelical emphasis upon personal conversion, and Christian involvement in social concern should never be polarised; the one flows out of the other.

If such factors do, indeed, lead to the conclusion that evangelistic preaching does have a certain priority in the scale of biblical values, then, there is no question but that preachers have to take time to think very carefully about the sermons Scripture requires them to preach if their hearers are to believe in the Lord Jesus Christ and be saved. It is, of course, axiomatic for us here, something on which I trust we are all perfectly agreed, that the Holy Spirit alone can convert a soul. None can enter into the kingdom of God except they be born from above. Preachers must not take to themselves any credit for the result of a work that so sovereignly belongs to God. But, equally, they must never forget that the Spirit does this work through means, and one of the chief means appointed by infinite wisdom is evangelistic proclamation.

The question of means is important to our whole understanding of what evangelistic preaching – or any other kind of preaching, for that matter – is all about and what it is calculated to achieve. It is the Bible itself which teaches us that preaching of the

evangelistic kind is the ordained means through which the elect
are, generally speaking, effectually called. To set that truth aside
or deny the Confessional theology that others may be outwardly
called by the ministry of the Word[4] and that Christ is freely offered
to us in the gospel[5], is to divorce what God has joined together
and fall into hyper-Calvinism, a heresy just as dangerous to the
Church as its counterpart, Arminianism.

In reference to the gospel invitation and offer, the scriptural
appeal to sinners, without distinction, to repent and believe is what
we speak of as the call of God. That there are not two gospel calls
but one, which, in the regeneration of the elect is made inward
and effectual, is important to grasp. And it is worth noticing that
the distinction in terms of efficacy can only be made when the
call is defined in terms of the sinner's response. This means that
evangelistic preaching, with its commands and invitations to all
men everywhere to repent and believe the gospel, may never be
regarded as being addressed to men other than as lost sinners. It is
neither foresight in the preacher, nor ability to distinguish the
elect from the non-elect amongst his hearers, that constitute the
warrant for the free offer, but the command of Christ to preach
the gospel to every creature.

Theologically, the matter can be summarised in this way: The
effectual call is God's action and cannot be foretold; for that reason
the gospel call authentically embraces all who hear it, and does
so because it is addressed to men as sinners without further
distinction or qualification. 'If we have any reserve or lack of
spontaneity in offering Christ to lost men,' writes John Murray,
'and in presenting the claims which inhere in the glory of his
person and the perfection of his finished work, then it is because
we have a distorted conception of the relation which the
sovereignty of God sustains to the free offer of Christ in the
gospel.' And then Murray makes this memorable statement: 'It is
on the crest of the wave of the divine sovereignty that the full and
free overtures of God's grace in Christ break upon the shores of
lost humanity.'[6]

---

4. Westminster Confession of Faith ch. X., iii and iv.
5. Shorter Catechism 31.
6. John Murray, *Collected Writings*, Vol. 1, p. 147.

Continual need of evangelistic preaching

One factor militating against evangelistic preaching is that most of us have to preach, today, to people who are already Christians. We do not live in times when unconverted people crowd the pews as they did in the Awakenings of last century. With this fact in mind, we have to say that it would be unhelpful folly to assault our regular, believing, Christian hearers with purely evangelistic preaching in every single sermon. That would be to leave the Lord's people untaught and frustrated and would do a serious disservice to the flock of God.

Nevertheless, at the same time we have to be extremely watchful not to fall into the opposite error, probably more serious – and widespread in Reformed circles today – than the first, and leave the evangelistic element out of our preaching altogether. The nature of Christian faith requires that believers hear evangelistic preaching. It is needed to keep them from carnal security. It is needed as an incentive to holiness. It is needed to make them watchful for their own souls, and the souls of others. Also, church history, and pastoral experience, teach the sad lesson that there will be some who are mere 'professors of religion' under every sermon we preach. Such need to hear the broad basics of the gospel reiterated and reinforced with all the intellectual power and spiritual warmth we can command.

But in addition to such considerations, the fact that the unconverted do not crowd our churches and that there is, therefore, no need for evangelistic sermons, calls for closer examination. We must ensure, for example, that the lack of unconverted people in our pews is not due to the lack of evangelistic preaching in our pulpits. Evangelistic preaching has always been one of the precursors of times of revival and true spiritual awakening. And it is such preaching that will attract the unsaved under its sound.

These are all factors highlighting the need for regular, stated, evangelistic preaching. There was a time when, in most of our churches, the evening sermon was exclusively given over to this work, the morning's to spiritual nourishment for the flock of God. That was a good practice. No doubt it was the changing patterns of attendance which halted it. But still there is need to avoid a situation where we cease to preach to, and for, the lost. Every congregation and every preacher should ask the question, Do we have at least one service a Sunday so structured, and one sermon so shaped, that our believing people are encouraged to bring along unsaved friends to hear the gospel preached?

I have no doubt that if we use this approach our believing hearers will not merely benefit spiritually, but understand and support us. Evangelistic preaching needs their prayers and their presence. They have a part to play in the work, and their participation creates the spiritual atmosphere in which the Lord is likely to be present, accomplishing conversions. Some of our best people will say to us, then, 'Well, I felt tonight that if I had never trusted the Saviour before, I would gladly do so now.'

Persuasive evangelistic preaching
An evangelistic sermon is characterised by an urgency, a warmth, and a love that lays aside all thought of technique and concentrates on speaking to the heart from the heart. There is a passion to invite men to trust in Jesus, and a freedom to give clear, cogent, compelling reasons why they should, why they may, why they must trust Jesus. In a word, there is proclamation of Christ, rather than mere preaching about Christ.

Let me dwell on that for a moment. All preaching of the Word should tend to encourage and foster trust in the Lord Jesus. Trusting in Jesus is all important. Let me illustrate, again, from one of the master preachers of the ages who knew how to build sermons that helped God's people and which, at the same time, always had enough saving truth in them to leave the ignorant without excuse before God. Although almost two centuries separate him from Boston, the same earnest spirit imbued him: 'Very seldom do I finish a sermon,' he says 'without going over this simple matter of trusting Christ.' 'Trust Christ,' he continues 'and you are saved. We have heard in our church-meetings, that, on several occasions, when at the close of the sermon I have merely said as much as that, it has been enough to lead sinners into life and peace; and, therefore, we will keep on at it.'[7]

That, of course, is C.H. Spurgeon. The remarks were made while he was actually preaching and as he drew near the end of a powerful sermon on Hosea 11:4, 'I drew them with cords of a man, with bands of love'. Its thrust was really to encourage Chris-

7. C.H. Spurgeon, *Trumpet Calls to Christian Energy*, p. 77.

tians in the work of evangelism but he goes on to apply what he
has just said in a very powerful and personal way that is worth
noting. 'My heart yearns to bring some of you to Christ tonight,
but I do not know what arguments to use with you. You surely do
not want to be damned. Surely you cannot make the calculation
that the short pleasures of this world are worth an eternity of torment. But damned you must be except you lay hold of Christ.
Doth not this cord draw you?'

That is very direct appeal – stark, blunt, and yet strangely warm
and tender – and going straight to the point with great urgency.
Yet he is not quite finished, but goes on to strengthen his plea
particularly to his regular hearers. 'I do not know one among you
that I could spare. I would not like to miss you who sit yonder
(and he must have pointed very directly!), nor any of you who sit
near (and he must have pointed yet again!). Well, but we cannot
meet in heaven unless we meet in Christ Jesus. We cannot meet
father, and mother, and pastor, and friends, unless we have a good
hope through Jesus Christ our Lord. Will not that cord of love
draw you?'

It was such preaching, such pleading, such earnestness that
made the Metropolitan Tabernacle the birth place of many souls
all through this towering, Spirit-anointed ministry. And Spurgeon
is not afraid to speak of what God has done – he seems to be as
free of false piety as he was of false modesty. Listen to him again:
'Let us congratulate one another that the Spirit of God is with us
as a people, and with us in no mean measure. God has been pleased
to add to us year by year, *pretty nearly after the rate of 400 members in a year*, till it has swollen our numbers beyond our most
sanguine hopes.... *I do not think there has been a sermon preached
here which God has not blessed.*'[8]

The nature of evangelistic preaching
In conclusion, let me highlight five elements which should characterise evangelistic preaching, as follows:

1. Evangelistic preaching must *interest our hearers*. This is a
prerequisite. People have grown accustomed to listening to com-

8. I have italicised those words because they were underlined by the
pencil of the Rev. Kenneth MacRae of Stornoway, to whom my copy of
this book once belonged.

municators in the media whose skills in exploiting the voice, and utilising the power of language have been honed to near perfection. Christianity can no longer afford to have the biblical message preached in language incomprehensible to the average person, or in tones which prove soporific even to the godly. If there is one thing we need in our preaching of Christ today it is what Whitefield used to call 'market urgency in market language'.

2. Our preaching must *instruct our hearers*. The sermons most likely to convert are those full of truth; truth about the Fall; truth about the law; truth about sin; truth about alienation from God; truth about grace; truth about Jesus the Christ; truth about the Holy Spirit; truth about the Eternal Father; truth about the new birth and the obedience of life which flows from it. Evangelistic sermons have a host of such truths to proclaim; truths about which many today are abysmally ignorant.

3. Our preaching must *impress our hearers*. The fundamental thing here is that we preach, not as if, but *because* the truths we handle have impressed our own hearts and affected our own lives. We must always ask the question, Have I preached in such a way that every word, every gesture, and every tone of voice impressed upon my hearers how utterly in earnest I am about my subject, because my subject, ultimately, is Christ the sinner's Saviour?

4. Our preaching must *implicate our hearers*. We must not merely preach truth and leave our hearers wondering how it applies to them. This is the great difference, I think, between lecturing and preaching. Lecturing aims to inform. So does preaching. But preaching must also stir the emotions, and grip the heart, and persuade the will. We must do what the apostle did in Rome when we read that he spent his time 'persuading them concerning Jesus' (Acts 28:23).

5. Our preaching must *implore our hearers*. Here perhaps is where we fail most deeply of all. Very seldom do we hear sermons that really plead with men and for men. If the preacher is unmoved *himself*, it is highly unlikely that his *hearers* will be moved. This is something which must begin in our own hearts, as part of the preparation of our sermons. Spurgeon says, '... my very soul is moved, and my very heart is stirred within me, when I think of what I shall say to my people, and afterwards when I am delivering my message.'

The lesson is there for us all. If we fail to learn it, all else that our studies give us will leave us ill-equipped to be gospel heralds to our fellow sinners. We must learn to anoint our sermons with our prayers as we prepare them, and with our love as we preach them. We must take up the task as anointed men, preaching anointed sermons, that hold out to sinners, the Anointed Saviour. We must learn to preach for the souls of hearers, and the glory of Christ. Those, in every age, are the compelling objectives which should motivate our preaching of the good news entrusted to us in the gospel.

2

The Place of 'Law Work' in Evangelism

One of the heartening signs of the times in which we live is a renewed and widespread interest in evangelism. Throughout the Western World churches are astir with questions about evangelism, with aspirations after renewal and with elaborate programmes for outreach. From the level of the local church through to the World Congress type of forum the subject is discussed and debated with deep sincerity and evident anxiety. One aspect of all this stir which serves as a measure of its intensity and extent is the plethora of literature and books on the subject which have been streaming off the press in recent years.

Now, as has been said, all this is heartening. The church and every person in the church must pray and long and work for the salvation of souls and the evangelization of the lost. Lack of concern about and disengagement from the work of evangelism is not merely a cause but a symptom of spiritual dearth; and spiritual decline and dearth have devastated the churches of the West for more than a century. But heartening though these signs may be, they carry within them an ominous note that should alert us to the fact that all is not well with present-day evangelism. This emerges when we take note of the singular fact that the first concern of almost every book being published on evangelism is with its methods rather than its message. The indication is thus strongly present that all the stir is achieving little success and that bewilderment is deepening among ministers, churches, missions and evangelists about the effectiveness of what is being done. It is a fact that each new book, after assessing and evaluating the methods of its predecessors, then proceeds to set out and elaborate some method of its own which will ensure greater success in outreach and church growth. But despite the advice given, whether that advice centres around 'three easy steps to faith in Christ', or

---

This chapter taken from the Banner of Truth magazine, issues 248 and 249.

'four' or even 'seven', the longed-for results are not forthcoming. In spite of the concern which has devoted itself to effective methods of evangelism we have to agree with Walter Chantry when he writes: 'After analysing, evaluating, praying and hoping, missions are not revitalised and sinners are not turning to Christ in great numbers. The questions are still being asked, "What's wrong with our evangelism? What is needed to win the world for Christ? Where is the power of Edwards and Whitefield?"'[1]

This is the state of affairs which alerts us to the fact that the first question we should ask is not about our method but about our message. If our message is wrong then our gospel is wrong; it is no longer God's gospel; and if it is no longer God's gospel then it is 'some other gospel', and it is not, and can never be, 'the power of God unto salvation'. A notable feature in the books which touch on the message of evangelism is the total lack of attention given to the subject of this study, i.e. the place of law-work and law-preaching in the proclamation of the gospel. I have been totally unable to find one modern book on evangelism which devotes even a chapter, or section of a chapter, to the preaching of law, of the place of that preaching, in our presentation of the gospel to sinners. Apart from Chantry, Pink, Packer and one or two other notable exceptions, present-day writers evince little concern about the claims and rights of God in the preaching of the gospel; not the law, but the love of God is to be the message, and all too often it is love as the antithesis of law, or love at the expense of law. The subject then, as I see it, is one of vital importance, for its impinges upon the very essence and character of the gospel; it posits searching questions about the message we have been commissioned to proclaim.

There are several ways in which the question could be approached. The ideal would be to consider it exegetically, then historically, and finally to treat it dogmatically. Limits of space forbid that approach and so I have chosen to deal with it dogmatically rather than exegetically or historically, and even then space requires a more scanty treatment than the subject really deserves and requires.

---

1. Walter J. Chantry, *Today's Gospel*, Banner of Truth, p. 10.

1. The Character of the Gospel

Let us begin, then, by looking, first of all, at the character of the gospel. We might suppose that it is very easy to define precisely what the gospel is. Most people today would probably say that the gospel is 'Good News for sinners'. That is fine. But it immediately poses the question, What is a sinner? And it is just here that the average person of our generation is in great darkness. A generation untaught in the Scriptures is a generation without any kind of adequate concept of sin or of sinnership. This fact points up the relevance and the importance of the place of law in modern evangelism, because the news held out in the gospel will certainly not be good news to the person who has no sense of sin or need; the news will then be irrelevant. That is why we have to look more closely at the question of how we define the nature and character of the gospel we are commissioned to preach, and paramount place must be given to the question of the relationship between law and grace.

John Murray pinpoints this for us in a very clear and cogent way when he writes: 'No subject is more intimately bound up with the nature of the gospel than that of law and grace. In the degree to which error is entertained at this point, in the same degree is our conception of the gospel perverted.'[2] After setting out the antithesis which Paul postulates between law and grace as the grounds of a sinner's justification in Romans and Galatians, Murray then proceeds to deal with the other side of the matter, the affinity and congruity between them. This is the facet of the matter which interests us here and Murray has this to say of it: 'But lest we should think that the whole question of the relation of law and grace is thereby resolved, we must be reminded that Paul says also in this polemic, "Do we then make void the law through faith? God forbid, yes, we establish the law" (Rom. 3:31). We are compelled therefore to recognize that the subject of law and grace is not simply concerned with the antithesis that there is between law and grace, but also with law as that which makes grace necessary and with grace as establishing and confirming law'. He then adds something that nails down the vital issue very bluntly and very clearly: 'It is not only the doctrine of grace that must be jealously guarded against distortion by the works of law, but it is

2. John Murray, *Principles of Conduct* (Tyndale Press, 1957), p. 181.

also the doctrine of law that must be preserved against the distortions of a spurious concept of grace.'[3]

Now, to read the literature which is poured forth on evangelism is to become conscious that precisely at this point present-day evangelism faces us with the very grave consideration that it may be seriously astray. It fails to ask the question, far less answer it, What place does law hold in the economy of grace? Murray's thesis that law is an integral part of the economy of grace is never raised. This is alarming. If the claims of law are neglected, muted, or even laid aside, the resultant message, no matter how earnestly proclaimed, is no longer the biblical gospel of God's saving grace. Preaching the true gospel involves what the apostle calls, 'declaring all the counsel of God' (Acts 20:27) and he says, 'I kept back nothing that was profitable unto you' (Acts 20:20).

The danger arises from the fact that, in much of the evangelism of our day, something is being 'kept back' from those being evangelized. The preaching of 'all the counsel of God' certainly involves a faithful declaration of the righteous demands of God upon all men, converted and unconverted alike. The omission, consciously or unconsciously, of any of the essential ingredients of the message with which God has entrusted us is serious and dangerous and can only lead to error in the understanding of our hearers. 'When a half truth is presented as the whole truth it becomes an untruth,' says Walter Chantry.[4]

The danger is that we tone down what we may think of as the 'rough edges' of God's truth. There is an emphasis in modern evangelism which flows from the desire that the gospel be made attractive to man's understanding, that it be 'respectable' and that it must not wound or offend the sensibilities of its hearers – especially of its cultured hearers! We are in danger of being in the place that Paul speaks of when he says, 'Then is the offence of the cross ceased'. No doubt the gospel is, indeed, 'good news to sinners'. But we must remember that it is only such when it is set against the background of man's lostness, his sin, sinnership and enmity against God. That surely is why the law is a very real and integral part of the economy of grace and has a very definite and important function and role in the proclamation of the gospel. The gospel aims to save, but it aims to save those who are lost.

3. Murray, *ibid*, p. 182. 4. Chantry, *ibid*, p. 17.

2. The Character of Law

Having thus brought into focus the gravity of the issue which is at stake, the very character of the gospel we preach, let us now go on, in the second place, to look at the character of law. Here, the whole question is, Why has God given the law? We are particularly concerned with its function and role within the economy of grace.

There are two things which are indispensable to true Christian life: first, a clear knowledge of duty; and, second, an obedience co-ordinate with that knowledge. Just as there can be no well-grounded hope of salvation without obedience, so we can have no sure rule of obedience without knowledge. Our Shorter Catechism beautifully defines the one, only rule of obedience for us: 'The Scriptures principally teach what man is to believe concerning God, and what duty God requires of man' (Answer 3). When sin and the Fall had ravaged what has been called 'the law of nature', then God, as ruler and judge of all the earth, was pleased to prescribe for us laws to regulate our lives and our actions. The nature and whereabouts of these prescriptive laws are again put very clearly and succinctly by the Catechism: 'The rule which God at first revealed to man for his obedience was the moral law' (Answer 40). This is the law with which we are concerned here, and as the Catechism again informs us, 'the moral law is summarily comprehended in the Ten Commandments' (Answer 41). The fundamental function of the moral law, then, is quite clear and explicit; it is the rule, and the only rule, of man's obedience to God; there is no other standard of obedience; conformity to this standard is obedience, nonconformity is disobedience. The moral law is the ultimate measure of what constitutes righteousness or unrighteousness, obedience or disobedience, holiness or sin. Says John Murray, 'Holiness is exemplified in obedience to the commandments of God',[5] and the corollary of Murray's statement is self-evident, 'sin is exemplified in disobedience to the commandment of God' or, as the Bible phrases it, 'sin is the transgression of the law' (1 John 3:4).

Here an important consideration arises. If obedience is the primary concern of the law, so it is also of the gospel. The Christlike life, the God-pleasing life, the holy life into which the gospel

---

5. Murray, *ibid*, p. 199.

ushers men in the power of saving grace is a life of obedience. At this point in their design and aim there is no antithesis, no disparity, between law and gospel: on the contrary, they are in full agreement and perfect harmony. Further, we should mark the fact that the obedience into which the gospel brings us has still, as its standard and rule, the moral law. In the measure in which Christian living falls short at this point – and it always falls short in greater or lesser degree – it is a shortfall from that standard. For the converted, as well as the unconverted, it remains true that 'by the law is the knowledge of sin' (Rom. 3:20).

Another consideration to be borne in mind here is that the law reflects the nature and character of God just as surely as does the gospel. In the Ten Commandments we have a transcript of the moral constitution of the Deity. 'It exhibits in all its parts,' says A. H. Strong, 'the nature of the one Lawgiver, and it expresses, in its least command, the one requirement of harmony with him.'[6] This means that the ultimate ground of all moral duty is that which lies back of, and is reflected in, the law, viz. the holiness of God. Not surprisingly, this point is made again and again in Scripture; for example, 'Ye shall be holy, for I, the LORD your God, am holy' (Lev. 19:2). And holiness in his people was invariably involved in his promise to be their God. The same principle finds repeated expression in the New Testament, for example, 'Without holiness, no man shall see the Lord' (Heb. 12:14), and is actually reiterated in Old Testament terms by Peter: 'As he which hath called you is holy, so be ye holy in all manner of conversation, because it is written, Be ye holy for I am holy' (1 Pet. 1:15, 16).

Were we dealing with our subject from the exegetical point of view it is at this stage of our study that we would wish to look at many of the texts which reflect the relationship existing between law and grace: for example, 'The law is our schoolmaster to bring us unto Christ' (Gal. 3:24); 'By the law is the knowledge of sin' (Rom. 3:20); 'Christ is the end of the law for righteousness to everyone that believeth' (Rom. 10:4). Having looked at that class of texts – and their range is surprisingly wide – it becomes clear that the real prelude to a conviction of sin is the conviction of God's holiness. It was a vision of the glory of that holiness which prompted conviction of sin in Isaiah and called forth the

---

6. A.H. Strong, *Systematic Theology*, p. 279.

confession, 'Woe is me! for I am undone; because I am a man of unclean lips, and I dwell in the midst of a people of unclean lips' (Isa. 6:5). On this basis Dr. James Buchanan writes:

> 'The principal means of conviction is the LAW, the LAW of God in its purity, spirituality and power .... The law in its holy commandment, the law in its awful curse, the law in its spiritual nature, as reaching to the heart ... the conscience is constrained to do homage to the law, and to acknowledge that "that law is holy and the commandment holy, and just, and good", while self-convicted and self-condemned, the sinner exclaims, "But I am carnal, sold under sin".'[7]

Too little attention has been paid to a further truth which follows on the fact that the law is the reflection of God's character: it reflects not only his holiness but his love. Had more attention always been paid to the preface of the Ten Commandments the antithesis between law and grace might not have been drawn as starkly as it often has been. 'And God spake all these words, saying, I am the LORD thy God, which have brought thee out of the land of Egypt, out of the house of bondage (Exod. 20:2). This confirms for us that whatever there be of awe-inspiring grandeur or solemn majesty attendant upon, and involved in, the giving of the law, it nevertheless is grounded in love. The law proceeded from, and is the revelation of, the God who is the gracious Redeemer of his people as well as the righteous Creator and Judge of all his creatures. And one principle which is clearly taught in this fact is that the love of God as Redeemer, the love which the gospel displays in its fulness, is a righteous and holy love. That principle is, no doubt, brought out in its clearest manifestation in the death of the cross, but it is enshrined and safeguarded also in the giving of the law. It follows, too, that all transgression of the law is not merely the breach of a rule of duty, but a sin against the God who has given the rule and so constitutes a violation of love as well as of holiness; all sin is sin against God's love. The very emphasis of the gospel requirement of holiness reflects the demand of law, for Jesus said, 'If ye love me, keep my commandments' (John 14:15).

Here we must ask ourselves the question, Does modern evan-

---

7. James Buchanan, *The Office and Work of the Holy Spirit*, Banner of Truth, p. 36.

gelism, and our own preaching of the gospel, really take these factors into consideration? Does our evangelism do justice to the demands of God's holiness as well as to his love, to a mercy consonant with perfect righteousness? Does it put the requirements of God before the needs of man? The nature and character of God's law indicates that 'man's chief end is the glory of God' and that this principle inheres in the evangelism of the lost as it does in everything else.

3. The Character of God

This leads us on, in the third place to look, briefly, at the place which evangelism must give to the character of God. We must seriously ask ourselves what sort of God our preaching proclaims to men?

The preachers of the Bible set before us a God who was to be 'feared'. They clearly worked on the principle that 'The fear of the LORD is the beginning of wisdom' (Prov. 9:10), and that this fear was a powerful element in the keeping of his commandments. The connection between those two things is set before us by the 'Preacher' when he says: 'Let us hear the conclusion of the whole matter: fear God and keep his commandments; for this is the whole duty of man' (Ecc. 12:13). There is, of course, a distinction to be made between the dread involved in an apprehension of God's wrath and the filial fear which is the basis of godliness. The first expresses itself in enmity and hatred, the second constrains adoration and love. But there is just as much real cause for the first kind of fear as there is for the second. 'God is angry with the wicked every day' (Ps. 7:11) and an angry God is one to be dreaded just as surely as a reconciled God is one to be loved.

This emphasis comes out strongly in the preaching described in the New Testament. The God proclaimed by John the Baptist, by the Saviour himself, and by the apostles, was a God who demanded repentance in order to the remission of sins; he was one whose curse rested upon sin and the perpetrator of sin; he was One who would by no means spare the guilty; he was one in whom all disobedience engendered righteous indignation. In other words, the preachers of the Bible did not pass lightly over the awe-inspiring attributes of God. New Testament preaching did not soften down or eliminate those characteristics of the Deity which make him a dread and a terror to the transgressor. Their gospel began with God and his glory. It extolled his honour and set forth his majesty and his greatness. It told men the kind of God they had offended. It sent them to sue for mercy and to beg for pardon from the High and the Holy One.

The preaching of our forebears in evangelism did the very same thing. To read the writings and sermons of Luther and Calvin, of Whitefield and Spurgeon, of M'Cheyne and William Chalmers Burns, is to be brought into contact with a God who is to be feared. The preaching of men whom God has most signally blessed in building up his church by evangelism has, uniformly, put the glory of God in the forefront of its aims and the character of God has been the foundation of its message.

Now, does this hold true for the present day? Does the preaching and the message of modern evangelism really set out the grandeur and glory of God's character? Does it do equal justice to all the attributes of the divine nature? Or is it more true to say, as Walter Chantry does, 'Love is set before sinners as the foremost characteristic of God.'[8] If as one fears, this charge is true – or very frequently is true – what damage is being done! What dishonour is involved towards God, and what danger towards the souls of sinners! 'To say to a rebel, "God loves you and has a wonderful plan for your life"', says Chantry, 'is terribly misinforming. The truth is that God is holy. Thus he is angry with the sinner at this moment. His sword of wrath already hangs over the head of the guilty and will for ever torment him unless he repents and trusts Christ. This plan is not so wonderful. God's redeeming love is found only in Christ, and the sinner is out of Christ.'[9] No doubt some will claim that Chantry is here stating the case in an extreme way, but that does not weaken the force of what he is saying. It nails into our minds the fearful danger of misrepresenting truth by bringing forth only a half-truth. And the half-truth is not only an untruth, it is a blasphemy in this particular instance, for it sets forth nothing less than a false image of the living God and gives a distorted picture of what he is like and what he does. That, surely, at the very lowest assessment, is no basis upon which to set about evangelizing lost men.

8. Chantry, *ibid*, p. 28.
9. *Ibid*, p. 29.

This, then, is one area where the preaching of the law becomes an essential in our evangelistic message. Lost sinners must be told that to know God is an essential of salvation: 'This is life eternal, to know thee, the only living and true God, and Jesus Christ, whom thou hast sent' (John 17:3). The law is a mirror in which the nature and characteristics of that God are very clearly reflected. We must hold that mirror up before men. To do so is intimately related to the salvation of sinners. Without a knowledge of God, the sinner does not know with any clarity whom he has offended, who threatens him with eternal destruction, or who is able to save him. To preach the love or mercy of God apart from the cross and the atoning death of Christ is of course to preach a mercy and love that are not in God at all. But, equally, to preach the cross or to apply its remedy apart from the law, which constitutes its necessity and provides its interpreting principle, debases the love it manifests and constitutes the cross as an arbitrary action of a capricious God. In other words, to know the God of the Bible is to understand why he has said, 'Without the shedding of blood, there is no remission of sin' (Heb. 9:22), and to be ignorant of him as he really is, is to be baffled by such a stringent demand. The law, then, as the reflection of God's character has a major part to play in the economy of grace.

4. The Character of Man

Evangelism must take stock of the kind of creature with which it is dealing. It sets out to impress truth upon fallen, sinful men, the truth about God and the truth about themselves. There was never a day when preaching needed to be more distinctly clear about the biblical teaching on the nature and condition of sinful man than our own day. Over against false and optimistic views of man, the truth of the Bible that he is a fallen, lost, condemned sinner needs special emphasis. Here, again, we need the law of God. By the law man can come to know God and he can come to know himself. Just in the very measure in which it exhibits the righteousness of God – and so, the righteousness which is alone acceptable to God – it teaches man of his unrighteousness, certifies him of his sin, convicts him of his guilt and condemns him for his ungodliness.

Until man begins to know his real character, until he is convinced of his real standing before God as under curse and condemnation, he cannot, and will not, appreciate the overtures of God's grace in the gospel. Here is one of the great functions of the law and, perhaps, one of the great failures of present-day evangelism. It is perilous in the extreme to forget, or neglect, the fact that 'by the law is the knowledge of sin' (Rom. 3:20).

Commenting on this biblical statement, Robert Haldane has this to say: 'Paul does not here intend simply to say that the law makes known in general the nature of sin, inasmuch as it discovers what is acceptable or displeasing to God, what he commands, and what he forbids; but he means to affirm that the law convicts men of being sinners.'[10]

'The law,' says John Murray on this same text, 'does perform this necessary and contributory service in connection with justification; it imparts the knowledge of sin and enables us to perceive that from the works of the law no flesh will be justified and therefore every mouth is stopped and the whole world rests under God's judgment.'[11]

'The apostle testifies,' says Calvin, 'that the law pronounces its sentence of condemnation in order "that every mouth may be stopped and all the world may become guilty before God" (Rom. 3:19). In another place, however, the same apostle declares that "God hath concluded them all in unbelief": not that he might destroy all, or allow all to perish, but that "he might have mercy upon all" (Rom. 11:32); in other words, that divesting themselves of an absurd opinion of their own virtue, they may perceive how they are wholly dependent on the hand of God; that feeling how naked and destitute they are, they may take refuge in his mercy, rely upon it, and cover themselves up entirely with it.'[12]

'In the precepts of the law,' says Calvin again, 'God is seen as the rewarder only of perfect righteousness (a righteousness of which all are destitute) and, on the other hand, as the stern avenger of wickedness. But in Christ his countenance beams forth full of grace and gentleness towards poor unworthy sinners.'[13]

Only preaching of the law will bring home to man the depravity and the spiritual inability of the unregenerate heart, the depth

10. Robert Haldane, *An Exposition of Romans* (Banner of Truth) p. 125.
11. John Murray, *The Epistle to the Romans* (Eerdmans, 1968) p. 107.
12. John Calvin, *Institutes II*, 7, viii. 13. *Ibid.*

of ungodliness and wickedness to which human nature has been subjected. These and similar truths are what the law enforces upon its hearers and they are calculated to humble the proud heart as nothing else can. Man needs to know today that only God in his mercy, by his Spirit, through the Son can deliver him from this helpless and hopeless state, but the very truths which teach him this solemn and soul-humbling fact are, in much of today's preaching and evangelism, almost wholly laid aside.

'Evangelicals are swelling the ranks of the deluded with a perverted gospel .... Many who have "made decisions" in modern churches and been told in the inquiry rooms that their sins have been forgiven will be as surprised as Tetzel's customers to hear, "I never knew you, depart from me".'[14]

5. The Character of our Message
In an age like ours, when men in general are ignorant of and indifferent to these solemn truths, there is little doubt that there is an urgent need of what might be called 'pre-evangelism'. Something that must concern us very deeply is that, all too often, evangelism stresses the remedy without first of all diagnosing the disease.

The mass evangelism of an earlier day could depend upon a people being fairly well instructed in, and holding to, the basic teachings of the moral law. This is no longer true. Hence, one of the priorities must be to present truths that will bring people to a conviction of sin and need. To be ignorant of one's need as a sinner is to be blind to the necessity of a Saviour. The righteous demands of God must be clearly set out. 'Contrasting our conduct with the righteousness of the law,' says Calvin, 'we see how very far it is from being in accordance with the will of God, and therefore, how unworthy we are of holding our place among his creatures, far less of being accounted his sons.' And he goes on, 'taking a survey of our powers, we see that they are not only unequal to fulfil the Law, but are altogether null. The necessary consequence must be, to produce distrust of our own ability, and also anxiety and trepidation of mind.'[15] Now, these two feelings, of guilt on the one hand and spiritual impotence on the other, are

---

14. Chantry, *Today's Gospel*, pp. 14-15.
15. John Calvin, *Institutes II*, 8.

precisely those that much modern evangelism utterly fails to instil.

From the Book of Acts we know that Paul could sum up his evangelistic preaching as a message of 'repentance toward God, and faith toward our Lord Jesus Christ' (Acts 20:21). Today, to judge from the literature on evangelism, the second element of that combination is proclaimed, almost to the exclusion of the first. Exhortations to 'accept Jesus as your personal Saviour', if they are not based upon and grounded in a clear demand for heart repentance, are just meaningless phrases, wholly inadequate to instruct a sinner in the way to eternal life. When Jesus began his public ministry, his message was, 'The time is fulfilled, and the kingdom of God is at hand: repent ye, and believe the gospel' (Mark 1:15). When the rich young ruler ran to him, he demanded that he 'sell all that he had' (Matt. 19:21); his gospel to the woman at the well insisted that she turn from adultery (John 4). On the day of Pentecost the message of Peter was a message of repentance (Acts 2). When Paul confronted the philosophers of Mars' Hill he preached, 'God now commandeth all men everywhere to repent' (Acts 17:30).

Repentance was neither a secondary nor an optional note in the apostolic message, it was primary and crucial. To exhort to faith in the Saviour without this prior imperative is not simply to fail to preach the gospel, it is to distort it into another gospel 'which is not a gospel'.

It is in the face of this lamentable failure that Walter Chantry writes, 'Today men are properly told to confess their sin and to ask forgiveness. But evangelists and pastors are forgetting to tell sinners to repent. Consequently, this misinformed age imagines that it can continue in its old ways of life while adding Jesus as a personal Hell insurance for the world to come.'[16] Chantry is right. Repentance, to be repentance at all, involves not merely the confession but the forsaking of sin. But in order to this repentance men must know what sin is. The law must be preached, not just in a general but a particular way. It must be brought to bear, in all its power, upon particular and personal and individual sins. It must be made relevant to the lives, and lifestyles, the sins and ungodliness of the people to whom we are preaching. To read the *Confessions* of an Augustine, or the feelings of a Bunyan under

---

16. Chantry, *Today's Gospel*, pp. 14-15.

conviction of sin, or the exhortations of a Baxter in his preaching for souls, is to feel oneself far removed from the atmosphere of much present-day preaching. To hear sinners being told just to 'decide for Christ', or 'to trust in him' because, if they do not they will be unhappy and maladjusted creatures, or will miss 'the real meaning of life' is to be aware of a terrific shift of emphasis in the message from these former times. To read the methods advocated in many of the books on evangelism is to feel that the gospel does not do much more than offer people some kind of magic formula that will really cure, once and for all, their many spiritual ills. Christ, one sometimes feels, is being reduced to some kind of clever psychologist who is able to straighten out all personal problems rather than being presented as the only Redeemer of God's elect, the only Saviour from sin and from hell.

To avoid giving such impressions in our evangelistic preaching we must, then, proclaim the law. Only against that background does the gospel have meaning and relevance. We must not be afraid of producing deep conviction of sin in our hearers. On the contrary, we should aim at it. Such conviction, and such conviction alone, will drive men to a sense of their need and their helplessness and make them seek a powerful and omnipotent Saviour. We are, perhaps, all of us, in too much of a hurry to apply the balm of the gospel to every wounded conscience. We must be willing, in some sense, to stand back and see the Spirit of God do a real, deep, lasting work in the souls of men. This, after all, is his office and we must not attempt to do a work which is wholly out with our remit as preachers and, in any case, totally beyond our power.

It is interesting and informative to note that, in the early years of his ministry in Sandfield, Dr. Lloyd-Jones wrote out fully, not his expository, but his evangelistic sermons. It was to these that he imparted, in a particular way, his careful thought and his most considered expression. The lesson for every preacher is simple but important: evangelistic sermons demand, and should always be given, careful and detailed preparation.

To sum up, let me stress that the doctrine of the law is really presupposed in that of the gospel, and the righteousness which is required in the one is revealed and supplied in the other. Law and grace are not opposites but complementary parts of the same gracious administration of the God of salvation. To neglect either, or to emphasize one at the expense of the other, is to distort and destroy both. Law work is a prerequisite of a grace work and, indeed, must be considered as an integral part of it. For the conviction of sin, and of righteousness, and of judgment to come are the fruits of the Holy Spirit at work in the soul and are the first signs that grace is stirring within and that the soul is being cast over into the arms of Jesus.

Let us preach towards, look for, and rejoice in, a real 'Law Work' in our hearers for, where the law is at work, there God is at work, just as surely as he is present in a 'Grace Work'; and Scripture assures us that, where 'God has begun a good work he will perform it until the day of Jesus Christ' (Phil. 1:6).

3

Justification by Faith: What It Means

Our understanding of justification by faith is fundamental to our proclamation and understanding of the gospel, so in this article I want to indicate what the preaching of the doctrine of justification is concerned to impart to others. This doctrine, then, will be discussed here in terms of its importance, its nature and its ground.

1. The Importance of the Doctrine of Justification by Faith
I want now to highlight the crucial importance of justification in the gospel scheme of salvation in three ways.

First of all, we can establish the importance of this doctrine by looking at its achievements in the history of the church.

We can begin the survey where the doctrine actually emerged in its clearest formulation. This doctrine has consistently and correctly been regarded as one of the two basic, controlling principles of Reformation theology. The authority of Scripture was the formal principle of that theology, prescribing its method and providing its sole touchstone of truth; and justification by faith was its material principle, determining its substance and directing its dynamic.

It was not, of course, a new doctrine discovered for the first time by the Reformers Martin Luther and John Calvin. We have to recognise that Christians right down through the ages discerned this principle, and in fact acted on it. The fact of acceptance with God on the merits of Christ, and by grace alone, was never really absent from the faith of Christ's church. There are many instances in which it finds expression down through the years, not so much, perhaps, as an articulated article of the faith, but certainly as a testimony of Christian experience. Now, that is to say just this: that no sinner can know Christ savingly apart from justification, and justification was known in the heart of every believer, even if it was not clearly formulated in his mind. While this fact must be

Originally published in the theological journal, Foundations (February, 1983).

remembered, yet it nevertheless remains true that it was the doctrine of justification by faith that was most clearly to mark the cleavage between the Reformation era and the ages that went before it. At the Reformation it found clarification, clear formulation, and very significant vocal articulation. It was at the centre of the preaching of men like Melancthon, Luther, Calvin and those who under God were entrusted with the revival that lay at the heart of the Reformation.

Now, the fact that the Reformation itself was in essence a re-discovery of the gospel way of salvation, and that the doctrine of justification by faith was one of the two major catalysts in that rediscovery, is proof for us of how closely it lies to the very heart of the gospel. So close to the heart of the gospel that I want to say this: where the truths of justification are held and proclaimed, there a door of hope is set before sinners; where these truths are neither known nor preached, then the way of salvation has been shut up, and the lost sinner can have no hope. It is because of this – and this is absolutely fundamental to our understanding of what the gospel is – that G.C. Berkouwer of the Free University of Amsterdam is right (and I don't always think Berkouwer is right!) when he says:

> 'The confession of divine justification touches man's life at its heart, at the point of his relationship to God. It defines the preaching of the church, the existence and progress of the life of faith, the root of human security, and man's perspective for the future.'

All these things are involved in the proclamation of justification by faith. Professor Finlayson tells us that these truths mentioned by Berkouwer really underlie the spiritual impulse of the Reformation and show us that the Reformation was in fact far more radical spiritually than we tend to think. He points out its historical importance when he says:

> 'It made faith,' (not just the Reformation, but the doctrine of justification) 'alone the sole contact between the sinner and the Saviour. It turned theology into religion; it proved to be the substitution of one religion for another of a totally different kind, of a divine religion for a human, of the supernatural grace of God for the blind and hopeless efforts of men.'

This is true. The emergence and the formulation of this doctrine lay behind the Reformation, and it was nothing less than the
substitution of one religion for another: the religion of God's grace
over against a religion that was couched in the blind and hopeless
efforts of men. And if there was one thing that was not said about
or by the Pope on his visit to Britain in 1982, it was this: the
doctrine of justification by faith was not mentioned.

Now, one of the men I have found most helpful on the doctrine
of justification by faith is Dr. James Buchanan, a theologian of
the Free Church of Scotland in the last century (and it's a comment
on evangelical understanding that his book is the last major treatise
that we have amongst evangelicals on justification by faith). He
pinpoints the importance of the doctrine to our own position like
this: 'The revival of the gospel doctrine of justification was the
chief means of effecting the reformation of religion in Europe in
the sixteenth century.' And we should never forget that if the
Reformation had not taken place, the history of the Western world
would be very different today from what it is. It is untrue to say
that the Reformation doesn't matter – it matters a great deal.
Professor John Murray confirms this opinion when he says: 'It
may be safe to say that the greatest event for Christendom in the
last fifteen hundred years was the Protestant Reformation.' He
continues: 'What was the spark that lit the flame of evangelical
passion? It was, by the grace of God, the discovery on the part of
Luther stricken with a sense of his estrangement from God, and
feeling in his inmost soul the stings of his wrath and the remorse
of a terrified conscience, of the truth and only way whereby a
man can be just with God. To him, the truth of justification by
free grace, through faith, lifted him from the depths of the
forebodings of hell to ecstasy of peace with God and the hope of
glory' (*Collected Writings*, Vol. 2, p. 203). 'The doctrine of
justification was the radical principle out of which grew the
reformation from Popery,' says R.L. Dabney; 'it was by adopting
this doctrine that the Reformers were led out of darkness into
light.' Let us never forget this and how vitally important,
historically, the doctrine of justification by faith is.

Secondly let me stress the importance of justification to the gospel scheme of salvation by referring to the spiritual effects which

this doctrine has produced in the lives of God's people.

The first and basic question in spiritual things is that of a man's relationship to God. All other questions of a religious nature take second place to that one. All religion – not merely the Christian faith – ultimately poses the query, 'How can a man be just with God? How can he be right with the Holy One?' And different religions pose a whole series of varied answers to that question. But when we come to the Bible the question assumes a far more serious and aggravated aspect than merely, 'How can a man be just with God?' The question now is, 'How can a *sinful* man be just with a *holy* God?' The gospel, which centres on the doctrine of justification by faith alone, supplies the only valid answer to that question. For this reason: in the final analysis sin is always against God; and the one who is against God can never be right with God. If we are against God then God is against us; it cannot be otherwise. God cannot fail to take account of that which is the contradiction of himself. His holy perfection required the recoil of righteous indignation to all sin and that recoil finds its expression in wrath. 'The wrath of God,' says the apostle, 'is revealed from heaven against all ungodliness,' and let us as ministers remember that in our own lives. 'The wrath of God is revealed from heaven against all ungodliness and unrighteousness of men' (Rom. 1:18). That is our actual situation; that is not theory, but fact. Because this is so, the gravity and complexity of the question is, 'How can a sinful man be right with a holy God?'

Man today really fails to face up to this reality. He is living in a cushioned vacuum of his own philosophical creation, and his understanding of reality is untrue. To efface not only God, but in addition the God of justice and of wrath who is angry with the wicked every day, is to distort reality, and to hide behind that which is untrue. This is one reason why the ground doctrine of justification by faith alone does not raise large 'Hosannas', either in our own hearts or in the hearts of the people to whom we preach. We fail to reckon with two vital things: with sin, and with the wrath of God. This is the reason why the gospel of grace will really be a mere sound in the world and church of our own day, for man has little sense of the reality of God and of the reality of his judgment; he has little understanding of the majesty of God and of his holiness, while sin is considered nothing more than man's misfortune out of which he is growing. If it's not his misfortune, it's merely a maladjustment to his environment, and proper education will sort it out. If we face reality in biblical terms we have to reckon with the fact that justification deals with lost sinners. 'The justification of a sinner,' says W.G.T. Shedd (and I would commend him to your reading), 'is different from that of a righteous person. The former is unmerited, the latter is merited. The former is without good works, the latter is because of good works. The former is pardon of sin, and accepting one as righteous when he is not so; the latter is pronouncing one righteous because he is so. The former is complex, the latter is simple.' That is how he makes the distinction between the justification of a sinner and the justification of one who is not a sinner. 'Holy angels, for example,' he says, 'are justified before the bar of God on the ground of their own righteousness; they have not sinned.'

Now we can go on to this: the plain fact stands before us that sin has involved man in guilt, while guilt, in turn, involves divine condemnation. To state the matter in this way points out for us the necessity of a complete reversal in our legal standing before God. That is where justification begins; it is where it must begin. Because of sin, and the condemnation that sin's guilt involves, man's standing with God is wrong. The real question that justification confronts is, 'How can that standing be put right?' Our salvation must involve not merely a change in our inward attitude to God, but before that a change in God's judicial relationship to us. How can that standing and that judicial relationship ever be changed? Justification is the answer; and justification is the act of God's free grace. Paul says in Romans 8:33: 'It is God that justifies, who is he that condemns?' So vital and fundamental, then, is justification, that its importance to salvation cannot be highlighted too strongly. Wherever men have come to an understanding of the doctrine of justification by faith in Christ alone, they have come to a wonderful, spiritual emancipation. Wherever it is lost or obscured, men enter in various degrees into spiritual bondage. The spiritual achievements of justification by faith tell us that it lies at the very heart of the gospel.

Thirdly, we'll now turn from the historical achievements of the doctrine and its spiritual effects to its theological implications. It is vitally important here to recognise the relationship that justification bears to all other doctrines involved in an evangelical and biblical scheme of theology. The biblical doctrine bears, for example, not merely on the application of redemption to sinners, but it bears even more strongly on the *nature* of the redemption which is to be applied to sinners. In other words, it ties in not merely with the application of redemption but with the accomplishment of redemption. Or, to put it differently, it ties in with what kind of salvation a sinner can find when he finds salvation in Christ.

Now, we know that the justification of a sinner is inextricably bound up with his regeneration, with his union to Christ, with his faith, his repentance and his conversion. That is, it stands in intimate relation to all the doctrines involved in the application of redemption. But that is not all. We must remember that it also stands intimately related to the person and work of Christ, and especially to the atonement. Was Christ's death a work that laid the basis upon which sinners could be accounted righteous before a holy God? Did he bear the guilt of sin? Did he safeguard the divine rectitude in the pardon and remission of sin? All these, and many other vital questions of theology, will not only affect, but they will in turn be affected by, our understanding of the doctrine of justification. Now this is very clearly spelled out for us by a theologian whom I admire very much, namely, R.L. Dabney:

'When we consider how many of the fundamental points of theology are connected with justification, we can hardly assign it too important a place. Our view of this doctrine must determine or be determined by our view of Christ's satisfaction. And this again carried along with it the whole doctrine concerning the natures and person of Christ. And if the proper deity of him be denied, that of the Holy Ghost will very certainly follow along with it, so that the very doctrine of the Trinity itself is destroyed by extreme views concerning justification. Again, "It is God that justifies"; how evident then that our views of justification will involve those of God's law and of his own moral attributes. The doctrine of original sin is also brought in question when we assert the impossibility of a man so keeping the law of God as to justify himself.'

I'm quoting Dabney to show the range of doctrines that will be affected by what we believe concerning the doctrine of justification by faith. Perhaps you never knew it was as important as that – but it is. Arianism, Socinianism and Unitarianism can all be traced back in their origins to a departure from the simple doctrine of justification by faith in Christ alone. Justification by faith, the more you study it, becomes a key in the whole archway of evangelical doctrine. So vital is it that where it is lost or obscured, perverted or misunderstood, the entire provision of God's redemptive accomplishment for the salvation of sinners is, in the same measure, lost or obscured or perverted or misunderstood. The importance of justification was not being misrepresented in the least when Luther declared it to be the article of a standing or a falling church. You can determine the health or otherwise of the doctrine of any church when you know its doctrine of justification by faith.

2. The Nature of the Doctrine of Justification by Faith

Now I want to go on to look at the nature of justification by faith. I am assuming that you are already well acquainted with this doctrine, so all I want to do is to clarify briefly the nature of justification by faith. How do you define it? I have looked at many books on this doctrine, and the best definition I have found is in the Westminster Shorter Catechism: 'Justification is an act of God's free grace wherein he pardons all our sins and accepts us as righteous in his sight, only for the righteousness of Christ imputed to us, and received by faith alone.' Could you better that?

Now let's look quickly at this definition. First of all, justification is an *act* of God. That might not seem very important – but it is. It is an act of God, and not a *work* of God; and the act is of a legal, judicial or forensic nature, and the terminology of Scripture about justification can only be understood in a forensic sense. Because it is a forensic act it has to do with our legal standing before God. It is not a work within the person being justified, but it is a declaration about the person being justified. Regeneration, to take one example of what God does in the application of redemption, *is* a work of God in us; but justification is purely and solely a judgment of God concerning us. The difference is crucial to a correct understanding of what justification is.

The distinction is similar to the difference between the action of a surgeon and the act of a judge. The one, when he removes some diseased part of the body, does something *in* us; the other doesn't do that, but he gives a verdict concerning our legal status, our relationship to law and our standing in the eyes of law. The declaration is either concerning our innocence or concerning our guilt – either of these two things and nothing else. Now, that declaration has nothing to do with making us inwardly good or inwardly bad. It is not a work that can make us either holy or evil; it is a declaration not about our inward condition, but about our actual legal standing.

Justification, therefore, means that the sinner is declared as being free from guilt and, in the sight of God, as sustaining a relation which meets all the requirements of his holy law and his inflexible justice. This difference is critical because many make the mistake of confusing justification with sanctification. This is done in a variety of ways and by a broad spectrum of religious opinion, ranging from the Romanists with their doctrine of infused grace on the one hand, to the Perfectionists with their doctrine of complete holiness on the other. There is always a confusion of two things which differ: justification and sanctification.

Now, in essence, this type of teaching which confuses these things simply puts the work of the Holy Spirit into the place which should be occupied by the work of Christ alone. This kind of teaching looks to the work of the Holy Spirit within the sinner as the basis of justification, rather than to Christ's work *for* the sinner as that basis. James Buchanan writes: 'There is, perhaps, no more subtle or plausible error on the subject of justification than that which makes it rest on the indwelling presence and the gracious work of the Holy Spirit in the heart.'

It's worth noting how damaging this kind of thought can be to biblical teaching, and how destructive of spiritual peace in personal experience. For if we are justified solely on account of what Christ did and suffered for us, we can rest upon a completely finished work, a righteousness already accepted by God. But if we are justified in the least measure at all by the work of the Holy Spirit within us, we are called to rest on a work that is still taking place, which is subject to resistance from our own depraved hearts, and which, in the case of the renewed sinner, is not even begun until that sinner is safely past the point of regeneration. Any such scheme of justification strongly detracts, not merely from the freeness of grace, but from the fullness of the atoning work of Christ. We must be careful, therefore, to distinguish between justification and sanctification; they are closely related, but distinctive.

It is, in fact, just at this very point that many evangelicals today lamentably fail to preach a full, clear, biblical message. They do this in a variety of ways and often, I like to believe, without realising it. They put forward faith or repentance, or prayer or even 'coming to Christ' as the basis for becoming right with God. Do you do that when you preach? I have to ask myself, do I? In fact, none of these things is the basis on which a sinner can come to God or become right with God. All of these things are only involved in us being made right with God; but it is true that any doctrine that over-stresses the activity of the sinner, or even the work of God within the sinner, as the basis for justification, has failed to grapple with the very nature of the justification it is seeking to proclaim. Justification is no more a work of God than it is the work of us men. It is an *act* of God in which he makes a declaration about the sinner's standing before the law.

The second thing to note from this definition is this: that the act is one of God's free grace. It couldn't be anything else. This is what marks the gospel method of justification as being absolutely unique. Justification has to deal with a sinner under condemnation. 'Condemnation' is the only sentence which can really belong to him before justice and law; and condemnation is, of course, the exact opposite of justification. The nub of the matter is that because he is dealing with sinners God is required, as the apostle says, 'to justify the ungodly'. The amazing thing about the gospel is that God can remain God and do that. He can be just and the justifier of the ungodly. This is precisely the truth which the gospel method of justification is concerned to proclaim. God's declaration proceeds upon his legal regard to what his free grace has already done, and what it has already achieved for the sinner in the finished work of Christ. God acts upon the basis of a provision which he has himself made, and which adequately meets all the exigencies of the matter in hand; a provision which is there because of his gracious love, and for no other reason at all. It is there because, in the words of the apostle, 'God spared not his own Son but delivered him up for us all' (Rom. 8:32). It is there because 'God *so* loved the world ....' What a gospel! It's rooted in the free grace of God. It's an act of God's free grace.

And the third point is this: 'In that act,' the Catechism says, 'he pardons *all* our sins.' This is a vital and important, but not the only, part of justification. The pardon of sin consists in the removal of sin's guilt; and that involves the absolving of the sinner from the obligation to punishment which was his just due because of his breach of God's holy law. He is absolved from it. This element of justification regards particularly, though not exclusively, the passive obedience of Christ, i.e., his suffering and death on the cross in the place of his people. The pardon granted here applies to sin because of the cross. Now listen: it applies to *all* sins: 'Wherein he pardons all our sins.' Sins in our ignorance, sins in our enlightenment, sins past, sins present, and sins future; 'wherein he pardons all our sins.' It involves the removal of *all* the guilt of God's people, and it brings them out from under *every* penalty. Any chastisement that the believer knows in relation to his sin is not, and never is, the chastisement of a judge. It is the chastisement of his Father God upon the child whom he has adopted into his family. Note in passing that Scripture always brings the pardon of sin into the most intimate relation to its punishment in the person of Christ. In the gospel the death of the cross brought about the situation where mercy and justice rejoiced together; where both were conspicuously displayed – 'When we were enemies,' says the apostle Paul (not, 'When we were friends'), 'we were reconciled to God by the death of his Son.' And he goes on to say, 'If we were enemies when we were reconciled by his death, much more we shall be saved by his life' (Rom. 5:10). In other words, if God grounds our justification as enemies and sinners in his death, he'll carry our sanctification on upon the basis of his life.

Now, although pardon is an important element in justification, it's not the only element. 'It is a mistake,' writes Dabney, 'not only of Romanists but of nearly every school of Arminian thought to teach varying shades of the idea that justification is merely exemption from penalty.'

There is something even more wonderful than pardon, for he also accepts us as righteous in his sight. It is positive as well as negative. Now this is a vital element in justification: acceptance with God in Christ. We are accepted 'in the Beloved'. Justification must not only deliver from the penalty incurred by guilt and disobedience, it must also provide a sinner with an equivalent of personal obedience. Whereas a holy being owes only obedience to God's perfect law, a sinful creature owes both penalty and obedience. When the sinner is justified, his justification must provide not merely for his deliverance from hell, but for his entry into heaven; and justification comprises not only pardon but entitlement to heaven. Heaven is only for the righteous, and it is ours because God pardons our sin and also accepts us as righteous in his sight. Because of his divine substitute who suffered 'unto death' for the sinner, the believer obtains not only release from punishment that his sin entails, but he also obtains a reward which he does not merit because his substitute *obeyed* for him. It is not only the passive obedience of Christ in his death which is important, but also the active obedience of Christ in his whole life, where he wrought out a righteousness for his people. He obeyed God not only for himself but also for us. I'm not happy with the division between the active and passive obedience of Christ for it has its weaknesses; yet it helps, too, in clarifying the true aspects of Christ's work for us.

3. The Ground of the Doctrine of Justification by Faith

On what basis does God do all this in his act of justification? Well, the Catechism goes on to say: 'Only for the righteousness of Christ imputed to us.' Why does God accept us? How can he do it? Because of the righteousness of Christ imputed to us. Now, we shouldn't be afraid to use the word 'imputation'. Listening to preachers when I'm on holiday in different parts of Britain, I seldom hear this word used in the pulpit, nor do I even hear the truth of it being preached. When did you last preach on imputation and counter-imputation to your people? Would they know what you were talking about? If not, they're not well taught.

To impute sin, or indeed to impute righteousness, in its scriptural usage is a perfectly straightforward, unambiguous concept. Charles Hodge writes, 'There is no necessity to go into a prolonged study of the Hebrew or Greek original to understand what imputation means. It means simply to set to one's account, to lay to one's charge or to one's credit; to credit as the ground of judicial process".' In many scriptures like Isaiah 53, Galatians 3, Hebrews 9, 1 Peter 2, our sins are said to have been 'laid on' Christ because the guilt was so charged to his account that they became his, and could be justly punished in him. 'He bore our sins,' says Peter, 'in his own body on the tree' (1 Peter 3:24). Now in a similar way Paul teaches us that Christ's perfect righteousness is laid to our account: 'God has made him to be sin for us who knew no sin, that we might be made the righteousness of God in him' (2 Cor. 5:21). There is imputation, and there is counter-imputation. Let me put it like this: imputation and counter-imputation, when they are clearly understood, just mean this: that as Christ stood over into the shoes of the believer in relation to sin, so the believer stands over in the very place of Christ in relation to righteousness. Let's remember, too, as Dabney points out, that 'imputation is not a transfer of moral character but of legal relation'. The imputation of our sin to Christ *never* made him a sinner. Not at all. Do you see any theological distinction in my saying that Christ was made sin, and Christ became a sinner? I wouldn't let you into a pulpit to preach if you could not see this distinction! Imputation is no transference of moral character. Christ was still the eternal God when your sins and mine were imputed to him. He was still the holy, sinless and perfect God. But it was a transference of legal relationship; as the sinless and obedient one, he was standing in the room of sinners. It is because of his sinlessness that he can be made sin in the sense that he was regarded as *the* sinner in the eyes of God when he was imposing penalty and punishment.

It is important to realise what this means. Christ, in his person and work, is the real basis and ground of our justification. We tend to think, perhaps, that something we ourselves can do will really help to make God much more considerate of us, it will help him to pardon and forgive us, or help us to become Christians. This is to go away from free grace to man's work and endeavour. God cannot justify on the sinful endeavour of a sinful creature. God can justify only on the basis of the ground which he himself, in his mighty grace, has laid: the finished work of Christ.

There is the other danger that we look to faith as the ground of justification. Now, faith is not the ground upon which God justifies. It is true that he will not justify until faith is there; it is the sinner who believes that God justifies. God is just and he justifies the ungodly, but only the ungodly who believe in Jesus; yet it is not because of, or on the ground of, his believing that God justifies. Professor John Murray declares: 'While no one is justified apart from faith, faith is not the ground upon which God justifies ... he justifies by, through, or in, faith. But he never uses the expression that God justifies on account of faith.' That is worth noting. Sometimes I think that what became the war-cry of the Reformation has led to a misapprehension and a misunderstanding about the ground on which God justifies. 'Justified by faith alone' is true yet it carries an inherent danger in it, because it makes people think of the faith of the believer as the ground of justification rather than the finished work of Christ. That shows how theological slogans or popular slogans can often, although correct in themselves, be theologically misleading; and it's one of which we should be careful. We are justified by faith in the Lord Jesus Christ alone.

Now, on the other hand, we must not minimize the role of faith in justification and salvation. Justification does not occur irrespective of any activity on our part. The Bible makes it clear that while God justifies the ungodly, it is always the ungodly who believe that he justifies. John Murray writes: 'Justification is on the event of faith, and not faith on the event of justification.'

Finally, remember that justification is not an end in itself. Men are justified in order that they may be sanctified. That's the biblical order: they are not sanctified in order that they may be justified. Remember this when you feel plagued with your inward corruption and sin. But remember, too, that redemption is not fully achieved with justification. In justification, however, the foundation has been laid upon which the whole edifice of redemption will yet stand complete. 'For,' says the apostle, 'whom he justified, them he also glorified' (Rom. 8:30). That's how closely justification and heaven are linked together. While, therefore, we are justified by faith, that faith includes all that will carry us home to the place which Christ is preparing for us.

Once we understand the fullness, freeness and utter graciousness of God's act in justifying sinners on the ground of Christ's perfect, finished work, and have ourselves been touched by the amazing love that's couched at the very heart of this doctrine, then I believe the foundation has been laid for the powerful, passionate, preaching of a doctrine that nestles at the very heart of the gospel of God's saving grace. This is not cold doctrine but something that should set our hearts afire and make us persuade men by all means to rest on no other foundation.

4

The Children For Christ
His Covenant Seed and their Covenant Sign

A powerful and attractive aspect of the ministry which this book[1] celebrates has been its focus on the welfare and status of the church's children. It has been bold enough, and biblical enough, to see them not merely as the church of tomorrow but as the church of today.

As the years went by it seemed to many of Mr. Still's friends that his appreciation of federal or covenantal theology enlarged itself and that it was his grasp of the place of children within that theology, and the practical questions which flow from it, that imparted a vital dimension to his ministry and the congregational life which it produced. Children were restored to the place which they had once held in Scottish churches; federal theology was not only believed, it was practised.

The healthy emphasis on 'family' religion which has characterised Gilcomston, generations of the congregation's children retained in the Christian faith, and published work on infant baptism are indicators of the prominence given in his ministry by Mr. Still to the biblical teaching on how the church should care for the children born within her fold. As one who shares his convictions and admires his action in this area, I would like to explore, by way of tribute, some aspects of the Bible's teaching on the children of believers as covenant theology interprets these, and in particular, their covenantal right to the sacrament of baptism.

---

1. A reference to *Pulpit & People*, Essays in Honour of William Still (Rutherford House, Edinburgh, 1986) in which this chapter originally appeared.

Getting the Question in Focus

It is a fact that no single passage or text in the New Testament can be pointed to as affording undisputed evidence that the New Testament practice was the baptism of children.

The fact that we are without express command to baptise children and that we are unable to cite any explicit case of infant baptism from the New Testament does not, however, mean that we must immediately abandon it. That would be no answer to the problem at all. It would merely be a simplistic solution to a difficulty which, viewed from a wider perspective, proves to be more apparent than real.

The first step in assessing the reality of the difficulty is to set it in context. Is it in fact the case that whenever there is no express or explicit injunction requiring a duty to be performed then that duty is either unlawful or may safely be neglected?

That question brings us face to face with two principles that must govern and regulate our approach to the biblical teaching on any specific question of Christian doctrine or Christian duty. These principles are given clear and cogent expression in the Westminster Confession of Faith where it is declared that, 'The whole counsel of God, concerning all things necessary for his own glory, man's salvation, faith and life, is either expressly set down in Scripture or *by good and necessary consequence may be deduced from scripture*' (Westminster Confession of Faith, 1:6 italics ours). In his comment on this article of the Confession, Robert Shaw sets out its implications in a way that really dissolves the difficulty we have posited. He says: 'We do not insist that every article of religion is contained in Scripture in so many words; but we hold that conclusions fairly deduced from the declarations of the Word of God are as truly parts of divine revelation as if they were expressly taught in the Sacred Volume'.[2] Two principles, then, one of 'Express command', the other of 'Necessary Inference', are to be applied in establishing the biblical basis of any Christian doctrine or duty. And where one fails in any specific instance, as the first one does in the case of infant baptism, then the second one must become the determinative factor in deciding the issues

---

2. Robert Shaw, *The Reformed Faith, an Exposition of the Westminster Confession of Faith*, repr. Christian Focus Publications, Geanies House, Fearn, Ross-shire, IV20 1TW.

at stake in that particular instance. Into this category, then, of 'good and necessary consequence', the New Testament itself forces us to go with our study of the biblical basis of infant baptism. This fact must also be accounted for, and our evaluation of what is called the New Testament 'silence' on the issue must take account of its historical and theological context. The sacraments were not instituted in a vacuum but against the background provided by Old Testament teaching and practice. Further, the Bible itself makes it clear that the sacraments are to be understood within a covenantal framework.

Having clarified the principles that must guide our approach to the biblical teaching on our topic, and having identified the context from within which that teaching may be traced, we can proceed to set out the data which provide the biblical mandate for child-baptism.

Preliminary Considerations

Before we do this, however, I wish to pave the way into that study by stating some considerations that bear upon an evaluation of these data and the conclusions to which they point. These are merely the brief statement of certain concepts of covenantal theology which can be established on Scriptural teaching but which, here, in the interests of brevity, are elucidated only in their immediate bearing upon our theme.

(i) The Unity of the Old and New Testament Scriptures

Each of these sheds light upon the teaching of the other and both are so linked as to make one, indivisible rule of faith and life for the Christian church.

(ii) The Essential Unity of the Covenant of Grace

The covenant administered under the gospel is the same covenant in its essential terms as that revealed in various outward forms to the church of God under the Old Testament dispensation. It is the final unfolding of what was embraced in the first promise to post-Fall Adam, and its progressive revelation under various forms to Noah, Abraham, Moses and the prophets can be regarded as the republication and the amplification of God's initial free promise of grace through the one covenant Mediator, the Lord Jesus Christ. This unity is given express statement by Paul when he says that

'The gospel was preached before unto Abraham' (Gal. 3:8), and when he elaborates that by going on to say, 'The covenant confirmed of God in Christ was given to Abraham four hundred and thirty years before the giving of the Law' (Gal. 3:17). 'Language,' as Bannerman remarks, 'fitted to mark both the identity of the covenant of Abraham with the gospel covenant, and its independence of the Mosaic ceremonial institutions.'[3]

(iii) The Unity of the Church of God in Old and New Testament Times

God has had a people on earth since the Fall. These people were graciously dealt with by God on the basis of the covenant which can be regarded as the charter of the church in every age. Those who have made up the church in every age have, by the same God, been called from the same lost state to the same Saviour and Mediator, Jesus Christ. Since the beginning he has been the Prophet, Priest and King of the church. The church – in the days of Noah, in the days of Abraham, in the days of Moses and the church under the gospel – while it was formed in various outward patterns according to the particular dictates of the developing covenant revelation, was in all its essential elements one and the same church. Galatians 3:7 reads, 'Understand, then, that those who believe are children of Abraham.' This establishes the essential spiritual relationship which exists between New Testament believers and Abraham. Verse 9 goes on to say, 'So those who have faith are blessed along with Abraham, the man of faith,' and this establishes that the New Testament church inherits and enjoys the very same blessings that were Abraham's in the covenant. And the essential unity between the two is brought to the fore yet again when Paul states, 'If you belong to Christ, then you are Abraham's seed, and heirs according to the promise' (Gal. 3:29). That it was essentially the same church even under the period of the Mosaic ceremonial is evident from the speech of Stephen in Acts 7:38 where, having quoted the prophecy of Moses concerning the coming prophet, he says, 'This is he that was in the church in the wilderness.'

---

3. James Bannerman, The Church of Christ, (Banner of Truth, repr. Edinburgh, 1974), ii, p. 70.

(iv) The Importance of the Family Unit in God's Dealings with Men

Man was created in the 'image and likeness of God'. That involved not merely man's individual personality but his circle of relationship with his kin. God himself ever exists in the fellowship of trinity and he it was who 'set the solitary in families' (Ps. 68:6). The trinity is the prototype of the family and, in this sense, the fact that the family fellowship was the sphere in which man was to bring forth children in his own likeness, thus imaging forth the creative power of God, makes it eminently fitting that the family should be the basic unit in God's covenant purposes for man; a unit of which the father is the representative and head.

(v) The Covenant of Grace under the Old Testament made Provision for the Children of Believing Parents

From its first free promise of grace to Adam, every fresh revelation of the covenant has highlighted this fact. An early instance in Scripture of the child's covenant status being in direct relation to its parent's faith, is that of Noah. His salvation was one of the first great illustrations of God's redemptive grace at work in a sinful world. In that act he demonstrated what was to be one of the great principles of his covenant activities towards man. The Genesis record makes clear the principle upon which God acted in saving, not only Noah, but his family from destruction. 'The LORD then said to Noah, "Go into the ark, you and your whole family, because I have found you righteous in this generation" ' (Gen. 7:1). The New Testament commentary on that act of God's grace confirms the principle of operation very simply but altogether sufficiently, 'By faith Noah prepared an ark, to the saving of his house' (Heb. 11:7. Note also 1 Peter 3:20-21). It is beyond question that it was upon the basis of the father's faith that this whole family was saved. Noah is thus made a witness to future ages that the faith of a believing parent secures a blessing, not for himself alone, but for the children as well. It is no surprise to us, then, that when the covenant was established in more fully elaborated terms with Abraham, its provisions include not merely Abraham, but his children as well. 'I will establish my covenant as an everlasting covenant between me and you and your descendants after you for the generations to come, to be your God and the God of your descendants after you' (Gen. 17:7).

Some Necessary Consequences
Now, the positions which we have set out thus far, along with the
bare indications of the line that the establishment of their full Scriptural validity would follow, dictate to us certain 'good and necessary consequences' which can now be asserted and supported by
various strands of biblical teaching.

*(i) The first assertion which we make is, that the Old Testament must
be brought to bear upon the issue of infant baptism*
It is rich in its teaching of the place and privilege of believer's
children in the church of God during that dispensation. It was
over against that teaching and under its guiding influence that the
New Testament church was established. The Old Testament
provided the norms by which the New Testament church organised
its life and expressed its faith. To confine the study of infant
baptism to the New Testament Scriptures – as is so often urged
upon us – merely because baptism is a New Testament ordinance
is to beg a high and vital part of the question. It is to leave out of
consideration a fund of evidence which is absolutely germane to
the biblical basis of baptism, and more particularly so when the
baptism in question is that of the children of believers. Here we
must insist, and insist in the strongest possible way, that, 'All
Scripture is God-breathed and is useful for teaching ... for
correcting and training in righteousness' (2 Tim. 3:16). The unity
of the covenant, and the unity of the church of God established
through the covenant, demand that the place of children in the
Old Testament church regulate our whole approach to, and
understanding of, the place of children in the New Testament
church.

*(ii) The second assertion we make is, that the covenant of grace
has always included infants in its provisions, and still does under
the gospel*
Each time the covenant was revealed to man it included the
child with the parent. This was the case, as we have seen, with
Adam, Noah and Abraham. It was also the case with Israel through
Moses. 'All of you are standing today in the presence of the LORD
your God ... together with your children ... to enter into a covenant
with the LORD your God ... to confirm you this day as his people,

that he may be your God as he promised you and as he swore to your fathers, Abraham, Isaac and Jacob' (Deut. 29:10-13). The very same keynote was struck in the opening sermon of the gospel era. Men were exhorted to believe for the specific reason that 'the promise is for you and your children' (Acts 2:39). At the beginning of the New Testament church we find that the title-deeds of its covenant life ensure, still, a covenant status for children of those who believe.

The nature and character of that status is confirmed for us in an interesting answer which Paul gives to a question which was posed to him by the church at Corinth. His reply to the problem given him is to be found in 1 Corinthians 7:14, where we read: 'For the unbelieving husband has been sanctified through his wife, and the unbelieving wife has been sanctified through her believing husband. Otherwise your children would be unclean, but as it is they are holy.' The word *holy* is the very same word that he uses earlier for church *members* and which we translate *saints*. The primary meaning of the word is 'to be set apart', and it is invariably used in Scripture of something set apart to God. It was used, for example, of Israel in the sense of their being a people set apart to God. They were a *holy* people, not because every individual amongst them was regenerated in heart, but simply because they were set apart by the covenant of grace to a holy purpose among the nations of the earth. This meant that they had special privileges through the covenant, one of which was, for instance, that 'they have been entrusted with the very words of God' (Rom. 3:2).

Now the context of 1 Corinthians 7:14 makes it clear that Paul was dealing with the specific problems of Christian converts married to unbelievers and the status that children of such a marriage should have in the church. Were they to be accepted with the believing parent or were they cast off with the unbelieving parent? Paul declares that the unbelieving partner and the children were 'set apart' to God in virtue of the faith of the believing partner and parent. He is not, of course, teaching that the children of such a marriage are 'saved'; but he does say that the faith and church membership of one parent sets them apart, and the term he uses implies some spiritual privilege. In this lies the whole force of his statement. For a people familiar with the covenantal teaching of the Old Testament this, of course, made perfect sense and Paul takes this familiarity for granted. His statement answered what was to them a very real problem. But outwith the framework of covenant principles it is difficult, not only to make complete sense of Paul's answer, but even to appreciate the problem to which his answer was the reassuring solution. Within that framework this Scripture simply reaffirms the spiritual privileges of children who have even one believing parent. It demonstrates also that the children of believers are in a different category, respecting their relationship to God, than are children who have no Christian parentage. 'There is,' says John Murray in a comment on this passage, 'a status or condition which can be characterised as "holiness", which belongs to children in virtue of a parental relationship.' And, he goes on to say, 'It is a "holiness" that evinces the operation of the covenant and representative principle'.[4]

(iii) The third assertion is that: the church of God which is the same under both dispensations, has always included infants among its members, and still does

There is no doubt that the church in the Old Testament was the church of Christ just as really as the church of the New Testament is. In prophecy, type, symbol and promise, faith laid hold of Christ and the benefits which, in the fullness of time, would be actualised by his atoning sacrifice. The spiritual realities enjoyed were, in essence, those which the believer under the gospel enjoys. It is equally sure that into the Abrahamic church infants, as well as their parents, were admitted as members. Circumcision was given as the seal of the covenant and as the badge of membership in the church which began to take a formal, outward structure from the Abrahamic covenant. This import of circumcision is not to be traced to the Mosaic administration of the covenant, but to Abraham. Jesus said to the Jews that this ordinance 'did not come from Moses, but from the patriarchs' (John 7:22).

In the New Testament there is not the slightest indication of a change with regard to the place of children in the church – but rather the opposite. Let us glance at some of the evidence that supports that claim, noting two things in particular.

First, Jesus and the little ones. It is reported in all three of the

---

4. John Murray, *Christian Baptism*, Philadelphia, 1962, p. 68.

synoptic Gospels that Jesus rebuked his disciples because they hindered little ones from coming to him. Luke makes it clear that 'People were bringing babies to Jesus' (Luke 18:15), and the word he uses to describe those so brought is *brephe – brephos* which does indeed mean infants or babies. Note that all three Gospels mention that Jesus 'laid hands upon them' or 'touched them' (Matt. 19:15; Mark 10:16; Luke 18:15); that Mark says, 'he took the children in his arms, put his hands on them and blessed them' (Mark 10:16). And Matthew makes it clear that there was a very specific purpose in the minds of the parents who brought these infants to Jesus, when he gives the reason, thus, 'For him to place his hands on them and pray for them' (Matt. 19:13). This is all too often understood as a kindly, sentimental 'recognition' of children by the Lord. It was far more than that.

Laying on of his hands – prayer – taking up in his arms – blessing – these are the terms used, and they are each significant. The words, 'Do not hinder them, for the kingdom of God belongs to such as these' (Matt. 19:14) seal the solemn nature of what Jesus did. While we do not rest infant baptism upon these passages we do claim that, at the very least, they are strongly indicative of continuing covenant favour for little ones, and mark their standing in the new administration of the covenant as no different from what it had been in the old. They make clear also, as G. W. Bromiley puts it, that Jesus 'does not seem to share the rationalistic view that the Holy Spirit cannot do his work of illumination and regeneration except in those who have at least the beginnings of an adult understanding. He does not endorse the idea that small children are not the proper subjects of his kingdom and therefore of the sacraments or signs of the kingdom.'[5]

Secondly, the place that Paul gives to children in his letters (e.g. Eph. 6:1-4; Col. 3:20). Paul addresses children as though they not only have a place in the church but in the discipline and privileges which are exercised in and by the church. In Colossians, where he is exhorting certain types of behaviour upon church members and where the members are classified – wives, husbands, masters, servants – one group is, 'children' and they, like the others, are exhorted to do all 'In the name of the Lord Jesus, giving thanks to God the Father through him' (Col. 3:17).

5. G. W. Bromiley, *Children of Promise*, Edinburgh, 1979, p. 5.

These citations are perfectly natural and easy to understand given the continuity of the New Testament church with the Old, and the inclusion of children of the believers amongst its membership. The children of Christian parents, in virtue of belonging to the believing community and sealed with the sign of the covenant, are to be taught the covenant obligation and privilege of obedience to parents in the Lord.

(iv) The fourth assertion is that: the ordinance of outward admission to the church has not changed, in its inward character and meaning, under the gospel.

Here we identify as essentially one and the same in their use, meaning and character, the Old Testament rite of circumcision and the New Testament rite of baptism. This lies close to the crux of our entire discussion and if it can be shown that the two ordinances held the same place, meant the same thing and performed the same function in the one church of God under both dispensations of the covenant of grace, then it is difficult to evade the conclusion that the one ought to be administered to the infant members of the one church under the last dispensation, as the other was under the previous one. Three points can be made.

First, both ordinances signal membership of the one church. That circumcision was the ordinance admitting to outward membership of the Old Testament church will not be questioned. There was no access to the privileges of that church except through the door of circumcision. By express command all male infants born into the fellowship of that church must be circumcised. In virtue of his birth and the privileges it carried, the infant was sealed in circumcision as a member of the visible church. And it was as a member of the church that he was ceremonially and spiritually qualified to receive the outward privileges and the inward blessings that were held out, or conveyed, through that church as a means of grace. There was no further qualifying ceremony of admission. This is indicative of the fact that, while circumcision was the outward badge of the visible church, it was also what it had been to Abraham himself in its first administration, the seal of admission to the true gospel church.

Baptism as the seal of membership in the New Testament church requires no elaborate proof. The great commission along with the apostolic practice with converts to the faith amply demonstrates it to be so. As seals of membership in the church of God, circumcision and baptism perform the same function and mean the same thing. They hold in this respect one and the same place, at different periods in time, in one and the same church. The biblical affinity between the two goes even further, though, as our second point shows.

Secondly, circumcision and baptism are signs and seals of the same covenant blessings. The great blessings held out in the covenant of grace are justification from the guilt of sin and renewal by the Holy Spirit. That circumcision was expressive of justification by faith and sealed it to the true believer is stated by Paul: 'And he (i.e. Abraham) received the sign of circumcision, a seal of the righteousness that he had by faith while he was still uncircumcised' (Rom. 4:11). That circumcision was expressive of heart renewal and heart-cleansing is also clear: 'The LORD your God will circumcise your hearts and the hearts of your descendants, so that you may love him with all your heart and with all your soul, and live' (Deut. 30:6). The inward reality symbolised by circumcision was a work of saving grace in the heart. New Testament usage confirms this. 'A man,' says Paul, 'is a Jew if he is one inwardly; and circumcision is circumcision of the heart, by the Spirit, not by the written code' (Rom. 2:29). It is hardly necessary to elaborate the fact that these same, inward, spiritual blessings are deeply embedded in the meaning of New Testament baptism.

Thirdly, baptism replaces circumcision as the covenant sign of inward renewal in the New Testament era. Read against its Old Testament background the New Testament makes it clear that the sacraments which Christ instituted, baptism and the Lord's supper, correspond to the two covenantal signs of the Old Testament; the Lord's supper to the Passover, baptism to circumcision. The point of discontinuity between the old signs and the new is self-evident and interprets the replacement for us. The old signs both involved blood-shedding, a feature which pointed forward, in type and promise, to the atoning work of Christ. By way of contrast, the new signs look backward to the 'one sacrifice for sin' (Heb. 10:12) which has taken place and the fulfilment of which is emphasised by the bloodless nature of the signs. This outward discontinuity emphasises not the disjunction between the facts symbolised but, in a very positive way, their spiritual continuity.

The continuity, in both cases, is spelled out in the New Testament in a clear way. The institution of the Lord's supper marks it quite strongly, but Paul actually spells it out for us: 'Christ our Passover lamb has been sacrificed for us' (1 Cor. 5:7). In the case of the other signs, which are our particular interest here, the link is established by Paul in Colossians 2:11-19. Expositors differ in their detailed interpretations of this passage but the focal fact it proclaims is quite clear. Over against those wishing believers to have the Old Testament sign of the covenant, circumcision, Paul urges, very cogently, that they have already been circumcised: 'In him you were also circumcised, in the putting off of the sinful nature, not with a circumcision done by the hands of men but with the circumcision done by Christ' (Col. 2:11). If we ask, when was that inward work sealed to these believers the answer is emphatic – 'having been buried with him in baptism and raised with him through your faith' (Col. 2:12). In terms of the Old Testament teaching it would hardly be possible to find a more positive rebuttal of the need for circumcision or to find a more accurate and fitting description of what had happened to those people than is couched in the phrase 'the circumcision of Christ'.

(v) The fifth assertion is that, the principle of the admission of children as church members was, and still is, the covenant status of their parents

It was to the faith of the parent that the promise was made and the sign given in the cases of Noah and Abraham. Right through the history of the Old Testament church the family unit was the pivot around which God's dealings in covenant grace turned. The promise was unvaried in its terms – 'you and your seed'. The faith of the parent conditioned the Godward standing of the child. In the light of that fact it is instructive to note the precise vocabulary used by Peter when the covenant terms are republished to the New Testament church. The vocabulary of Acts 2:38-39 is that which any man would use in summarising the covenant terms proclaimed to Abraham in Genesis 17. There, the covenant promise of God embraced three things: blessing to himself; blessing to his seed; blessing to many nations. How succinctly and cogently

Peter puts these three elements forward as he unfolds the covenant promise and holds out to his hearers the blessing which it assures to repentance and faith. 'The promise,' he says, 'is to you, and to your children, and to all that are afar off.' In Acts 2:39, then, it is clear that infants are not only placed in the same relation to their parent's faith as they are in Genesis 17, but that they are placed in precisely the same relation to baptism as they were to circumcision; and they are placed there by the identical terms of an identical covenant promise.

Concerns in New Testament Practice

Having looked at some of the basic factors which have to come into our consideration of child baptism and at the way in which these establish the correlation between the Old Testament covenant sign and that of the New Testament, it remains now to look a little more closely at what did take place in the New Testament church. Do the baptisms spoken of there strengthen or weaken the link we have been following? Do the New Testament facts encourage us to see baptism as a suitable replacement for and fulfilment of the sign of circumcision? Of twelve cases of baptism cited in the New Testament – and only twelve are mentioned out of the thousands that must have taken place – no less than four, perhaps five, are cases of what we generally refer to as 'household baptism' but which, for reasons that will follow, I prefer to call 'family baptisms'.

The fact that at least four out of twelve baptisms are recorded as taking place within a family situation is interesting on statistical grounds alone. But it is even more so on linguistic grounds.

The New Testament uses two Greek words for house and household – *oikos, oikia*. In every instance in the New Testament it is said that the *oikos* was baptised, never the *oikia*. This is significant because of the different connotation of the two words. The literal meaning of *oikos* is the inside of the house, or the rooms in it which are used by the family which lives there. The literal meaning of *oikia* is the ground around the house – or the immediate setting of the house. Both words, however, seem to have a similarly differentiated figurative meaning. Figuratively, *oikos* is used of the immediate family, *oikia* of other persons who go to make up the wider household, or of people who are assembled there in a meeting. A house, in this sense of *oikos*, implies family lineage, but the figurative distinction between 'house' and 'household' is not so clear to us in English – if, indeed, it is there at all – and so the distinction tends to be obscured in our English translations. The Greek text of Acts 16:31-33 illustrates the distinction quite clearly. 'And they said, Believe on the Lord Jesus Christ, and thou shalt be saved, and thy house' – and there 'house' is *oikos*; then in verse 32 we read, 'And they spake unto him the word of the Lord and to those that were in his house' – *en tae oikia*. And then when it comes to the actual baptism, and to those who were baptised, they are denominated, *autos kai hoi autou pantes* – 'he and all his'. Now, had the English translation taken note of this distinction and translated *oikos* as 'family' it would have followed the sense of the Greek text more closely and avoided the confusion that tends to arise in the mind of the reader about the precise connotation of 'house' and 'household'.

Noting these distinctions Dr. Alan Harman goes on to say: 'It is interesting that in the two references to the family of Stephanus, in the first in 1 Corinthians 1:16 *oikos* is used but in 1 Corinthians 16:15 ('You know the household of Stephanus, that they were the first fruits of Achaia, and that they have devoted themselves for the ministry of the saints') the wider word *oikia* appears.'[6]

Irrespective of the linguistic argument, however, the baptism of families or households provides evidence that the 'representative' or 'family' principle, so deeply embedded in Jewish practice, was in operation in the New Testament church just as it had been in the Old. That fact lends its support to our entire thesis.

Enough has probably been said to demonstrate that, 'by, good and necessary consequence', a broad spectrum of Scripture teaches that infants of believers are to be admitted as members of the visible gospel church and that the seal of their membership in that church is baptism. Let us summarise the situation, however, with a closer look at the actual instances of baptism in the New Testament and by examining the data they give us against the background of all that has been said already.

As we have seen, the New Testament gives us only twelve instances of actual baptism. Of these twelve, four are clear in-

6. Alan Harman in *Hold Fast Your Confession*, ed. Donald Macleod, Knox Press, 1978, p. 209.

stances of household baptism – and, if the household of Crispus be included on the grounds of 1 Corinthians 1:14, allied with Acts 18:8, the number is five. Here the number of family baptisms is high enough to indicate such baptism as a frequent occurrence in the apostolic practice and one can only agree with John Murray when he says, 'It would be practically impossible to believe that in none of these households were there any infants'.[7] But further, of the remaining seven cases cited, four were of 'group' or 'crowd' baptisms and the presumptive case for children being a part of any, or of all of them, is of the strongest kind.

That leaves only three stated cases where we can be absolutely clear that no child was involved and where we have the baptism of individuals being baptised upon the profession of their own faith. These are Simon of Samaria, the Ethiopian eunuch and Saul of Tarsus. Let us note too that these were baptised within the context of a missionary situation. In a similar situation today, any paedobaptist minister or missionary would require the same profession before baptising any similar adult convert, and in such a situation he would expect a good number of such baptisms. But, once the missionary situation was no longer the predominant one, such cases of baptism would not, in a paedobaptist church, be so frequent. And, although the New Testament writings extend for a period of more than thirty years from the inception of the Christian church, it is surely a very significant fact that not one single case of the baptisms instanced in the New Testament was that of an adult who had grown to the age of maturity within the gospel church.

On the inference that children were baptised along with their parents the absence of 'second generation' baptism is not surprising; but apart from that thesis it is inexplicable in a record that covers the first thirty/sixty years of New Testament church-life so extensively. On the other hand, the existence of even one such instance would be a stronger counterpoint to the continuity of the covenant principle in the New Testament church than any other factor which can be brought against it. But the fact of the matter is that the baptism of people who have grown up within the church is a practice which cannot be demonstrated from the New Testament.

7. John Murray, *Christian Baptism*, Philadelphia, 1962, p. 69.

Finally, we must remind ourselves of the background against which the New Testament writings are to be set. They are to be set in the perspective of the total teaching of the Old Testament and the place of the child within the covenant, and within the church which the covenant terms established. Hence, it need not surprise us that none of these writings should carry an express command or contain an explicit example about administering the sign and seal of the covenant to the child. The Old Testament teaching was so clear, the warrant so deeply woven into its warp and woof, that no new command was necessary. The New Testament silence at this point, far from being a weakness in the whole case, is one of its best pillars of support. The practice was perfectly clear and it was to remain what it had ever been in the covenant dealings of a gracious God with his people. The federal theology which we have inherited in Scotland provides a cogent framework within which to demonstrate that the practice of baptising the children of all Christian believers is firmly rooted in the teaching of Scripture, and that the duty of every Christian church and the privilege of every Christian parent as to the baptism of their children is made very clear by 'good and necessary consequence' from principles which lie richly widespread through the Old and New Testaments.

It is the unity of the covenant, taken along with the covenantal solidarity of the parent/child relationship, which establishes, we believe, the right of the believer's child to the sign and seal of the covenant just as surely in New as in Old Testament times.

The baptism of our children is a perpetual seal to us that God is not only a God to his people but also to their seed after them. When this is understood, who is the Christian parent or the Christian minister but will say, 'Can any man forbid water that these should not be baptised?' (Acts 10:47).

5

Eldership Today

The Bible magnifies the office and work of the elder: 'Let the elders who rule well be counted worthy of double honour...' (1 Tim. 5:17). This should encourage a biblical approach to the principles and practice of the eldership. What is so evidently important in the Lord's eyes should be important in ours also.

Realism suggests that the work of the elder is neither clearly defined, nor well understood, in the church of today. Views moulded by tradition rather than Scripture dominate the scene, and the eldership functions along lines that have little semblance to, or respect for, biblical patterns. So it will be useful to begin by clearing our minds of some inbred attitudes. It is dangerously easy to cherish concepts of the eldership to which we may not, perhaps, have given sufficiently detailed attention.

What the elder is not

The New Testament teaches us that the elder is not just a figurehead in the church. He is there to work. We dare not think of his role as a mere convenience – structured over long periods of time – imposing order into the church's life, or welding God's people into a well run, highly organised community. That belongs to his role but does not explain the elder nor how he came to be part of the church's life and structure.

Nor will New Testament light on the *kind* of person the elder is to be allow us to regard the eldership as just a convenient way of promoting useful Christians. No matter how diligent or zealous people may be (and all believers should be both) the eldership is not there merely to give them prominence amongst the people of God, nor in order that their example can be seen and their good points emulated. Spiritual worth, usefulness and diligence should characterise the elder, and his life certainly should

Chapters 5-7 are taken from *The Monthly Record of the Free Church of Scotland* (February, March, April 1988)

set godly standards for others, but none of those things defines or explains the biblical view of the elder or his role in the church.

Still less does the Bible permit us to think of the eldership as a way of sorting certain people into social ranks in the community, or of slotting specially qualified people, such as bankers, lawyers or schoolmasters into a position where professional ability and status appear to make them particularly suitable. (Of course, such *will* be in the eldership and their professional qualifications may prove useful, but it is another set of criteria altogether by which their suitability for eldership must be assessed.)

Biblical teaching discourages any idea that the eldership evolved under the pressure of pragmatic necessity alone. Functionally ideal though it is (when understood and organised along the lines of its biblical norms) for pastoring and caring for the people of God in a wide variety of circumstances, it is not a scheme devised by men at all, not even by wise and godly men. The most fundamentally important thing in the biblical view of the eldership is that it is not a human invention but a *divine* institution. It is there in the church of the New Testament, not because apostles and early church leaders thought it a convenient thing, but because God ordained it.

Why there is eldership

This involves conviction that elders are a very special *order* of people within the church with a specific, divine *calling* from Christ, the head of the church. That being so, it is crucial for the church to be clear in her own understanding of the eldership. Here two considerations are vital: the spiritual qualifications for the office, and the functions which the office involves. Today it is essential that the church re-examine the role that the Scriptures prescribe for the elder.

This is because the Bible emphasises that elders are called to leadership, service and supervision in the church. They are to *pastor* and *shepherd* the flock of God and to be responsible for its individual and corporate welfare. That makes the elder a key person in the good of the church. When he does his work well, she will be well. When he does not, she will do badly. The view that the health of a congregation depends solely on the minister reflects a shift away from the biblical view of eldership.

The need to establish clear biblical principles and have them determine perspectives and dictate practice can scarcely be over-emphasised. A biblically patterned, spiritually qualified, pastorally involved, working eldership is essential to the well-being of the church. The vitality and the health of every congregation is closely and intimately bound up with it. In the church's life today, renewed understanding and biblical application of the elder's duties and responsibilities are matters of pressing urgency. A functioning biblical eldership has seldom been more important to the church than it is at this particular juncture in her life.

The early church and the need for leadership

One of the most exciting success stories in history is the mush-rooming of the early church. From Pentecost on, the book of Acts makes it plain that the infant church had to cope with the very happy problem of swarms of newly converted people.

It is out of the heart of this lively situation that leadership issues first come into focus. Expansion and growth meant then what they would mean for us still, *organisation*; and good, careful, organisation along with wise use of resources led, in turn, to consolidation and to further rapid expansion. A spiritually healthy and well-nourished, wisely led, carefully pastored people provided the environment congenial to a quickly growing church. His church was being blessed by her risen Lord in a spectacular way, and the salient features of its life – namely, rule, guidance, leadership, pastoral care and effective evangelism – must be seen as both the means and fruit of that blessing.

From Pentecost onwards the disciples were under the pressure of ministering to huge crowds. Unless we have the concept of thousands of converts right from the beginning we fail to do justice to the facts of the biblical narrative. Those thousands of new converts had to be pastored and taught. They had to be nourished in the faith and built up into warm, lively, caring, loving communities and congregations. They had to organise for worship and service of all kinds. They had to be helped to express their experience of fellowship in Christ and live out the radical transformation that faith in him involves.

None of this was done in a vacuum. It was a process, and must have required a great deal of time, effort, prayer and patience on the part of the apostles. It is a process of which the book of Acts gives only glimpses. There was the pastoral care of newly converted crowds, enthusiasm (converts in the time of their 'first love' are always enthusiastic!) and spiritual energy had to be harnessed and directed into useful channels. How was it done? How were the apostles able to cope with such an enormous task? How was utter chaos avoided in a situation like this?

All this of course was of God. Scripture teaches us that God is not the author of confusion. His works are characterised by order and harmony. That is perfectly true. But Scripture also teaches us that God uses *means* in effecting his gracious purposes. He uses men. Church history underlines this principle for us. It confirms that one great hallmark of a true work of God's grace is the raising up of leaders to channel and control its effects. He does not leave his flock without shepherds, but calls and equips men to teach, lead and *shepherd* the converts under the direction of his Holy Spirit.

That is precisely what happened in the New Testament church. Blessing led to new structures and more detailed organisation. To look at these and how they were achieved, we turn to the period before Pentecost and the pressures its outrush of blessing brought to bear on leadership.

Although the biblical concept of leadership is broader than eldership the two cannot be separated; the eldership is part of the wider whole. This accounts for the presence of an eldership very early in the life of the New Testament church and helps us interpret its function. The simple fact is that from the beginning the biblical account centres on leadership. Its initial focus is on the *headship* of Christ himself, and this remains central to the New Testament witness. But even during his public ministry he delegated leadership to others. We must not overlook the fact of leadership, and so of form and structure, prior to Pentecost. These are considerations that bear upon the eldership, and we turn to them.

The earliest leaders, the apostles

Early in his public ministry the Lord Jesus chose 'twelve to be with him' (Matt. 10:1, 7, 8; Mark 3:14, 15; Luke 6:13) and sent them out at different times with authority to preach, heal and minister to people in his name. It is beyond question that those men, the apostles, were the earliest leaders of the church.

They received from Jesus a commission to continue his work. They were witnesses of his resurrection and formed the nucleus of the group who waited for the Spirit in the upper room. They were in the natural position of leadership for the larger community formed at Pentecost, but growing rapidly. In addition to the Eleven, and to Matthias, chosen to fill the place of Judas, James the brother of the Lord also came to occupy a position of leadership.

It is clear that the apostles were also elders: at least, that is the case if Peter and John are typical. 'The elders which are among you I exhort,' says Peter, 'who am also an elder' (1 Pet. 5:1). And John calls himself in several places 'the elder' (e.g. 2 John 1; 3 John 1). This fact lends its own dignity and importance to eldership and gives insight into some, at least, of the duties it involves.

The elections of deacons

The simple rule of the apostles soon became insufficient and they began to need help. Rapid growth led to increasing complexity which, in turn, demanded a division of labour. Apostles remained in control of spiritual matters but there were ministries that they had to delegate. To free them for the work to which they were specially called – prayer and proclamation of the Word – this new order of helpers was established. We should notice carefully that this is the work to which ministers are called still, and all too often it takes second place to another complex of duties expected of them in the average congregation.

It is interesting to see how God virtually forced the apostles into doing something about this situation. Action of some kind became necessary because of *complaints*! (Brethren in the ministry should take comfort that Christians complained even when the ministers were *apostles*!) There was cultural and racial feeling involved, for we read that 'There arose a murmuring of the Grecians against the Hebrews because their widows were neglected in the daily ministrations' (Acts 6:1). And, interestingly, the word underlying 'ministrations' is the Greek *diakonia*, from which we get the English word 'deacon'.

The New Testament and diaconal ministry

This word, in itself, does not specify what the duties of the seven men chosen in Acts 6 were, nor does it confine diaconal service within specified limits. Compared to its English derivative it has a wide range of application in its New Testament usage that deserves a moment's notice. In its *non-official* sense it means a *servant*, one who ministers to others regardless of the type of service. This is seen for example in Matthew 22:13, 'Then said the king to the servants (*diakonois*), bind him hand and foot.' It is frequently applied to the apostles and those who serve God in the ministry of the Word, as in Colossians 1:23: 'The gospel ... whereof I, Paul, was made a minister' (*diakonos*). Those examples help illustrate the richness of the word in the language of the New Testament.

It is worth observing, however, that when the service intended is a ministry in terms of Acts 6 and the choice of the Seven, that is, help to the needy or poor, the translators of the Authorised Version have uniformly translated *diakonos* as *deacon*, as for example, in Philippians 1:1. This underscores an important principle of interpretation for understanding the role of deacon – or elder, or preacher – in the New Testament. The *kind* of service cannot always be decided solely from the use of a particular word, but from its context and the particular circumstances to which it is applied. It was only when our translators understood the word *diakonos* as meaning a church *official* appointed to minister to the needs of the poor that they translated it by the English word *deacon*.

Most scholars trace the office and function of deacon back to this episode in Acts 6. If correct, this is highly significant because, for some at least, their diaconate became a very effective training ground for a wider sphere of service, a different type of ministry. All we know of their later life points to the importance of the diaconate as a preparatory office. It proved to be a splendid training ground for a useful, effective eldership role as well as for the work of an evangelist. While the diaconate has its origins in Jerusalem there is little doubt that it spread throughout the church and we find it in operation at Philippi, at Rome, at Cenchrea, and at Ephesus. Not only so, but the qualifications fitting a person for the office of deacon are detailed with such care that it was obviously meant to be a permanent part of the church's life.

The enormously significant thing for us today, however, is the delegation of duties involved. That speaks to the contemporary need of the church. Here is a development in the ordered life of the church: additional structuring, but based upon a simple division of labour. There is spreading of responsibility, a redeployment of preaching resources, a broadening out of the shepherding role to deal with the new situation, and the urgent need of teaching and evangelism. They are organising themselves to cope with new circumstances in a sensible and biblical way. And God is quite evidently in all this. The election of this new order of helpers and leaders is the implementation of his will. That is how they regard it and how the Scriptures would have us regard it as well.

The New Testament elders

It is in Acts 11:30 that the *elders* of the church are mentioned for the first time, and they are brought before us in an almost incidental way. It is simply said that the church at Antioch sent famine relief *to the elders* of the church at Jerusalem. Such men, such an office and function were already established. These elders are mentioned without explanation or definition. The narrative at this point gives no information about the where, when, or why of the elder or eldership. There is no elucidation of the appointment of these elders, no explanation of their duties. All this is taken for granted. In order to understand who, why or what they were, we have to look elsewhere. And, as we would expect in the face of this circumstance, the Bible comes to our help. So we must look briefly at the broader picture that can be built up from Scripture on the origin and function of the elder and eldership.

The origins of eldership

The origins of eldership are not totally obscure. It traces back into the Old Testament and the time of Moses. Jewish elders are mentioned quite frequently in the Gospels and Acts and, together with the chief priests and scribes, they were represented in the Sanhedrin. From those sources it is quite evident that 'elders' had important religious and social functions in Judaism and that their authority was both local and general. So from the time of Moses right up until New Testament times elders had held positions of authority in the Old Testament church and the Old Testament society. There are at least 27 citations in the Gospels and Acts which mention the elders of Israel and of the synagogue.

Those elders were the recognised representatives of the people. Sometimes elders and people are used interchangeably, implying that action by the elders was regarded as the action of all. Joshua *summoned the elders* (Josh. 24:1) and *said to all the people* (verse 2). Through Israel's history they appear in tandem with *judges, rulers, officers,* and it is important to note that sometimes they are to be identified with those posts. They also stood as representatives of the people before God, and had duties of instructing in the law and the commandments (Exod. 18:16; Deut. 27:1; 31:1-31). They had a responsibility for order and decorum in the public worship of God. 'Let them exalt him in the congregation of the people, and praise him in the assembly of the elders' (Ps. 107:32).

The place of eldership in the Old Testament would bear further elucidation, but the emerging picture should be clear. The ministry of Christ and the events of Pentecost and after did not take place in a void. They have to be understood against a specific background and interpreted within their historical setting. The New Testament church develops within this context and so what we have in the Book of Acts is the picture of this young, vigorous, church drawing its patterns and forming its structures from the Old Testament church of which it is the crown. There is continuity as well as disjunction with that church.

6

Eldership In Practice

Having looked at the biblical teaching on the origins of eldership, we move on to what the New Testament teaches about how the elders actually functioned, and the nature of the tasks expected of them in the New Testament church. We shall then draw some practical inferences and conclusions for our own day and situation. The purpose at that stage is to probe, particularly, what the contemporary church should expect of her elders if they are going to function according to the biblical pattern.

We have seen that the office of elder is taken for granted in the New Testament church. Unlike the beginnings of the diaconate, explained for us in Acts, the New Testament gives no details about the first elders in the church. The reason is that the office of elder went back into the Old Testament church, and was well known in the life of the contemporary synagogue.

The names and titles used of the elder

As the office of elder came into the church from this specific and familiar background it carried with it the names attached to it in the Judaistic system. It is helpful for our study that the New Testament elders are frequently described (and very beautifully) in terms of what they did: teacher, shepherd, leader, ruler, (Acts 15:22; Eph. 4:11; 1 Tim. 5:17; Heb. 13:7; 1 Pet. 5:1-4, etc.). These very designations begin to indicate their importance to a healthy, flourishing, witnessing church and it is worth noting that wherever we find the church in the New Testament we also find elders. This is one of the most significant factors about the New Testament scene and yet one which, perhaps because blended so constantly into it, is all too easy to overlook. For this reason it requires brief elucidation.

From a general point of view the facts are straightforward, but crucially important for our understanding of the eldership. We find that Paul established elders in all the churches which grew out of his missionary labours (Acts 14:23; Acts 20:17, 28; Phil. 1:1 etc.). We also find that Peter exhorted the elders in the congregation of the dispersion and takes their leadership of those churches for granted. James gives his spiritual exhortations and practical advice in the unspoken but implicit confidence that there will be elders in the churches to which he writes. Not only so, he clearly expects that these elders will work at their tasks. His letter visualises their genuine pastoral concern, and he exhorts them especially concerning the duties of visiting (and *praying* with) the members of the flock who are sick (Jas. 1:1; 2:1; 5:14).

The most common New Testament name for the person in the office is the one we are familiar with in the Scottish churches, 'elder'. It translates the Greek word *presbuteros*, from which we get our well-known words, 'Presbytery' and 'Presbyterian'. In its Old Testament usage it had reference to age (hence, *elder*) and experience; and so carried over into the church connotations of leadership qualities; irrespective of their age the elders, spiritually, were to be men of wisdom, knowledge, maturity and balance.

The word 'bishop' translates the Greek *episkopos* from which the word 'Episcopal' derives. It means 'overseer' (as in Acts 20:28) and is descriptive of the elder in his responsibilities for the general welfare of the church and all its members. Biblical scholars agree that 'bishop' is used synonymously, or interchangeably, with 'elder'. The grounds for this view became clear from a comparison of passages such as Acts 20:17, 28; Philippians 1:1; 1 Timothy 3:1; 4:14; 5:17, 19; Titus 1:5, 7; 1 Peter 5:1, 2. If we ask why there are two titles the answer, again, is straightforward; it is more than fitting that the term *overseer* is used when the emphasis is on their *work* (1 Tim. 3:1), the term *elder* when the emphasis is on the *honour* that is their due (1 Tim. 5:17). As we shall see, these titles are not without their own significance.

The plurality of the New Testament eldership
One of the first things to notice about the working of the New Testament eldership is that it functioned, wherever possible, on the principle of plurality. A key passage in establishing this is Acts 20:17-38. Paul was on his way to Jerusalem. From Miletus he invited the *elders* – not *the* elder – of the church at Ephesus to meet with him there for consultation. Interestingly enough, this is

also one of the passages where both New Testament titles for the elder are used of the same persons, and which illustrates that the *presbyter* (presbuteros) and the *bishop* (episcopos) are not two different people, nor two different categories of people, but one and the same (compare verses 17 and 28).

In this passage and, it would seem, uniformly through the New Testament, the title Presbyter is used of the 'office', and the title Bishop of the function, or work, in which the office obliges the person to engage. In verse 17 we are told that Paul called for the elders from Ephesus (literally, the *presbyters*) and then in verse 28 when he is exhorting these elders as to their work and duties in the church at Ephesus, he speaks of them as overseers (literally, the *episkopoi*) set apart by the Spirit for shepherding the flock of God. His exhortation is framed to emphasise the fact that their *oversight* consists in and is to be exercised by *shepherding the flock of God*. The title he uses is exegetical of function, expressive not so much of what those men *are* as of what they *do* in the office of the eldership.

In other words, as Paul reminds these Ephesian elders that God has called them to be 'bishops', he quite deliberately uses, not the word which highlights their status in the church, but the one that emphasises their work. He employs the title which illustrates their calling to serve within it. The fact is that the word 'bishop' (overseer) effectively describes them in terms of their pastoral responsibilities as *elders*. He does not have two different species of church officer in mind but is talking *to*, and about, the same persons. There can be no question about this. The message is beautifully simple, the position crystal clear. The function of the elder is a *pastoral* one; it involves caring for, looking after, being concerned about, the welfare of the people of God – the *flock* – that God has called him to superintend, care for, nourish, cherish and feed. Those officers clearly had the oversight (as our old translators recognised) of the flock that was entrusted to their care. They had to provide for it, govern it, and protect it, as the very household of God.

What I want to emphasise particularly here, however, is that those men did not act independently of one another. The very nature of the eldership forbids unilateral action in the rule and pastoral care of the church. They acted in unison and not merely as individuals. They must have had specific duties which involved each of them on the individual level, of course, but at the same time they were part of a team and so their responsibilities were basically corporate rather than individual. In practical terms this meant that the care of the flock was not committed to *one* person, but to a number of persons. There was a division of labour within the critically important sphere of pastoral responsibility and pastoral care. The awesome task of shepherding God's people in New Testament times was not, and is never spoken about as though it were, the sole responsibility of any one individual within the church.

This is one facet of the biblical pattern of eldership which should receive earnest attention in our day and its prevailing circumstances. The care of God's people lays a great burden upon the elders. They themselves are only men. The frailty of human nature belongs to them, no matter how godly, how holy, how single-minded they may be, nor how earnestly or solemnly or passionately they may fulfil their task. When all has been said and done, they are only men. From a purely practical point of view sole oversight is an intolerable burden to lay on the shoulders of any one man.

Let us reflect that the truth confronting us here is not merely that oversight by one man is burdensome, but that it is also quite unscriptural. The idea of a *one-man-oversight* (or a one-man-eldership) is alien to the New Testament. It really has no place in a healthy church, or one which is run on classical Presbyterian (i.e. biblical) patterns. John Murray summarises the position accurately when he says: 'Plurality is written in the boldest letters in the pages of the New Testament, and singularity bears the hallmark of despite to Christ's institution.'

How wise of God that no single man should be, or is meant to be, left with the sole care of the flock in any locality, no matter how big or how small numerically. At the smallest, it is too much for one man to shepherd on his own. One of the most solemn lessons of church history is the havoc wrought by individuals who came to believe that their contribution, or their teaching, or their correction and rule, was the one factor that could save the church from error, or unbelief, or apostasy. But the New Testament indicates that God never does leave the shepherds on their own. There is to be more than one of them involved in what is an enormously solemn and responsible task.

The parity within the New Testament

The New Testament does not know anything of one elder being higher in rank than another. All are on the same footing, the same platform, with equal status and equal responsibility for the flock. The apostolic exhortation of 1 Timothy 5:17 illustrates this parity very well and, from this point onwards, we will concentrate attention on what it has to say. It is illuminating not merely on this issue of parity, but on other elements of our study which call for notice or comment.

Let us look, initially, at how the text elucidates the thought that all the elders enjoyed equal status. It says, 'Let the elders who rule well be counted worthy of double honour.' This focuses on the elders' general pastoral responsibility and marks out for special mention (as well as for special respect) those who do it 'well'. The wording of the Authorized Version may pose the question as to what particular function of the eldership is actually in view here? What is it to 'rule well'? The New International Version clarifies this, even if at first glance it appears very general: 'The elders who direct the affairs of the church well are worthy of double honour.' If that does seem vague to us, then it is almost certainly because we are pouring extraneous ideas into the word 'church' as Paul uses it here. In its most fundamental, but not its only New Testament usage, the word 'church' speaks of the church at the local level, as the readers know it and are part of it.

Now, if we think of the 'church' at this level, rather than the denominations of our own day, or the wider church of New Testament times, or even of the church as an entity right through history, the wording of this text loses its vagueness and sharpens up into a very clear picture. Who are the elders worthy of double honour? They are the elders who, taking their task seriously, give their time and energies to it in such a fashion that they direct the affairs of their church for the spiritual and temporal good of everyone in it.

These are the elders that Paul has in view in this exhortation. Irrespective of where their church is, they look after God's people as carefully and as tenderly as they would their own family (1

Tim. 3:5). The church is not a vague, far-off entity that need not concern them; the church, for them, lies first of all in the congregation in which they are called to serve. The message conveyed becomes needle-sharp as it is personalised and brought home to us in terms of the concrete and specific situations of which we, ourselves, are a part.

When we stop to consider the elder and his work in these terms then the practical application of Paul's words becomes quite specific and highly unexpected in our present-day context. Or, to put it another way, where we tend to ask today, What kind of pastor is your minister?, Paul is asking, What sort of pastors are your elders? The first question is a commonplace in our churches; the second generally goes unthought and unasked. This, in itself, is a sad indicator of how far removed we often are from the biblical view of the eldership. It should also be a solemn reflection for us that an unbiblical view of the eldership carries along with it a distorted view of the ministry, or more correctly, of the work of the ministry.

The minister a preacher, the elder a pastor

Let me illustrate a distinction involved at this point, and one which, shortly, we will probe more fully. Clearly formulated views on the work of the eldership, as well as that of the minister, provide us with one good, biblical reason why Scottish Presbyterianism has always spoken of the 'minister' rather than the 'pastor'. In doing so it conserved not only the idea of the specially called 'preaching' elder, but also the parity of the eldership in pastoral responsibility. The custom emphasised that one 'pastor' over a flock is not a biblical concept, and that the principle of the 'minister' (servant) devoted to preaching the word (while working with and being part of the pastoral oversight) followed the biblical pattern. Some of us may feel that the teaching of our text has sharp barbs when applied like this but, in fact, it has to be brought to bear on specific situations even more rigorously than we have applied it so far.

As it stands, the 'affairs of the church' is a very general term, quite deceptively vague. The danger is that we live with it happily. We can do so for a very simple reason. The realities represented are so nebulous that we feel them to be the responsibility of others. We may even think those others far more competent to look after 'the affairs of the church' than ourselves. We are content to leave these concerns to better equipped people; they will be done efficiently and well. We can relax, and settle back in our chairs and chatter on about what the church should be doing in the places which are not our immediate concern.

But if we stop to ask what Paul actually means here, it becomes impossible to think in this way. He is speaking of a real church that has real elders with a real concern for God's people. Their concern ensures that they pastor God's people well. That includes making sure that they have a preacher, and that their preacher is supported, kept free from distracting worry, and encouraged to preach to the peak of his ability and power. They enable him to 'give himself to prayer and the preaching of the Word'.

7

Ruling Well

In our final study, we concentrate on Paul's thought in 1 Timothy 5:17, 'the elders who rule well', asking what such elders are like, and probing how this singular, biblical commendation should inform our concept of the eldership and illumine its duties. When speaking of those who 'conduct the affairs' of the church, Paul is not thinking in terms of denominations, or organisations, or finance, as we might all too easily imagine in our contemporary Scottish scene.

Paul's framework of reference is quite different. He is talking about the people in our street, or our village; forcing thought to our particular congregation and the people in it. It is always people, not organisations, who need our love and pastoral care. He is not inviting attention to well-run denominations, or well-heated, well-painted buildings (laudable, but purely diaconal responsibilities), but to people who need pastored, counselled, helped, visited and loved in Christ. His concern is for people who require to know that their elders 'care for their souls' and 'keep watch over them', as well as providing them with polished, varnished pews (that mostly belong to the discomfort of 150 years ago!); people who, in all the contemporary pressures upon their faith, need to be made to feel a part of the local 'body of Christ'.

The sphere of eldership responsibility
Only in a pastoral context can this exhortation to the church about her elders be understood. The scene envisaged, the questions prompted, are neither vague nor general but quite specific. How are the *people* over whom God has made *us* overseers? Are they walking with God? Are they worried or discouraged? Are they out of work, frustrated, afraid? Are there elders who have to answer such queries with another one of their own: 'Who knows?' Are there elders who know how much certain homes contribute to the treasury each week, but who have never been in those homes, and are dumb before the questions their pastoral responsibilities

actually pose? Are there elders who never exercise the work of hospitality, or people who have never been helped or encouraged (perhaps even converted!) by the influence of the warm, caring, Christian atmosphere of their elder's home?

The shepherding role inherent to eldership explains why Presbyterianism insists that the elder be inducted into a specific sphere in which to exercise his oversight. Elders, once ordained, remain elders, but if they leave the congregation in which they exercise the pastoral oversight of their office they are no longer recognised as 'acting' (working!) elders and must wait induction into another Session before they can do the work of an elder again. This feature of Presbyterian life should imprint upon our minds that eldership is exercised in regards to people; not denominations, finance, buildings, or organisation in the first instance, but God's people.

This is the point our text drives home when we put the type of question asked above. The *elders who rule well* will know the answers to the questions which concern those over whom God has set them. Is it the case that needy believers have to turn to the 'professionals' of our day, the doctors and psychiatrists, the social workers and police (who all serve our society in a very dedicated way) to get another human ear to hear and a human heart to share their problems? Can church members be ill, be in hospital, have surgery, go through traumatic experiences, and never have the pastoral care of an elder? Can homes in our churches be bereft of mothers, or fathers, or children and not be visited by the elders as an expression of the Church's (and the Lord's) concern and compassion? Has our Scottish eldership forgotten what Scripture says about, 'pure religion and undefiled before God and the Father ...'?

If we take Paul's word seriously, it is impossible to escape the *specific and concrete*. In effect, it deals with the elders we know, the churches to which we belong. Its message is cogent only in terms of the situations in which God's people live and his church witnesses. Only there can we know our elders, only there can we assess them, only there can we 'honour' those (and there are such!) who meet the standards of the text and 'rule well'. Let me insist upon and illustrate this important fact by asking a few more sample questions.

In our (my) church: Who is pastoring the people, visiting them, praying *for* them, praying *with* them, helping in spiritual matters? Who is training and leading them in outreach evangelism? Who contacts the young, the students, or workers newly into our localities? Who calls on the sick and the aged, or the home-bound 'carers' looking after elderly relatives? When we put such pastoral queries to our text we do *not* get the answer present-day practice would anticipate. Today's pastoral norms would make our text answer with two words, *the minister*. (That is, if he's not at a committee, or too busy, or in hospital with a heart attack or depression.) But that is not the thought of our text. Its answer is: (does it surprise us?) '*The elders* who direct the affairs of the church well.'

Particularity within the eldership

Another aspect of eldership in this text requires mention. Paul adds to his exhortation about honouring *the elders who rule well* a little phrase that marks further demarcation, even amongst them: *especially those whose work is preaching and teaching*. This is the distinction between the 'minister (servant) of the word' and the 'ruling (oversight) elder'. All elders are to be 'apt (able) to teach' (1 Tim. 3:2), but *there are those called*, as the apostles in Acts 6, to give the *preaching* of the word, the proclamation of the gospel, the place of priority in *their* oversight of the church.

This critical distinction within the eldership was probably more clearly appreciated when the minister was known as 'the teaching elder'. It was in tandem with that usage that the title 'ruling elder' came into use in the Scottish churches. We have to come to grips with the fact that *all* elders rule (exercise pastoral care and oversight duties), and all who exercise rule are elders. But among the elders, all of whom share in this generic notion of oversight, there is a further functional distinction, a solemn calling *not* shared by all. There are elders for whom preaching is the primary pastoral obligation. We must recognise, in this instituted order of things, that preaching and shepherding both belong to the work of the minister but that, for him, preaching must take priority.

That all elders are to be 'able to teach' does not mean that all elders are to be preachers, or *labourers in the Word*. They are to be able to help those they pastor in understanding the Word, and to teach the people in the homes they visit or at the hospital bed-side, but that they are *all* required to climb the pulpit and preach is not taught here. The very opposite is the case. While the text recognises no elders whose call is *simply* to preach, it knows of elders who are not called to preach, but to pastoral care of other sorts. Disregard of this distinction poses a threat to preaching, and a grave danger to ministers, in Independency today. It does its own despite to Scripture, and its own damage in the church.

Taken in conjunction with the fact that the apostles felt called to give themselves fully to prayer and preaching, this distinction undergirds the practice of a full-time ministry of the Word, called by God, trained and maintained by the church (verse 18 makes it clear that part of the 'honour' Paul has in mind is financial care of the preaching elder!). But it does more. It lays upon the church the obligation to ensure that such men, ministers, teaching elders – whatever we wish to call them – be free to give themselves to their calling. Such men are elders with responsibilities of 'over-sight' in the church but for them, the priority lies, in their call to *preach*.

This means that such freedom from other pastoral duties as is required for preaching must be guaranteed from within the over-sight (or eldership) of any church or congregation. In fact, one of the first ministerial duties of the eldership, as a body and as indi-viduals, must be to care for the welfare of the man they have called as their preacher. Wise godly encouragement at the right time, as well as gracious correction and *brotherly* counsel (also given at the right time – and *that is never* immediately after a sermon!), may well rescue a ministry from mediocrity, save it from depressingly unhelpful, or wearisome, patchy, despondent performance and direct it into increasingly useful channels.

Probably few elders realise the potent influence they can exert, for good or ill, upon the *minister of the Word*. It is all too easy, and perhaps all too common, for potentially powerful ministries to be hindered, even destroyed by bad, unsympathetic, unspiritual and even unchristian attitudes in the eldership. I am personally quite convinced that, as a general rule, no preacher will minister the Word in power if his eldership does not support him with prayer, pastoral concern and personal encouragement. He should know that he is not fighting the battle entirely on his own.

Here is where the principles of parity and plurality must both come into play. There must be sufficient flexibility in the eldership to ensure not only the pastoral care of the flock, but the ability of the preacher to pursue his special calling in a gracious and caring *Christian* environment.

Structuring for pastoral care
One of the priorities for urgent attention in the contemporary church is a renewed interest in the pastoral care of our people. The first concern for every Kirk Session should be organising the eldership for this work. It is a sad reflection on the eldership that people still think, as I did when I was a little boy, that the elder has two main tasks in life; one, to stand by the church door and see that everyone puts something into the collection plate, the other, to serve the elements to God's people around the Communion Table. That, of course, is a complete travesty of the elders' role. No doubt elders, and deacons and others, should be organised to welcome people as they come to worship God, extend the hand of friendship and fellowship to visitors to the church, see that people are able to worship in comfort, and that all present have praise books. These are all matters which should be discussed and organised at regular meetings of the elders.

Another area requiring drastic overhaul amongst us is the frequency with which Kirk Sessions meet. Deacons' Courts or Finance Committees meet every month to supervise business affairs. All too often, however, Kirk Session meetings take place only two or three times a year, to appoint communion or examine for baptism. Surely the spiritual welfare of our people demands far more care and attention than buildings or finance. If anything, the elders should meet for prayer, discussion of the spiritual state of the congregation, the work of outreach, the pastoral care of the flock, the visitation of homes, the hospitals, the sick, the elderly and so on, more frequently than the deacons do to discuss the roofs and the rhones, and other such matters.

Only in continual discussion of the work and in ongoing exposure of need on this practical, pastoral level will elders ever discover what the eldership involves. They need to be encouraged, and to encourage one another, in fulfilling the pastoral tasks that come under their jurisdiction. Calvin in Geneva met with his elders every week to discuss the wellbeing of the flock. So did John Knox when he was minister of the High Kirk in Edinburgh. Such regular meetings of the eldership would ensure that every elder had his own sphere of pastoral care mapped out in agreement with his fellows: his own district, or hospital, or Eventide Home. His regular reports on the encouragements or discouragements met with would stimulate praise and prayer amongst his fellow elders as the case might be. It would also help to create and maintain a spiritual, prayerful watch over the congregation or community in which the church is set. If the elders do not 'watch and pray' over their places, who will?

Pastoral work by elders and deacons

Where possible, elders should carry out their pastoral visitation along with a deacon. The pattern of 'two' going and working together is that of the New Testament. With two people present, home visits would be much easier, and useful spiritual conversation more likely. It would also be a safeguard for both the eldership and the ministry. People would be less likely to speak disparagingly of the minister, or his sermon (he was long last week, wasn't he? He's not spending much time in his study just now, is he? Don't you think he shouts too loud?) with two visitors than with only one, and they would certainly be less likely to acquiesce and unwittingly 'stab the minister in the back' (and the ministry of the Word) while doing so. In other words, such a practice might allay the fears that the spectre of an actual working, pastoral, biblical eldership seems to raise in the minds of all too many ministers.

It could also be an invaluable training ground for future elders who had learned from godly men how the pastoral side of the eldership should be conducted. We give no training of any kind to elders and even conferences on the eldership, or the work of the elder, are novel in the Scottish context. If what I am saying sounds like the 'counsels of perfection', and impracticable for some situations, it should still be regarded as the biblical norm towards which we begin to strive, and for which we work and pray in all our varied situations.

Discussion at regular Kirk Session meetings could allocate homes in the congregation to each elder (not too many; ideally

perhaps 10, but in some situations, 15 or 20?) and circumstances
would dictate how often visits take place. Regularity is of greater
importance than frequency. The Free Church of the last century
ordained that each elder must visit his district once a month! A
minimum number of visits per annum should certainly be set for
each working pair (elder and deacon) and adhered to strictly. They
should also be responsible for praying for the people under their
care and for keeping the minister informed of any special need
for his pastoral attention.

The eldership and evangelism

One further area of eldership work requiring renovation amongst
us is evangelism. Here, if anywhere, the church suffers from the
'one-man-band' or 'clerical' mentality which has gripped it
through this century. How many Kirk Sessions up and down our
land regularly discuss the needs, or the possibilities, of ongoing
evangelism in their communities? The general needs will be similar everywhere but with specific aspects particular to each locality. These demand, and should have, the prayerful concern and
practical planning of every Kirk Session. The congregation *not*
evangelising its community has forfeited its right to exist.

As our Scottish Reformers and their successors brought the
gospel to bear on their own particular day, so we must bring it to
bear upon ours. In all too many cases the local church is out of
touch with its community, or its witness is so ineffective, or unbiblical, as to be almost irrelevant. The eldership must carry its
share of the blame for such situations.

A few days ago a friend gave me an address by Horatius Bonar
at the ordination of elders in his Kelso Congregation last century.
Some of his wise words gather up the essence of our studies and
give it memorable expression.

'Let me press upon your notice this most important truth, *that your
office concerns the souls of men.* It is not for any earthly or temporal
purpose that you are thus solemnly set apart; it is for the care of that
"flock over which the Holy Ghost hath made you overseers ... the
church of God, which he hath purchased with his own blood." To
this extent the office of the elder and the minister is the same. The
design of both is the *oversight of souls.* I am the more anxious to
give prominence to this, because for many years past the office of

the eldership has fallen into decay .... I beseech you, my dear brethren, keep the *spirituality* of your office continually before your eyes, in the daily discharge of your momentous duties .... How much God blessed the zealous exertions of godly elders, the history of our church bears ample witness.

8

Evangelical Religion in the Scottish Highlands

1. From the Roman Legions to the Reformation

The beginnings of vital Christianity in the Scottish Highlands go back such a long way that they are hidden in the mists of antiquity. All the indications are that although the trained legions of Rome could not subdue the warlike tribes of ancient Caledonia with the sword the gospel of God's grace brought them, early in our era, into obedience to the Prince of peace.

When and by whom the Evangel was first brought into our northern glens is not clearly known. However, it is not unlikely that among the Roman soldiers left to defend the great wall which extended from the river Forth to the river Clyde, there were earnest Christians who, as opportunities arose to talk to the people of those northern tribes, would tell them the message of 'Jesus Christ and him crucified'.

The Celtic Church

The first certainties that the early history provides for us focus upon a fine Christian missionary called Ninian. Born around the middle of the fourth century, he was actually a native of the region and, before the Roman Legions had taken their final departure, he had visited Rome, spent some time in Gaul with the famous Martin of Tours, and set up a Christian centre on the shores of the Solway. From its famous White House – the Candida Casa – Whithorn takes its name still.

While the Whithorn church was being built, news came of the death of Martin, and the new building was dedicated to him. As the death of Martin occurred in 397 it helps date the time of Ninian's mission and the erection of the first known Christian church in Scotland. The monastery at Candida Casa was known as the 'Great Monastery' and it became a college for the training of missionaries.

This chapter originally appeared as an appendix to *Gleanings in Highland Harvest* by Murdoch Campbell (Christian Focus Publications, 1989).

Students flocked to it from all quarters and men who trained there went out and missioned in Ireland and into the North of Scotland. They have left traces of their work in local place names as far north as Glenurquhart on the shores of Loch Ness and Navidale in Sutherland.

Columba

Though many earnest missionaries worked northwards from Whithorn in the fifth century, the name which stands out most prominently in the emergence of the Celtic Church is that of Columba who landed on the island of Iona on 12th May, 563. The teaching of this zealous missionary, who with his disciples had crossed over the Irish sea, was warmly evangelical and under his labours the north and the west of Scotland became the cradle of a robust, literate church which in its best days sent many Christian scholars and preachers out across Europe.

This is not the place to dwell on the forces which eventually obscured, and almost extinguished, the witness of that old Celtic Church. It is enough to say that under the invasion of Norse paganism and medieval Roman Catholicism, the darkness of a long spiritual night settled over the Scottish Highlands. The Word of God became a closed book to the people, and many of their instructors in spiritual things were not only ignorant of Scripture in the letter, but were without any experience of its sanctifying power.

Precisely how the gospel made its way back into the northern region of Scotland after the Reformation is also a perennially interesting question but one to which the answer is not easily determined. While much that is instructive and thrilling has been recorded about the reintroduction of the gospel and the noble figures involved in the process to the south of the Grampians, all too little is recorded in this connection by those who lived to the north of that great mountain range. The psalmist of Israel could say:

O God, we with our ears have heard,
Our fathers have us told,
What works thou in their days hadst done,
Ev'n in the days of old (Ps. 44:1).

Today, we can only deeply regret the silence of our Highland forefathers of the immediate post-Reformation period on this important subject. It would seem that those who had the ability to write up the history largely lacked the opportunity, and however desirable they themselves may have regarded such a work, they were intent rather on the practical tasks which lay to hand and demanded their energy. So our knowledge of the Highland church has to be gleaned from sporadic writings and a wide variety of scattered and, for the main part, secondary sources.

Wycliffe's Bible

The time came when the deep spiritual darkness that had overlain Scotland through the medieval period was pushed aside and a new day of gospel light began to dawn over the land. But unlike the beginnings of the Celtic Church, when the light had come out of Ireland in the west, it was from the Continent in the east that the brightening rays of a new day took their rise. With the establishment of the Reformed Church in Scotland in the summer of 1560 the new day had come. That church faced an enormous task and not the least of its difficulties was that it had still to reach westwards and northwards into the remote and mountainous regions of the Highlands before the Reformation of religion in Scotland was complete.

Over the previous thirty years, however, it would seem that Wycliffe's Bible and Tyndale's translation of the New Testament, as well as the powerful Protestant tracts and theological writings of Martin Luther, were penetrating the land along the commercial routes from Germany and the Low Countries. The ports of the Eastern seaboard such as Leith, St. Andrews, Montrose and Aberdeen gave the Reforming literature access to the Scottish Lowlands. In the same way, those of Inverness, Cromarty, Tain, Wick and Thurso gave it entrance to the north-east Highlands. When the great evangelical doctrines that informed, and gave impetus to, the Reformation process began to impress the English-speaking people of those regions, it was natural they would tell their Gaelic-speaking neighbours what they had learned and experienced of God's grace. In that way, gospel light began to penetrate the districts around the northern seaports.

Patrick Hamilton
Tertullian, one of the great theologians and writers of the early church, gave us the dictum that 'the blood of the martyrs is the seed of the church'. The Scottish Reformation brought martyrdom to a number of Christians and among the earliest of them was Patrick Hamilton. An aristocrat by birth, he was given the income from churches in the north to help finance his studies and was Provost of the church of Tain and Abbot of Fearn from the age of twelve.

The young Hamilton went to Paris University about 1515 and graduated five years later, soon after Luther had taken his bold stance for the gospel. He returned to work in St. Andrews University, but coming under suspicion of Lutheranism there early in 1527 he fled to Wittenberg and for a period actually worked alongside Luther. He was at the opening of Philip of Hesse's new Evangelical University of Marburg (May 30th, 1527) and drafted the theses for the first academic disputation. Later that year he returned to Scotland, intent on preaching the gospel, but was enticed to St. Andrews and burnt at the stake there on 29 February, 1528 while still only in the 25th year of his life.

While there is no evidence to show that Patrick Hamilton ever preached in the churches of Tain or Fearn, the people of that area, like those in the Lowlands, must have heard of his martyrdom and the memorable words uttered by him in the flames: 'How long, O Lord, will darkness cover this realm, how long wilt thou suffer this tyranny of men? Lord Jesus, receive my spirit.' His death certainly had a different effect from that anticipated by those who caused it, for one man is reported to have observed that the 'reek (smoke) of Master Patrick Hamilton had infected as many as it blew upon'. His death would raise many questions in the north-east and stir a special interest in the book and the doctrines for which their brilliant young Abbot was willing to give his life.

2. From Reformation to Covenant, 1560-1638
The history books inform us that men of high position gave their influence to establishing Reformation principles in Scotland. This was true not only in the south but in the north as well. Thus, in the Scottish Parliament of August 1560, all the Commissioners from the Grampians right up to the North Sea voted for the disestablishment of the old, moribund Romish Church and the ratification of

the new, Reformed Confession of Faith prepared by John Knox and his fellow-Reformers.

Prominent among them was John Grant, chief of that clan, and Commissioner for the county of Inverness-shire. For the county of Ross, there was Robert Munro, 17th Baron of Foulis, and also chief of his clan; William Innes of Innes; Sutherland of Dufus, the Abbot of Fearn; the Commissioner for the Burgh of Banff; and the Commissioner for the Burgh of Inverness; the Earl of Caithness; and John, 15th Earl of Sutherland. We also know from Knox's *History of the Reformation* that Lord Lorne, or Argyll, was very active in support of the Reformation. Such men were linked, by ties of blood, with leading families right through the Highlands, and the clan chiefs in those days wielded a mighty influence for good or evil among their people.

Another person whose influence must have affected the area north of the Highland line was the Regent Moray, half-brother to Mary, Queen of Scots. He was thoroughly committed to the Reformation cause, and with vast landed interests in Moray and Ross, must have exercised a strong influence in those areas. The enthusiasm of the people of Easter Ross for Protestant principles at this early period finds unusual testimony from him, for he presented an oak pulpit to the parish church of Tain sometime before his assassination in 1571.

Donald Munro of Kiltearn

At the Reformation there was a great dearth of Reformed ministers in the Highlands but the new Church showed real enterprise and, as early as 1563, special Commissioners were appointed to plant churches and schools. By 1567 there were 257 ministers in Scotland, 455 readers, and 151 exhorters – 863 in all.

The northern Highlands shared the benefits of those special measures and one of the commissioners selected in 1563 was the Rev. Donald Munro, the minister of Kiltearn. He is said to have been the first minister to have preached the Reformed doctrines in the north at a service which, traditionally, is said to have taken place 'in the old Church of Limlair, between Dingwall and Foulis'.[1] This famous minister is described by the historian of the

1. Dr. Donald Munro; *The Monthly Record of the Free Church of Scotland*, July 1918, p. 116.

period, George Buchanan, as a 'learned and godly man'.[2] We have only a meagre knowledge nowadays of the men who occupied the Highland pulpits prior to the beginning of the 17th century but one historical record again involves the burgh of Tain, and interestingly, confirms the beneficial influences that trace back to the Regent Moray and Patrick Hamilton. Of the nineteen ministers that were present at the famous Aberdeen Assembly which met, under the frown of King James VI, on 2nd July 1605, one was the Rev John Munro, the minister of Tain. He must have been thoroughly Reformed and thoroughly Presbyterian into the bargain to have risked incurring the royal displeasure in such bold fashion.

Robert Bruce in Inverness

In the year 1605 another event took place which was to strengthen and advance the spread of the gospel in the north in an unusual and unexpected manner. The minister of St. Giles, Edinburgh, was the famous Robert Bruce of Kinnaird, a masterly theologian, a powerful preacher and probably the most popular minister in the Scotland of his day. His preaching was greatly owned of the Lord and one of his converts was none other than the great Alexander Henderson, architect of the National Covenant of 1638 and a Scottish Commissioner to the Westminster Assembly of Divines in the following decade.

Bruce was undoubtedly one of the greatest men of his time, and even King James himself professed the highest esteem for him. In 1590, when James went to Denmark for his Queen, it was Bruce who was left in ultimate control of national affairs and James acknowledged his obligations to him. Perhaps Bruce had demonstrated his leadership qualities only too well, however, for a few years later when he opposed the introduction of prelacy into the Scottish Church by the King, he was banished north of the Grampians and 'warded' in the town of Inverness. Bruce entered Inverness on the 27th August, 1605 and was to spend almost eight years there. He had freedom to preach every Sunday forenoon and every Wednesday evening. There is little doubt that he attracted many people to those meetings and that his preaching was blessed

2. The quotation comes from the Moderatorial Address of Dr. Gustavus Aird, in the *Proceedings of the Assembly of the Free Church*, 1888, p. 5.

to some. Released in the spring of 1613, he was forced into a second exile in Inverness on 18th April, 1622. It was while he was setting out on this last journey to the Highlands that he had one of those remarkable moments of prophetic, spiritual insight which various writers speak of in connection with his ministry.[3]

The following account of this particular incident has been well attested by one of his successors in Larbert and recorded by the historian, Wodrow.

> 'When Bruce was going to Inverness on one of these occasions, several gentlemen and relatives accompanied him part of the way. Ere he entered the saddle he stood looking up to heaven musing for a few minutes: after he had mounted, a friend asked him how he was engaged when musing? Mr. Bruce replied, "I was receiving my commission from my Master to go to Inverness, and he gave it to me himself before I set my foot in the stirrup, and thither I go to sow a seed in Inverness that shall not be rooted out for ages".'[4]

On this second visit the effects of Bruce's preaching were remarkable. Dr. Aird is clearly surprised, but deeply impressed, by the impact made on this occasion far to the north and west of Inverness. He writes:

> 'It is upwards of half a century since I heard a tradition which astonished me then, that during part of Mr. Bruce's ministry in Inverness, persons from Sutherland and Ross were in the habit of going there to hear him, through bridgeless streams and rivers, and across ferries; but years thereafter I found it verified in *Blairs Autobiography*.'

He then goes on to quote Blair as follows:

> 'June 29, 1700 – The memory of that man of God, Mr. Bruce, is sweet to this day in this place Inverness. He in the day of James was confined in this town and country about, for multitudes of all ranks would have crossed several ferries every Lord's day to hear him, yea they came from Ross and Sutherland: the memory of the just is blessed.'[5]

---

3. Chapter 19 in 'Seeing Visions and Dreaming Dreams', D.C. MacNicol's fine biography, *Master Robert Bruce*.
4. Wodrow, *Life of Bruce*, p. 146.
5. Proceedings of the General Assembly of the Free Church, May 1888, p. 6.

Speaking also of this second period of Bruce's Inverness ministry, Donald Munro says:

'A great revival of religion took place under his earnest, evangelical preaching. A few of his converts in the faith, it is said, were alive at the Revolution (1688). Sometimes it happened that men who came to Inverness on business were drawn by irresistible force to Mr. Bruce's meetings. On one occasion a drover from a Highland glen was led to attend the weekday service, where a barbed arrow entered his heart, which forced him to cry out in his broken English – "I'se gie two coos [all he had] to 'gree God and me." But the Lord also gave his devoted servant souls for his hire among the nobility. It is said that the Covenanting Earl of Sutherland was one of the fruits of his ministry, as also his Countess, a daughter of Lord Fraser of Lovat – one who was eminent for her deep piety.'[6]

Alexander Munro of Durness

One of those converted through the ministry of Bruce at Inverness was Alexander Munro, son of the Laird of Katewell, Kiltearn. This fine young man was ordained into the ministry in the extensive parish of Durness in the north-west of the county of Sutherland. He found his people illiterate and ignorant of the gospel but he persevered in teaching them and Dr. Aird says, 'Wodrow in his *Analecta* states that, At his entry there the people were almost heathen, but his labours had great success, and a large harvest of souls'.[7]

One interesting feature of this ministry has come down to us and it well illustrates how ready those early Highland ministers were to turn every facet of life to spiritual advantage. Noting how fond the people were of singing Gaelic songs their young minister capitalised on their aptitude for poetry and began to versify portions of the Scripture into their native Gaelic, setting them to popular tunes and teaching them to the people through the winter evenings. In such interesting fashion were his parishioners made familiar with the fundamental doctrines of God's Word, and many of them came to experience its power.

---

6. *Monthly Record,* July 1918, p. 116.
7. *Op. cit.* p. 7.

Highland soldiers in the Netherlands

Yet another influence upon the emergence of evangelical life in the Highlands can be traced to the wars of religion on the Continent. As early as 1586, 1603 and 1628 Scottish soldiers were being enrolled into what eventually became known as The Scots Brigade. The Stuart policies of imposing Episcopacy made it easy for such military contingents to get good Scottish ministers to serve as chaplains. The practice can be illustrated from the fact that Rev. Andrew Hunter, minister of Carnbee, Fifeshire, was one of the early chaplains listed on the payroll of the Scottish regiment serving in the Netherlands.[8]

The armies involved on the Protestant side were often favoured with some of the finest of the English Puritans – great biblical scholars and warmly evangelical men – as their chaplains. One fine study of this fascinating connection informs us, for example, that, 'In spite of some unworthy chaplains, the religious situation in the seventeenth-century Netherlands army was better because of the well-motivated refugee Puritans available for service, some of considerable theological eminence (William Ames, Robert Parker, John Burgess, John Paget, Thomas Scott)'.[9]

It was actually from the northernmost point of the Highlands that Sir Donald MacKay of Naver, afterwards known as the first Lord Reay, mustered the initial expedition of Highland soldiers for this purpose. In 1626, along with Munro of Foulis, he gathered over 2,000 men, composed of MacKays from his own lands in the west, Sutherlands from the eastern parts of the territory, and Rosses and Munros from the county of Ross and town of Inverness, and embarked at Cromarty for the Continent. After fighting with the forces of the King of Denmark, this regiment entered the service of the 'Lion of the North', as the godly Swedish King was known, and in his service they so distinguished themselves that throughout the Netherlands they were spoken of as 'the right hand of Gustavus Adolphus'.

It seems to have been under the influence of the Puritan chaplains that a great many of those Highland soldiers were converted to Christ and large groups of them returned to their native counties as ardent Christians. In this way, the evangelical

---

8. Cf. A.L. Drummond, *The Kirk and the Continent*, p. 78 ff.
9. Keith L. Sprunger, *Dutch Puritanism*, p. 263.

life of the northern Highlands came under the influence of English Puritan theology, with its emphasis on personal, experimental and spiritual religion, as well as its strongly reflective and doctrinal character. The link is further illustrated in the common occurrence of the Christian name Gustavus throughout the northern counties; Dr. Gustavus Aird, the Free Church minister of the parish of Creich through the latter half of the nineteenth century, is said to have had several elders named Gustavus on his Kirk Session through that period.

Dr. Donald Munro, noting this Puritan influence and its impact in the North, goes on to say:

'When one of those pious soldiers, as was sometimes the case, lived at a considerable distance from the parish church, he considered it his duty to conduct a Sabbath evening meeting, which the people in the neighbourhood attended. These gatherings are said to have been instrumental in the conversion of sinners, and in the refreshing of God's heritage.'[10]

3. From the Covenant to the Revolution 1638 to 1688

It is not surprising to find that the strong evangelical testimony implanted in the north through the labours of Robert Bruce, and the influence of the godly amongst the returned veterans of the Continental wars, eventuated in the National Covenant of 1638 being largely and heartily signed in those northern counties. Though there may have been strong political motives for the excitement that this event precipitated through the country, yet its basic movement was undoubtedly that of a strong spiritual current; it was more the work of religion than of politics. And the Lord did not leave his people without gracious tokens of his evident approval, for the signing of the Covenant in the Highlands, as elsewhere, was followed by great spiritual prosperity.

We know very little about the ministry in the north in the years immediately following the famous Covenanting Assembly held at Glasgow in 1638, yet there appears to have been spiritual stirrings in many areas in the north, and these were fostered by the influences we have already noted, and in special meetings and conferences which multiplied through the next few decades. In the

10. *Monthly Record,* August 1918, p. 132.

short memoir of Thomas Hog of Kiltearn, one of the famous ministers who was 'ousted' at the Restoration, we have almost the only record of that period in the north. Great success evidently attended his own short ministry before his ejection, and probably the same happy results flowed from the ministries of other faithful men.

There is an interesting reference to prayer and fellowship meetings amongst the Christian people of the north at this moment in their history which has come down to us in the correspondence of one of Cromwell's soldiers. It is part of a letter dated 8th January, 1651, in which the writer, while mentioning some of the troop movements through various Highland areas, remarks:

> 'I perceive by Captain Simpson and others that came from thence that there is a very precious people who seek the face of the Lord in Sutherland, and divers other parts around Inverness, which but that I have had it by so good hands, I should have much questioned, considering how few all the Southern parts have afforded ... and though there were very few in any part of this nation wherever we came that would be present at any private meetings, yet the people in these parts will rather leave their own ministers and come to private houses, where our officers and soldiers meet together.'[11]

This illuminating comment is a fairly clear indicator, not merely of the spiritual hunger of those people and their desire for teaching and fellowship, but also of the scarcity of evangelical and Bible teaching ministries in the north as compared with the south of Scotland where believers would not leave their ministers, and the regular, stated means of grace which they already enjoyed.

Of the 400 ministers who refused to conform to the demands for acceptance of Episcopacy in the wake of the Restoration of Charles II in 1660, few more than a tenth were to survive the Revolution which restored Presbytery and closed the Covenanting period. Of eighteen ejected in Argyll, only seven survived; of eleven in the north, eight, among them Thomas Hog of Kiltearn. By that time this godly man, and most of the other survivors as well, were not capable of carrying on their ministries, not so much from their age as from the permanent effects of rigorous persecution.

---

11. Donald Munro, *Monthly Record*, August 1918, p. 132.

Notable Highland Conventicles

Such occasions were greatly used of God in encouraging Christian believers and in the conversion of sinners. It would seem that the sacrament of the Lord's Supper was seldom observed in the north by the 'conforming' ministers who, to a very large extent, held the parish pulpits after the ejections of 1661. But there are two places which, traditionally, have been connected with great Sacramental gatherings in the north during the dark days of the Covenanting persecution.

One of these was at a place called Obsdale in the parish of Rosskeen in Easter Ross. There, on a fine September day in 1675, a huge number of earnest Christians gathered to observe the Lord's Supper. Three of the ousted ministers led the services, John MacKilligan of Fodderty[12], Hugh Anderson of Cromarty, and Alexander Fraser of Daviot. Dr. Kennedy writes of this event:

'Mr. Anderson preached the preparation sermon on Saturday, Mr. MacKilligan officiated on Sabbath in the forenoon, and Mr. Fraser in the afternoon, and Mr. MacKilligan preached the thanksgiving discourse on Monday. During this last service, there was such a plentiful effusion of the Spirit, that the oldest Christians then present declared they had never enjoyed such a time of refreshing before.'[13]

The other such occasion has an added interest for us today because of the unusual circumstances which led up to it. Although all the parish ministers in Sutherland had actually conformed and so, to a large extent, had lost the confidence of the people, a minister from Warwickshire found his way to the Cape Wrath district of Sutherlandshire. He was, in fact, the great-great grandfather of Dr. Gustavus Aird, who has been mentioned already and on whose work this present narrative has drawn at various points.

The English minister, George Squair, himself a fugitive from Charles II's religious policies, became so concerned with the spiritual needs of the people that he set himself to learn Gaelic and became an accomplished preacher in the language. His preaching through the northern districts was greatly blessed and the time

---

12. His wife had a small estate in Alness, where he preached through the years of his ejection; cf. Kennedy's *The Days of the Fathers in Ross-Shire*, Christian Focus Publications, footnote p. 37.

13. *Op. cit.* pp. 38, 39. Cf. also Wodrow's II, pp. 284, 285.

arrived when he proposed to hold a Communion.

The place selected for the purpose was, according to Dr. Donald Munro, 'an isolated spot among the wild hills of the parish of Eddrachillis'. Another historian speaks of this Communion and tells us:

> 'The whole service was a memorable one.... Not only was there no interruption of the service, but all there felt so much of the Lord's presence, and their bonds were so loosened, and their fears so dispelled, that all, without a single exception, felt constrained to say with Thomas, "My Lord and my God," and without exception, commemorated the dying love of their Redeemer.'[14]

Such occasions will be mentioned again, for writers on the religious life of the Highlands recognise that, right through from these Covenanting days until the great Evangelical Awakening of the nineteenth century, the sacramental gatherings and the district 'Fellowship' or 'Question' meetings as they were called (and they were an invariable element of evangelical Communion seasons) were amongst the main agencies in evangelism. 'To one or other of them,' says MacInnes, 'we can trace all or most of the awakenings and revivals which have quickened the spiritual life of the people'.[15]

4. Out of Moderatism to Evangelical Awakening, 1730 to 1830

The revivals of the 1740s in Cambuslang and other areas of Lowland Scotland worked northwards into the Perthshire Highlands, and on beyond Inverness into the area of Easter Ross, Nigg, Fearn and Tain. While the north had its own share of Moderate ministers, who tended to be orthodox in theology but, as the name suggests, always very chary of religious enthusiasm or any emphasis upon spiritual life or personal godliness, there were also earnest gospel ministers of the best kind to be found in many parishes.

On the western seaboard of the Highlands there were fewer instances of spiritual awakening through the first half of the eighteenth century than in the north, and by all accounts forthright evangelical ministries are few and far between in those parishes during that time. It was to be into the late 1700s and even the first

---

14. Quoted by John MacInnes in *The Evangelical Movement in the Highlands of Scotland*, p. 15.
15. *Op. cit.* p. 155.

decades of the 1800s before the gospel was to make its strongest impact in the west, and before many of its ministers could properly be reckoned amongst the great Highland evangelicals. One exception is the saintly (and physically huge) Aeneas Sage.

Ordained to the ministry in the parish of Lochcarron in 1726, this rugged man of God was destined to become one of the great folk-names in the history of Highland evangelicalism, and was regarded by many with something of the awe of an Elijah. But his work, although ultimately greatly blessed, was never easy and must, at least initially, have been extremely difficult and exacting. On his very first night in his parish, his new flock tried, literally, to burn him out. He survived this attempt on his life and went on to change his people through his powerful, biblical preaching. 'He found the people,' writes his grandson, Donald Sage, 'sunk in ignorance, with modes of worship allied to Paganism. Before the close of his long and efficient ministry, the moral aspects of the people were entirely changed.'[16]

Another powerful and influential ministry was also conducted in this same parish over the closing years of the eighteenth century and it had beneficial effects over an astonishingly wide area. Writing in 1861 Dr. John Kennedy, Dingwall, in his well known book *The Days of the Fathers in Ross-Shire* says, 'Of all the eminent ministers in the Highlands, none is more famous than Mr. Lachlan Mackenzie of Lochcarron. Owing to his genius, his peculiar Christian experience, and his great acceptance as a preacher, he has retained a firmer hold of the memories of the people than any other besides.'[17] Lachlan Mackenzie was settled as the minister in Lochcarron in 1782 and his ministry was greatly blessed there, and all over the Highlands, until his death on 20th April, 1819.

5. The Ministers in the Evangelical Awakening
The solid foundations which underlay the spiritual revivals of the mid-nineteenth century, and the evangelical ministries that were able to guide and channel the masses of new converts into the paths of godliness, trace back into the early years of the century. As well

---

16. *Memorabilia Domestica*, p. 2.
17. John Kennedy, *The Days of the Fathers in Ross-Shire*, Christian Focus Publications, pp. 57,58.

as the great ministries of John Kennedy, Redcastle (father of Dr. John Kennedy, Dingwall) and Dr. John MacDonald, Ferintosh (known as The Apostle of the North because of his wide-ranging, itinerant, evangelistic labours) which attuned the ears and the hearts of thousands to powerful, doctrinal gospel preaching, there were also other factors at work.

Not least amongst these were the strongly doctrinal, theologically informed, and intellectually stimulating ministries of Dr. Andrew Thomson in Edinburgh and Dr. John Love in Glasgow. These great city preachers were making evangelical teaching tell on the student world of their day, having their respective city charges crowded with divinity students, and the future preachers of Scotland's pulpits hung on their every word. Great preaching shapes men and influences future ministries, and of course amongst these students were many young Highlanders whose preaching, in turn, was to transform the lives of countless numbers in years to come. The famous brothers, Archie and Finlay Cook, for example, sat at the feet of Dr. Love through their student days in Glasgow.

Varied types of gospel ministries

The lengthened perspective from which we are able to look back and survey the Highland religious scene through the first half of the last century helps in assessing the ministries that led to the Awakening. It is quite clear that many of the pulpits, especially in the district then covered by the Synod of Ross, were filled by able, biblical preachers. They were men who, for deep experience of a work of grace, for habitual nearness in their walk with God, and for clear, full and powerful proclamation of gospel truth have seldom had their superiors in any Christian church.

That those ministers had their favourite themes is quite clear, yet they all took particular care to cover the entire spectrum of biblical truth and to declare, very faithfully, the whole counsel of God. Among them, as their sermons and history show, were men such as Dr. Angus MacIntosh of Tain who gave great prominence to the breadth and spirituality of God's holy law, and the dreadful peril of the impenitent sinner as transgressor of its righteous demands. Yet it was said that this man was never harsh in his preaching or statements of such solemn truths. Kennedy of Dingwall, himself a masterly preacher, made a wisely critical and discerning hearer of sermons, and he remarked of MacIntosh, 'If he sometimes used a sharp razor, it was always well oiled.'[18]

The fact is that one of the most luminous features of Highland preaching in that era was its *tenderness* and many of the recorded sermons, or fragments of sermons, which have been preserved and have come down through the oral traditions of the people bear ample testimony to this fact. Those men were true 'pastors' of the flock of God and took individual and personal spiritual needs into their preaching.

Other preachers such as Dr. MacDonald, Ferintosh gave particular prominence to the glory of Christ's person and the richness and freeness of the way of salvation. He was a masterly exponent of the doctrine of justification by faith in Christ alone. To this special emphasis, apparently so perennially present in his sermons as to be a characteristic of his popular preaching, Dr. Chalmers, for one, attributed MacDonald's great evangelistic success. There were men also of the Rutherford stamp who were masters at preaching gospel comfort and consolation to downcast Christian believers. Such a man, it is quite clear, was the Rev. Charles Calder, MacDonald's predecessor in Ferintosh, for it is said that he never wearied of 'speaking from a full heart of the *love of Christ which passeth knowledge'*.[19]

The highs and lows of Christian experience were also given thorough treatment by the outstanding preachers of the north as well. In fact experiential preaching was perhaps the department above all others where the great masters of the northern pulpits excelled. The marvellous minuteness with such specialists in spiritual analysis such as John Kennedy, Redcastle, and his son, John Kennedy of Dingwall, John MacRae (known as Big MacRae), Knockbain, and Archie Cook of Daviot, could describe and illustrate, not only the past history, but also the present feelings of exercised souls was, to their hearers, plain proof that they were true messengers of God.

The preaching of some of these Highland fathers was almost invariably characterised by apt illustration and a natural gift for figure of speech. They painted vivid word pictures which came alive in the minds and hearts of their hearers and remained with

18. Donald Munro, *Monthly Record,* September 1918, p. 132.
19. *Ibid,* p. 162.

them long after the preacher's voice had stilled. Those familiar
with the literature, or traditions of Highland religious life last
century will readily think in this connection of names like Porteous,
Kilmuir; Lachlan Mackenzie, Lochcarron; Finlayson, Helmsdale;
and Francis Macbean of Fort Augustus, who was in many ways the
Christmas Evans of the Highlands. Listening to such preaching
was a moving and memorable experience and the stories,
illustrations and even the framework of their sermons lived on
amongst the people for many years after they had been preached.

6. The Spreading Flame

One great disadvantage under which the western Highlanders
laboured for a long time was the lack of the Scriptures in their
native Gaelic. The first translation of the New Testament into
Scottish Gaelic did not appear until 1767, and the entire Bible was
not published until 1801. The only way in which the people could
have the Word of God read to them in their own language until
those dates was by immediate, oral translation. This the evangelicals
amongst the Highland ministers trained themselves to do, and it
speaks well of their linguistic abilities that almost all of them could
readily translate in this way. They had mastered the technique of
reading directly from English into Gaelic in a very accomplished
and informative fashion.

Such facility, of course, lends testimony to the truth that those
men were very familiar with the Word of God. It is also a salutary
reminder that most of them were well educated and compare more
than favourably with present day ministerial accomplishments in
the fields of language and literature. John MacKay, the famous
seventeenth-century minister of Lairg, was deeply read in Dutch
theology and so was able, during the Covenanting period, to carry
on a theological seminary for young men going into the ministry.
The MS sermons of John Balfour of Nigg reveal his constant use
of the Greek New Testament and James Fraser of Alness, author
of *The Scripture Doctrine of Sanctification*, was a theologian of
high repute.[20]

---

20. Cf. MacInnes, *op. cit.* p. 70.

Two helpful societies

The Evangelical Awakening also owed a great debt to two societies whose members, over many years, took a deep interest in the moral and spiritual welfare of the Highland people. One of these was formed into a corporate body as early as 1709 under the title, 'The Society for Propagating Christian Knowledge'. The other was instituted in 1725, and was popularly known as the 'Royal Bounty'. These societies succeeded in establishing, even in the most remote corners of the north, schools and mission stations which were the means of teaching the people to read and write and of bringing the gospel to them. Many of the men who became well known ministers actually served their ministerial 'apprenticeship' in such stations and the combination of teaching and preaching combined to form them into extremely skilful communicators.

To mention only one such mission station, that of Achreny in the heights of the parish of Halkirk, it is worth noticing that its name is associated with some of the best known ministers in the evangelical life of the Highlands. Alexander Sage, Kildonan; Hugh MacKay, Moy; John Robertson, Kingussie; John MacDonald, Ferintosh; John Munro, Halkirk; and Finlay Cook, Reay, all served in this station and, as young men, gained the practical pastoral experience from its varied missionary tasks that was to shape their later ministries along very useful lines.

Schoolmasters and catechists

In addition to the preaching of the Word there was also the widespread practice of catechising. With the financial support of the societies mentioned earlier, catechists were appointed to many of the northern parishes and did excellent work in teaching the Bible and the fundamentals of Christian doctrine as set out in the Westminster Shorter Catechism. These men generally visited all the families in their district and would frequently gather the people into one home where meetings for prayer, discussion and preaching were held to round off the evening.

It was usually the case, however, that the evangelical ministers never wished to have this part of their pastoral and teaching work done for them entirely by others, for it was a labour they regarded as particularly important, and which they often spoke of as being especially profitable and enjoyable for themselves. The godly

James Calder, minister of Croy, records in his diary, under the date of 24th October, 1762: 'This day had a diet of examination. The house was crowded, the Lord was present, the duty delightful and edifying.'[21]

The Highland schoolmasters also made a great contribution to laying the groundwork of evangelical life in the north and west of Scotland. There were three types of school in the Highlands last century. The oldest and longest established was the parish school, often spoken of as the 'legal' school, and in the main centres they did a very good work educationally and spiritually. Future ministers, such as John Balfour of Nigg; Dr. MacIntosh MacKay, Dunoon; and Dr. George MacKay, Inverness all served such schools in their student days.

Then there were the schools, in more remote areas, supported by the Society for the Propagation of Christian Knowledge. For years, the men serving those schools also worked as preachers or catechists in the mission stations, and so part of their support came also from the Royal Bounty, and the instruction of the older people as well as the children of the district was in their hands. From 1811, special Gaelic schools were instituted where instruction in the medium of their own language could be given to the young Highlanders. Many of those Highland schoolmasters, serving the different types of school, were men of outstanding godliness whose labours were wonderfully blessed both in the conversion of sinners and the upbuilding of believers.

So keen were many of the people to take advantage of the facilities provided by the Gaelic schools of 1811, and the opportunity afforded to learn to read the Word of God in their own language, that sometimes the grandmother and the grandchild sat on the same bench. In this connection Dr. Donald Munro has recorded a fascinating story.

'The teacher who conducted the Gaelic School in Glencalvie, in the parish of Kincardine, Ross-shire, in 1815, had an experience that was probably unique. One of his scholars, a man of the name of Iverach, had seen three centuries. He was a young soldier of seventeen years at the time of the Jacobite rising of 1715, and such was his desire to have access to the treasures of God's Word that in his 117th year he

---

21. Quoted from Munro, *Monthly Record,* September 1918, p. 163.

joined the Gaelic class, and became an enthusiastic, and not unsuccessful pupil'.[22]

7. Times of Refreshing

The half yearly (in some circumstances, annual) commemoration of the Lord's Supper became a major feature of Highland religious life and, especially in the nineteenth century, was a major factor in spreading spiritual blessing. These sacramental 'seasons', as they were called, developed into a carefully structured series of services designed to help foster spiritual life and Christian fellowship in people who often had to live in isolated places, and maintain their Christian witness under difficult providential circumstances.

Such occasions, and the enormous crowds they attracted, provided a high point in the Christian calendar of these people, and served a similar purpose to the Christian conventions and conferences which have featured more and more in the Evangelical world of the late twentieth century. In the eyes of ministers and people, they were such a rich means of grace and blessing. They were frequently linked, also, to times of revival and spiritual awakening as at the famous Kirk o'Shotts revival in 1640, when the Holy Spirit was poured out during the thanksgiving service on the Monday, the final meeting of a Communion season.

The Fellowship Meeting

In the Northern Highlands the Friday of each Communion season was devoted to 'The Men's Meeting', so called because the elders and leading Christian men spoke at it rather than the ministers. This was also known as the 'Fellowship Meeting' or, following its Gaelic title, the 'Question Meeting', so called because a passage of Scripture was given out by one of the men, who each then spoke to the *question* of one's standing before God. This would be dealt with in a practical fashion and 'marks' or 'tokens' of those who were the subjects of a genuine work of saving grace were brought from personal experience and deliberated on.

Such meetings were frequently the means of removing the perplexities of anxious enquirers and seekers after the Saviour. As they heard the inward workings and experiences of God's people being discussed, so their own spiritual questions and strivings were often dealt with and explained for them. The topics handled

---

22. *Ibid.*

varied enormously from speaker to speaker and, as most of them were mature, exercised believers of long standing, the richly experimental quality of the individual contributions provided a means of comforting and assuring sorely tried or downcast Christians.

The origin of those meetings has never been clearly traced but is generally associated with the ministry of Thomas Hog, the Covenanting minister of Kiltearn mentioned earlier. He is known to have come under very deep distress of mind when a student at the University of Aberdeen. He was greatly helped in his difficulties when he and some other young men developed the practice of meeting together for theological discussion and Christian fellowship. It has been thought that this habit suggested the idea of the Fellowship Meeting to him, and that he inaugurated them in the early days of his own ministry in Kiltearn. The similarity to the Disputation or 'Quaestio' (the Latin term by which it is known), an oral and sometimes written exercise in scriptural exegesis for divinity students which might well have been familiar to men like Hog, is also too striking to ignore. However all that may be, those meetings certainly became a prominent and valuable feature in the spiritual life of the Highlands.

It would appear that the meetings, in their earlier format at least, were held in each evangelical congregation on the first Monday of each month at noon, and were rather in the nature of a family or private character than a public meeting; that is, they were purely for Christian believers aiming to help those who had professed their faith in Christ and were in the full communicant membership of the congregation. In some cases where there were real spiritual strivings or soul concern, seekers after peace in Christ were permitted to attend at the discretion of the eldership. The Fellowship Meetings on the Communion Fridays probably also took this same form at their first appearance, but eventually they were open to all who wished to come and, indeed, became so popular they had to be held in the open air, as the church buildings could not accommodate the crowds which attended after the years of the Awakening.

The Communion seasons

There is little doubt that the Communion seasons were a means of deepening spiritual life in the northern Highlands, and did much to foster a rare type of godliness. As in other times and countries through the history of the Christian church the Spirit of God, poured out in revival blessing, brought people through very vivid spiritual experiences both in their conversion and in their walk with God. Many maintained a lifetime of intimate, daily, close communion with their Lord and knew what it was to have his will made wonderfully clear to them through the Scriptures. This aspect of spiritual life, so common then, is so rare now.

The sacrament week was the great event in a northern parish through the middle years of the last century. It was anticipated with great interest, not only by the elderly and the more serious in the neighbourhood, but even by the young and such people as otherwise took scarcely any active part in the spiritual life of the parish. All was preceded by days of special preparation. Not only were arrangements made for entertaining the visitors but, in the case of the Lord's people, there was a looking to God for the preparation of heart they wished for, as well as earnest prayer for the coming of the Spirit of God in power.

We shall allow Dr. Donald Munro, whose early spiritual nurture was amongst Christian people who had lived through and personally participated in such times of awakening, and who had seen something of their sunset glory himself, to describe the scene of a Highland Communion Sabbath service to us in two of his wonderfully moving paragraphs. They provide descriptions which could only have been written by one who was a deeply appreciative eyewitness, and was himself a participant in the solemn enjoyment of all that was taking place.

'Seldom could one witness a more inspiring sight than the immense concourse that assembled on a sacramental Sabbath in the days of the fathers. Under the canopy of heaven they met, in some wooded dell, at the famous 'Burn' of Ferintosh, on the grassy seashore, or on the hillside in some natural amphitheatre which seemed to have been created for the purpose. The very surroundings often seemed to lend impressiveness to the solemn service, for sometimes there was no sound to break the stillness which brooded over the secluded spot save the sighing of the gentle breeze, or the boom of the waves as they rolled on to the pebbly strand. In front of the preaching-tent stretched two long rows of Communion tables, with their snow-white linen, around which a dense mass of people, sometimes amounting to several thousands, sat. The picturesque appearance of the vast gath-

ering might appeal to the superficial observer, for some of the
venerable-looking men were attired in blue cloaks, and others had
wraps and plaids of various shades, while over the caps of elderly
matrons were large muslin kerchiefs.

'At the appointed hour, generally 11 o'clock, the presiding
minister entered the tent. He was generally one of the most outstanding preachers in the north, for as a rule only men of weight and
experience, such as Dr. Angus MacIntosh, Mr. Kennedy, Killearnan,
and Dr. MacDonald, were asked to preach the Gaelic Action. This
was what the sermon prior to the participation in Communion, was
called and, generally, it dwelt on some aspect of the atonement. The
preacher came direct from the ivory palaces of secret communion,
and the fragrance which accompanied him was diffused around. The
very reading of the opening Psalm had a subduing effect on the
assembled thousands, while the singing of it to one of their plaintive
melodies, led by a choice precentor as the leader of the praise was
called, was most thrilling. The prayer which followed, so fervent and
unctuous, found a response in many a contrite heart. It must have been
a most cheering sight which met the eye of the preacher as he stood
up to announce his text. An earnest, expectant look was depicted on
many a countenance, for not a few came there to hear a message from
God. The prayerful atmosphere which pervaded the congregation
was intense, and the preacher was conscious of it. From the very
beginning of the sermon, in which the glory of Christ's person and the
merits of his atoning sacrifice were treated with rare clearness,
fullness, and tenderness, the interest of the hearers was aroused; and
as the subject was unfolded their riveted attention showed how nice
[that is, precise] doctrinal distinctions and apt illustrations were
appreciated. But as the service proceeded, the breathless silence, the
awed look, the deep sigh, or the trickling tear indicated how profoundly the hearers were being impressed. Sometimes a wave of
emotion would pass over the congregation, under which they would
be bowed down as the ripe corn before the autumn breeze. At other
times, as the preacher became more absorbed in his theme, and rose,
as it were from peak to peak, in his upward flight, some in the
congregation were carried away in ecstasy of soul – the things of time
were receding, eternal things were so real that they felt as if trans-
ported to the very gates of heaven, and seemed to gaze through
shining vistas into the celestial city.'[23]

---

23. *Monthly Record*, November 1918, pp. 178,179.

There were times when the Communion services were very long as relays of believers came forward, sat at the long Communion table, and then rose to give way to another waiting group. Each 'table', or 'sitting', was spoken to in a 'pre-communion address' and then, having partaken, they were encouraged to faith and godliness in a 'post-communion' word of encouragement. Dr. Munro says that, 'an outstanding feature of the day's service was the concluding address, which followed the administration of the ordinance. That was a part of the day's duties in which many of the noted ministers of the north excelled. Most moving were the appeals to the unconverted, for they flowed from a glowing heart in a molten stream. Many of the Christians in Easter Ross in Disruption times (1843) could trace their first serious impressions to the concluding addresses of Dr. Angus MacIntosh.'[24]

8. Alexander MacLeod, Uig, and the Lewis Awakening of 1826

Alexander MacLeod was a native of Sutherland, being born in the Stoer area of Assynt and so entering into the rich spiritual heritage of these northern parts in which, as we have seen, the gospel had been powerfully at work for upwards of 160 years before his birth in the year 1786. His mother was a very godly woman and he was reared in a home where the fellowship of godly people was always warmly welcomed. His conversion to Christ took place while he was still only fifteen years of age, and he traced it back to a sermon preached by the Rev Charles Calder of Ferintosh. It is on this he reflects as he writes, 'Remember the feast you had in Dingwall, on a sacrament occasion, when you could not deny that you got Benjamin's portion of 300 pieces of silver and five changes of raiment.'[25]

Earning his livelihood for some years in crofting and fishing, he eventually heard, and heeded, the call of God to the ministry and to that end took up study in Aberdeen in 1808. On completing his education he was licensed as a ministerial probationer in 1818 and ordained and inducted as minister of the Gaelic Chapel, Dundee, in 1819. From there he moved in 1821 to the parish of Cromarty. He then received and accepted a presentation to the parish of Uig in Lewis, and was inducted to the Charge on the 21st April, 1824.

---

24. *Ibid,* p. 179.
25. *Memoirs and Sermons of the Rev. Alexander MacLeod,* p. 5.

That date was to go down in the spiritual annals of Lewis, for Alexander MacLeod was to prosecute a powerful and wonderfully fruitful evangelistic ministry in the Island over the following fifteen years and, as a result, it was never to be quite the same again. A new day had dawned in its history. He left Lewis for Lochalsh and after seven years there, in 1846, was called to Rogart, a parish in his native county of Sutherland, where he died on 13th November 1869 at the age of 83, after 50 years in the ministry of the gospel.

On his arrival in Uig he was the first evangelical minister the people had known and he found them, although for the greater part in church membership, sunk in gross spiritual darkness. On the first occasion of observing the Communion he noticed that practically every person in the parish, irrespective of belief or behaviour, sat freely at the Lord's Table, and became profoundly disturbed at such an unbiblical state of affairs. So deficient in spiritual knowledge and saving experience did he find his parishioners, despite their public profession of being followers of Christ, that he took quite drastic measures to try and jolt them into an awareness of their true condition. He deferred the observing of the Lord's Supper in the parish for two years and began to preach sermons on the necessity of regeneration and true godliness. His pulpit emphasis became very specifically and specially evangelistic and, it appears, he was especially gifted at this type of preaching. Gradually at first, and then more frequently, he began to see people becoming very deeply moved under the gospel message and in about two years' time he found himself in the midst of a great spiritual movement.

When next the Lord's Supper was observed amongst his people, matters stood very differently. By then his preaching of righteousness, his emphasis on the need of the new birth, and his powerful expositions of the doctrine of justification by faith in Christ alone had, under the blessing of God's Holy Spirit, revolutionised the spiritual values and the religious perspectives of almost all in his parish. On this occasion, so great was the change that only six people came forward to sit at the Communion table though he judged that, by then, many more were truly converted and should have been there. Such were the beginnings of a spiritual Awakening in the Island of Lewis which has persisted, in ebbs and flows, until the present day.

9

John Knox – Preacher of the Word

There is little doubt that John Knox was best known to his generation as a preacher. There is equally little doubt that in his own view preaching was his divine calling in life and for that reason had primacy of place in his order of priorities. A high view of the proclamation of the gospel has characterised all the great preachers of the Christian era. No matter how they may differ in other respects they have all, without exception, been convinced that, under God, the preaching of his Word is the most influential and dynamic factor in the spiritual transformation of men and their times. Knox had that essential ingredient for a preacher from the time he first set foot in a pulpit and it never seemed to forsake him.

Two flashes of his thought have come down to us which illustrate how other things, important enough in themselves, were always subordinated to his preaching. The first is in the preface of one of the few sermons he actually had printed himself:

> Considering myself rather called of my God to instruct the ignorant, comfort the sorrowful, confirm the weak, and rebuke the proud, by tongue and lively voice in those most corrupt days, than to compose books for the age to come; seeing that so much is written (and by men of most singular erudition) and yet so little well observed, I decreed to contain myself within the bounds of that vocation, whereunto I found myself specially called.[1]

The other is a little phrase which was constantly on his lips and came frequently from his pen and betrays, in a quite unselfconscious way, how preaching was a passion that mastered this man; it also inspired the happily chosen title of one of the best

---

This article is taken from the November 1987 issue of *The Reformed Theological Journal* (published annually by the Reformed Presbyterian Church of Ireland).
1. John Knox, *Works*, ed. D. Laing, 1864, VI, p. 229. Cf. also John Knox's *History of the Reformation in Scotland*, Croft Dickinson's 1949 ed., ii, 159-60.

biographies of Knox to appear in recent years, W. Stanford Reid's, *Trumpeter of God*. The phrase? 'I love tae blaw my Maister's Trumpet'. In a very real sense this tells us everything about Knox's view of preaching. Like another great preacher called John, he regarded himself as just a 'voice crying'. He was merely the instrument of vocalising, sounding forth, trumpeting the message entrusted to him by God.

Commenting on Knox's strong sense of calling and linking it into this theme, Stanford Reid writes:

It runs throughout his life and work from the time he entered the ministry at the insistence of the congregation in St. Andrews until his death some twenty-five years later. He believed that he was called in the same way Jeremiah and Amos, his two favourite prophets, were commissioned to bring God's word to Israel. He was to blow the trumpet in Zion, summoning men back to repentance and faith in Jesus Christ as Saviour and Lord. This was his chief purpose in life.[2]

The thesis of this short study, and what it seeks to illustrate, is that this attitude, this passionate attachment and total commitment to preaching and to what preaching alone can achieve, provides the real key to understanding Knox as a man, a Christian and a Reformer. To underestimate this aspect of Knox's life, his work, his character or even just to ignore it, is to get all the other events and achievements completely out of focus. Knox, of course, as we are being continually reminded by writers of this century, was only human. But he was also regenerate. And while regenerate humanity is not yet perfect, we believe that his regeneration and his conversion to a lively faith in Christ was the main factor in his magnificent achievements in various fields and to all of these his preaching and his passion for it made the single greatest contribution.

Something else is worth noting on the threshold of our study. When we stand back from the theories and the themes, the misconceptions and the distortions that have gathered around this great man – who has been spoken of as vain, inconsistent, uxorious, and a jackal[3] on the one hand, and on the other, described as

---

2. W. Stanford Reid, *Trumpeter of God*, 1982 ed. by Baker, Preface xiv.
3. See, for example, G. Donaldson, 'Knox the Man' in *John Knox: A Quarter-Century Reappraisal*, ed. Duncan Shaw, pp. 18ff.

'the one person as "God's trumpeter" who seemed capable of maintaining and strengthening the morale of the forces which were seeking to make the Reformation (in Scotland) successful'[4], when historical events are allowed to speak for themselves, then Knox's preaching gifts must be acknowledged as equally impressive with those of any of the great preachers of history. What he accomplished by preaching testifies that he was superbly equipped for the great task to which his Master called him.

A final factor to bear in mind as we go into our theme is that it was in the role of preacher that Knox emerged as one of the key figures in the Reformation process, not merely in the narrow focus of obscure little Scotland but on the wide spectrum of a much broader scene. His greatness as a preacher has to be estimated not only within a Scottish but a European context. And right across that broader front it is quite clear that his preaching left a strong impress upon the people and the events of his time. It was as a preacher that his many hundreds of converts and his various congregations admired him, and it was as a preacher that his enemies and opponents feared him most. And the fervour with which he was either admired or feared attests one thing; the preaching of Knox was a power to be reckoned with!

A Neglected Field

Over against what has been said so far, it seems strangely anomalous that Knox's preaching is the very thing with which, today, we are least familiar and to which his best biographers have paid but scanty attention. Why should this be so?

While there may be very complex reasons behind this anomaly those which immediately strike one are, in fact, very simple and straightforward. The first to mention is that any detailed study or analysis of Knox's preaching power and his splendid gifts of evangelism labours under the disadvantage that there are very few of his sermons in print. The writer who would study Knox's exegetical techniques, or his expository flair, or his sermonic structures has little to work with. The difficulty this poses is not small, and it has daunted many.

The fact is, though, that this difficulty is not insurmountable. We are aware that with any of the great preachers of the past the

---

4. *Trumpeter of God*, p. 289.

influence exercised, to a very large degree, belonged only to the transitory moment and, from one point of view, evaporated when the preacher's voice was stilled. All students of the subject would acknowledge that even verbatim reporting seldom captures the power and the thrill that accompany the hearing of truly great preaching. That kind of preaching has a dimension to it, a chemistry in it, which cannot be transferred to the permanence of writing. Yet, what has been written about such preaching, and especially its spiritual and moral effects upon men and its power to uplift and ennoble life, has reached down through time and impressed its reality upon following ages. So too, with John Knox. True, it is not now possible to recapture what is spoken of as a marvellous deep, melodious voice, nor the clarity of tone in its constantly changing register, nor the flow and fire of felt emotion and conviction, the energy of a lively delivery that drew eye as well as ear; all the factors that made his preaching a crowd-puller and a life-transforming power on the European scene of his day – these are all things we can only guess at now. But the effects and fruits assure us that they were there and that they were there in singular and unusual measure. Indeed it is all the greater tribute to Knox that, isolated from the eloquence which loomed so large with his contemporaries and of which we have but an echo, the memoranda which we do have of his sermons mark him as a man rarely gifted in the use of language and a preacher with the gift of making the truth he was handling relevant and practical to people in their present need. He was a masterly expositor and adept in the use of lively metaphor and luminous illustration.

Another factor making for difficulty in the study of Knox as preacher is the spread of his interests and the scope of his work. He was richly and variously gifted and he influenced so many spheres of life that they have clamoured for, and claimed, the attention of many of his biographers. For example, he was a statesman of no mean order and has been described by one of his better biographers, Jasper Ridley, as a 'consummate politician'. In this area, his interaction with Mary, Queen of Scots, while it has been grossly overworked by hacks and historians alike, is a testimony to his influence in matters of State as well as the Church. His administrative abilities were of a high order and his comprehensive grasp of biblical principles – as well as his experiences in

Geneva and France – help us pinpoint him as the man who laid down the lines along which the Presbyterian policy of the Scottish Reformed Church was to be developed. His thought and even his language are clearly reflected in the *Scots Confession* as well as in the *First Book of Discipline*.

Earlier writers on Knox clearly felt that preaching was the real place of his strength, his pulpit his throne, his biblical message the sceptre of his power. He has a central place in the Scottish Reformation, for example, in the thought of Dr. Thomas McCrie, and in that place his preaching power is paramount. Speaking of Knox's return to Scotland in May 1559, McCrie writes:

> He arrived ... at a period when his presence was much required, and at a crisis for which his character was admirably adapted. Possessing firm and high-toned principle, the foundations of which were deeply laid in sincere piety and profound acquaintance with the Scriptures; endowed with talents of no common order, and an *eloquence popular and over-whelming* (italics ours!); ardent in his feelings, indefatigable in his exertions, daring and dauntless in his resolutions, John Knox was the man, and almost the only man of his time, who seemed to be expressly designed by the hand of Providence for achieving the lofty and adventurous enterprise to which he now consecrated himself, spirit, and soul, and body.[5]

This is a side of the Reformer that has been largely lost sight of and it is good to recapture the perspective that this great student of Knox had. But at the same time it illustrates that, for men like McCrie, Knox's pulpit power was a self-evident truth which required no special or lengthy exposition or defence.

A great shift has taken place since McCrie's day. Preaching as such, and even the gospel that is preached, have all been thrown into the melting pot and, in the absence of the framework of biblical authority within which Knox operated and by which his work for more than two centuries was evaluated, subjective rationalism and unbelief have been unable to do much but shunt it aside as unimportant or irrelevant. This has meant that the basic criteria for a just estimate of the man, his character and his achievements have been left out of the picture. Not only so, but a positive element of distortion has inevitably crept into the process. Writers who

5. *Sketches of Church History*, Edin., ed. 1846, Vol. 1, pp. 55-56.

have been deeply, sometimes bitterly, prejudiced against Knox's views of Scripture and his doctrines of sin and salvation have allowed that bitterness to spill over into attack on the man himself.

Any interpretation of Knox which fails to come to grips with his preaching does the man an injustice. It was preaching that was the source of his power among men and that preaching was based upon the conviction that the Bible was God's Word and the gospel of Christ was a message of good news for men to hear. These are the elements in Knox which, under God, brought great crowds of his fellow-sinners out of gross darkness and into the marvellous light of the gospel. This man's preaching reshaped the beliefs of the Scottish Church along the lines of biblical Christianity. It transformed the faith of his nation and did so because it transformed the lives of so many individuals in that nation. We must not lose sight of the fact that he is at the centre, not merely of a reforming of doctrine and belief, but of a powerful spiritual revival. And revivals that have had lasting influences on the spiritual life of a nation or people, as this one did, have always had great preachers at the heart of the movement.

The Evidence of Contemporary Events

If the material for a detailed analysis of Knox's preaching is sparse, there is still a field of evidence available to us from which we can assess his preaching power by its effects. While all that we know of great moments and achievements related to his preaching cannot be looked at here, we can turn to one or two specific instances which illustrate the more general pattern.

(a) The First Public Sermon

This was preached, probably about the end of April 1547, in the Parish Church of St. Andrews.[6] High views on the calling of a preacher left him, like many other great preachers, slow to mount the pulpit steps. He was long in coming to his kingdom in the matter of preaching. Dating his birth at 1513-14[7] he was over thirty before he or anyone else – and he less than others! – suspected that preaching God's Word was his true vocation in life.

---

6. Cf. *Trumpeter of God*, p. 47.
7. Cf. *Knox*, Jasper Ridley, Appendix 1, pp. 531 ff., W. Stanford Reid, *op. cit.* p. 15.

Two leaders of the castilians at St. Andrews, John Rough and Henry Balnaves, privately asked Knox to help the Reformed cause by taking a share of the preaching. His first reaction warms us to him; this is how he tells the story: 'But he utterly refused, alleging "That he would not run where God had not called him"; meaning, that he would do nothing without a lawful vocation.'[8]

The leaders then took fairly drastic steps. They arranged that Knox be called to the office of preaching at the close of a public service at which Rough preached on the election of ministers.[9] The result of this must have been as surprising to Rough and the congregation as it was embarrassing to Knox himself:

> Whereat the said John, abashed, burst forth in most abundant tears and withdrew himself to his chamber. His countenance and behaviour, from that day till the day he was compelled to present himself to the public place of preaching, did sufficiently declare the grief and trouble of his heart; for no man saw any sign of mirth of him, neither yet had he pleasure to accompany any man, many days together.[10]

This reflects the spiritual awe with which Knox regarded the work of preaching and to read into it as some writers have done evidences of physical fear or cowardice betrays a woeful ignorance of what the preaching of God's Word involves for those who accept it as divine revelation.[11] Great and solemn issues hang upon faithful declaration; the glory of God and the destiny of men are not matters to be taken lightly. To enter the pulpit, open the book, and speak to men in the Name of Christ was for Knox, as for every great preacher, a painful and costly business. Bautain speaks for such men when he writes:

> There is an oppression of the respiration, a weight on the chest, and a man experiences, in a fashion sometimes very burdensome, what has been felt by the bravest at the first cannon-shot. Many a time do I remember having found myself in this state at the moment for mounting the pulpit, and while waiting for my summons. Could I

---

8. *History,* i, p. 82.
9. Cf. *History*, i, p. 81 ff., *Trumpeter of God*, pp. 47 ff.
10. *History*, i. p. 83.
11. Cf, for example, Stanford Reid's mention of G. L. Warr's view, *op. cit.*, p. 47; and G. Donaldson, *op. cit.*

have fled away without shame, most assuredly I should have done
so.[12]

The truth of the matter is that Knox, like Moses before him,
shrank from a task that he never sought; it sought him. The writings
of men like Augustine and Calvin, Luther and Latimer, Whitefield
and Spurgeon, all illustrate for us the sort of doubts and fears
which must have crowded Knox through those days. Even an
apostle of Christ, appalled at the task to which God called him as
preacher, had to say, 'Who is sufficient for these things?' (2 Cor.
2:16). But Knox was to know, from the outset, the fact that Paul
also proved: the preacher's sufficiency is 'of God' (2 Cor. 3:5).

Preaching from Daniel 7:24,25, Knox excelled even in his first
sermon. Preached before the University faculty – which included
John Major, his fellow townsman and former Professor of Theology – as well as the castilians, the sermon seems to have had a
quite electrifying effect:

> Of this sermon ... were there diverse bruits (reports; rumours). Some
> said, 'Others sned (lopped) the branches of the Papistry, but he strikes
> at the root, to destroy the whole.' Others said, 'If the doctors, and the
> Magistri Nostri, defend not now the Pope and his authority, which in
> their own presence is so manifestly impugned, the Devil have my
> part of him, and his laws both.' Others said, 'Master George Wishart
> spake never so plainly, and yet was he burnt: even so will he be.'[13]

The sermon and the reaction to it both shed light on Knox, the
preacher. He refuted error directly from the Bible and his ultimate reliance on that authority gave his sermon a great ring of
conviction and himself the assurance that he spoke truth. He
stressed the doctrine of justification by faith in Christ alone and
maintained Christ as Saviour of God's people and spoke confi-
dently as one who had, himself, trusted in Christ and who regarded him as the true shepherd of the church. Above all, his time
in the pulpit and the reception given his preaching stilled all his
initial misgivings and never again, as Laing notes[14], did he seem
to question his calling. He had put his hand to the plough and not
once did he look back.

---

12. *Art of Extempore Speaking,* Eng. trans., p. 204.
13. *History,* i. p. 86.
14. Cf. Knox's Works, III, 14.

He never forgot the months of preaching in St. Andrews. The love of his calling had captivated his heart even then. The oft-quoted remark, made when ill and chained to the oar of a French galley as it lay off the Fife coast, gives another insight into his view of what preaching is. Asked by a companion if he knew the place, the weak Knox replied:

> Yes: I know it well; for I see the steeple of that place where God first in public opened my mouth to his glory, and I am fully persuaded, how weak that ever I now appear, that I shall not depart this life, till that my tongue shall glorify his godly name in the same place.[15]

(b) A Visit to Scotland

In 1555-56 Knox paid a visit to Scotland from Geneva, coming as a fugitive, with a price on his head. He found shelter in the homes of some of the nobles who had backed the Protestant cause, Erskine of Dun, the Earl of Argyll and some others. He found he says a situation he had never seen in Scotland before, a general thirst for the gospel. The power of the Spirit was at work and Knox moved from Lothian through to Angus in the East and Kyle in the West finding everywhere people willing to risk their lives in order to hear the gospel. Many must have been converted. He gives a touching account of one woman, Elizabeth Adamson, converted when she came to hear Knox preaching what he calls the 'Evangel of Jesus Christ' in East Lothian. He was giving an exposition of Psalm 103 when, as she expressed it later, 'Began my troubled soul first effectually to taste of the mercy of my God.' Shortly afterwards, an illness from which she did not recover overtook her. As she lay dying in Edinburgh, she was visited by priests with their ceremonies and superstitions and all ready to administer the last rites. 'Depart from me, ye sergents of Satan,' she said, as she began to testify what Christ had done for her soul. The priests departed, 'alleging that she raved and wist not what she said. And she shortly thereafter slept in the Lord Jesus, to no small comfort of those that saw her blessed departing. This we could not omit of this worthy woman.'[16]

This narrative assures us of a fact that is seldom brought out in

---

15. *History*, i. p. 109.
16. *Ibid*, p. 120.

the literature on Knox and which, even when his preaching power
is recognised, we allow to drop out of sight. This man was an
evangelist. He had a burden to see people converted and, when
they were, he rejoiced with them. His preaching aimed at instruction in the truths and doctrines of Scripture, and that instruction
was given so that, God working with him, men might be delivered from consciences burdened with the guilt of sin. In other
words, Knox preached for informed decision and intelligent commitment to the claims of Christ and he was thrilled when he saw
men and women turning away from unwarranted ceremonies of
an outward and empty kind, that did dishonour to Christ and a
disservice to men, to find inward peace and spiritual reality through
faith in the finished work of Christ.

(c) The Famous Sermon of Stirling

Knox finally returned to Scotland in May 1559 and things
immediately began to prosper for the Reformers. However, in the
autumn of that year there was a period when, forced out of
Edinburgh by the superior number of French troops, they had to
retreat to Stirling, a dejected and depressed group. Here we see
Knox at his very best as a preacher. As a number of historians
have remarked, 'he never showed up so well as when in the midst
of defeat, for he could point to the Congregation's (i.e. the
Reformed Church which was emerging) complete dependence on
God for victory.'

That was his theme when he arrived to preach in Stirling on
the 8 November 1559, to this dispirited group, and took his text
from Psalm 80:4-8. Let us listen to Dr. A. M. Renwick as he described what must have been a stirring scene:

> It was a sermon for that dismal day. Its effect was notable and was
> spoken of for long afterwards. Knox assured his depressed audience
> that, although they were being punished for former sins, if they turned
> sincerely to God their sorrow would be changed into joy, and their
> fear to boldness. Whatever became of them and their carcases, the
> cause of God would finally prevail in Scotland. Under the burning
> words of the preacher each man became heroic. Of a similar sermon,
> Randolph, the English ambassador, wrote to Cecil: 'The voice of
> one man is able in one hour to put more life in us than five hundred
> trumpets continually blustering in our ears.' Although darker times

were still to come the sermon at Stirling was a turning point in the history of the Reformation.[17]

The upshot of this powerfully uplifting sermon was that the lords promptly met and, after inviting Knox to lead them in prayer, they authorised William Maitland of Lethington, who had just recently joined the Congregation from the side of the Queen Regent, to go to London immediately to inform the English Queen and Council of the rather desperate state of affairs in Scotland. Knox himself tells us that this sermon picked up the unfinished exposition of Psalm 80 which he had begun preaching in St. Giles and he felt that there was a providential purpose to be seen in the fact that he was, in any case, next due to preach at verse 4 of the Psalm. This exposition of portions of Scripture in ongoing sequence was habitual with Knox, as with Calvin, and it was part of the preaching pattern and usage of Scripture that he bequeathed to the Scottish Church. The sermon is well structured as we can see from the fairly full account he gives of it.[18]

It is worth mentioning, in passing, that George Buchanan, in his *History* writes of the same occasion:

> There John Knox delivered to them a splendid address and stirred in the minds of many a certain expectation of soon emerging from these troubles.[19]

It is worth noting, in fact, that Buchanan, on each of the four occasions on which he mentions Knox in his history, does so in connection with his preaching and about explicit sermons. The great scholar and historian of the day had felt the power and sway of Knox's eloquence and regarded him as the power of the Scottish pulpit. In each case when he touches on the subject Buchanan used the complimentary, if somewhat vague, description, 'luculenta concio' (sparkling address).

General Effects Of his Preaching Power
One of the most critical elements in the evaluation of preaching is the kind of gospel it proclaims. That, in turn hinges on personal

---

17. A. M. Renwick, *Story of the Scottish Reformation,* IVF, 1960, p. 83.
18. Cf. *History,* i. pp. 265 ff.
19. *Rer. Scot. Historia,* Bk. XVI, c. 49.

faith and personal experience. From his conversion to Christ onwards he seems to have enjoyed a rich assurance of his own salvation and his standing 'in Christ'. His servant, Richard Bannatyne, revered Knox for his godliness, and servants get to know people well! His description of John Knox's deathbed scene (again, a stern test of godliness!) helps us estimate the powerful, experimental Christianity out of which the passionate gospel message flowed. When asked what Scripture he would have read as the end drew near he asked for John chapter 17 where, he said, 'I first cast my anchor.'

That anchor had held the soul of this man firmly through great storms and his soul must have found rest in its great truths throughout his life as well as in death. It provides proof that Knox did not drift into a merely intellectual acceptance of Reformed doctrine but that there was a definite spiritual experience, a definite decision that was linked into a particularly luminous part of gospel teaching. Its stress on the deity of Christ, his priesthood, and salvation through faith in his name – the themes of this chapter inform Knox's doctrine and his message and were continually sounded out in his letters as well as his preaching. From the moment he came to know Christ as Saviour, John Knox was a 'man with a message'. Every great preacher has been. It is one of the prerequisites of great gospel preaching.

His Recognition As A Preacher

John Knox cared about people as well as doctrine.[20] This concern must have found warm expression in his pulpit work and it made him a preacher sought out by 'troubled believers' as well as 'seeking sinners'. One simple, but highly significant, fact is frequently overlooked by his detractors in this very connection. Christian congregations just do not ask men who do nothing but harangue, or scold them endlessly, to be their regular preachers or permanent pastors. Knox, even when hunted from his own land, never lacked a pulpit of his own. Christians seldom become warmly attached to preaching that does not help them live out their faith. His preaching did that and he was never in any danger of becom-

---

20. Cf. 'John Knox Pastor of Souls', *Westminster Theological Journal;* Vol. XL. No. 1, p. 1 ff. A fine study of this aspect of Knox's work by Stanford Reid.

ing what in his own land is still known as a 'sticket minister', one
who never gets a call to a pastorate.

In his wanderings as a fugitive in other lands Knox was eagerly
sought after and held congregations in Berwick, Newcastle,
Frankfurt and Geneva and his preaching was always highly
acceptable and useful. He was for part of his time in England one
of only six royal chaplains when the English scene boasted some
notable preachers. And back home in Scotland, once the
Reformation was established in 1560, he filled the principal pulpit
in the Capital where he exercised the most influential spiritual
ministry of the decade.

Preparation And Practice In Preaching

All his days Knox was a diligent student. In his letters he sometimes describes himself as 'sitting at his books' and as studying
the gospel by the help of the Fathers 'and among the rest Chrys-
ostom'. He had a competent knowledge of Greek and learned Hebrew during his years in Geneva. He never wrote out his sermons
but obviously studied them very carefully, as is witnessed by the
fact that he could reproduce their substance days and even years
after they had been preached. We learn from an incidental remark
in his 'Admonition to England' that his method was to speak from
a few notes made on the margin of his Bible.[21] The framework of
his sermon was thought out beforehand and, from his own memoranda as well as the reports of others, he clearly had premeditated
the precise words by which he would express his thoughts.

The one sermon he did print was written out thirteen days after
it had actually been preached. Relations between the Reformers
and Mary had been strained by her marriage to Darnley. Knox
was preaching one day on Isaiah 26:13-20, and his application of
the truth angered Darnley considerably. Gossip exaggerated
Knox's comments and twisted his meaning (as it does still!) and
to show that Darnley's objections and the Council's talk of treason
were all unjustified the sermon was printed. It provides standing
proof that Knox was not a 'rabble rouser' but a careful, if vivid,
preacher of biblical truth.

As minister of St. Giles he regularly preached twice every Lord's
Day and gave three 'lectures', as they were called, on weekdays.

---

21. Cf. Laing's Knox, iii, pp. 257-330

He met with his elders every week for the oversight of the flock and also met with the other city ministers every week for what he called 'the exercise on the Scriptures'. Add to all this the fact that there were constant demands for his preaching in other parts of the country and it is clear that he was a busy man. Little wonder that his people gave him a colleague to help him in 1563.

It was, perhaps, his time as a slave in the French galley *Nostre Dame* that left his French fluent enough to use as a medium for the powerful preaching of his gospel. His remarkable work in Dieppe for the weeks he waited there in the spring of 1559 would, in itself, mark the man as a preacher on whom God had his hand in a very special way. The work of G. and J. Daval,[22] published in 1878, sheds light on this episode of a brilliant preaching career:

> On February 19th (1559) there arrived in Dieppe the Sieur Jean Knox, Scotsman, a very learned man who had been received as a pastor in England in the time of Edward VI ... and preached at Dieppe for the space of six or seven weeks. He achieved a great result, and the number of the faithful (believers, converts) grew in such degree that they dared to preach in full day; whereas till this time they had only dared to go (to sermon) during the night.[23]

The astonishing blessing of this visit comes home to us when we learn that, a month after his departure, from six to eight hundred people celebrated the Lord's Supper in the Reformed way and that in 1562 no fewer than twelve pastors were being requested from Geneva for the needs of the Protestant cause in Dieppe.

As well as preaching in French, Knox preached in *English*! It is eloquent of his view of the importance of the gospel, and of the unity of the church that he preached and wrote, not in his own broad, Scottish accents but in the English of his day. He was even twitted with this fact by Winram and others but it speaks volumes for his basic, spiritual concern for men of all nations that he used language as a means of communication for winning them to Christ, refusing to let it become a barrier to the work he had so much at heart. Preaching was paramount.

Let the final picture in our study of Knox the preacher be taken from the sphere in which he most frequently and wonderfully

---

22. *Histoire do la Reformation a Dieppe.*
23. Cf. P. Hume Brown, i, pp. 218-219.

exercised his consecrated talents and the influence with which
they filled his preaching days, the pulpit. It comes to us from the
very scene of his first preaching, a pulpit in the university town of
St. Andrews, and from the pen of a student who, himself, was to
make a mark on the Scottish religious scene, James, nephew of
the more famous Andrew Melville. The picture belongs to 1571,
the year before Knox's death. Knox was not old, just around fifty-
eight. But he was worn, and ill, and getting so frail in body that he
had to be helped into the pulpit. But frail and ill though he was,
the maestro could still sound his 'Master's Trumpet' with its bugle-
notes of warning, its stern call to battle and its silvery, winsome
melody of salvation through faith in Christ. He sounded it that
day with powerful and dramatic effect. This is the quaint, but
lively and vivid description of Melville:

> I haid my pen and my little book, and took away sic things as I could
> apprehend. In the opening up of his text he was moderate the space
> of an half-hour; but when he enterit to application, he made me sa to
> grew (shudder) and tremble that I could nocht hold a pen to write ...
> or he haid done with his sermont, he was sa active and vigorous that
> he was like to ding (strike) that pulpit in blads and fly out of it.[24]

This is a picture of a man who has been mastered by the gospel he
is preaching. It fires his mind, moves his heart and animates his
whole body. Let another great preacher of our own era, who knew
the same gospel and had a similar passionate commitment to it,
impress upon us what is really happening here:

> his great characteristic as a preacher was vehemency. Great preach-
> ers are generally vehement; and we should all be vehement. This is
> not the result of nature only; it arises from the feeling of the power of
> the gospel. Vehemence is, of course, characterised by power; and
> John Knox was a most powerful preacher, with the result that he was
> a most influential preacher.[25]

On 14 February 1570 Knox preached the Regent Moray's
funeral sermon from the text: Blessed are the dead which die in

---

24. *Melville's Diary.* pp. 26, 33.
25. D. M. Lloyd-Jones, *The Puritans. Their Origins and Successors,*
Banner of Truth, 1987, p. 266.

the Lord (Rev. 14:13). 'He moved,' writes Calderwood, 'three thousand people to tears.' Whether he mentioned the closing phrase of that text the great historian does not tell us. But, without doubt they, also are true of this man – Scotland's greatest preacher – 'Yea saith the Spirit, that they may rest from their labours; and their works do follow them.'

10

CALVIN, GENEVA, AND CHRISTIAN MISSION

As the sun sank over Geneva on Saturday, 27th May, 1564, another occurrence was to give this daily happening a striking and strongly symbolic significance; John Calvin died in the city which, although only his by adoption, is forever linked with his name.

It was of the coincidence of these two events that Theodore Beza, Calvin's friend and biographer as well as his theological colleague and successor, made imaginative use as he pointed out the significance to the whole Reformed movement of Calvin's removal from the scene.

> Thus in the same moment that day the sun set and the greatest light which was in this world, for the direction of the church of God, was withdrawn to Heaven. We can well say that with this single man it has pleased God, in our time, to teach us the way both to live well and to die well.[1]

This high evaluation of Calvin's importance to his times is no empty eulogy. No matter how men may appraise his work, there is absolutely no questioning his significance for the theological world of his own day and since. Nor is the tribute to his example in life and death merely the hollow compliment of friendly kindness. Few men have been so single-mindedly industrious as Calvin. Fewer still have achieved so much in a lifetime, despite the fact that he died almost two months before his fifty-fifth birthday. If faith in God, commitment to Christ, compassion for one's fellow and a massive commitment to spiritual enlightenment are factors to be weighed in assessing what it is to 'live well', then Beza was right; Calvin *did* live well.

Beza was also right when he said that Calvin died well. Death

---

This article is taken from the November 1989 issue of *The Reformed Theological Journal*.

1. Theodore do Beze, *Vie do Calvin,* in *Calvini Opera,* XXI, 45. Cf. also *The History and Character of Calvinism,* (Oxford, 1953; Galaxy Paper, 1967) by John T. McNeill, p. 277.

had come slowly, lingeringly, painfully. Rumours of his dying had been filtering out of Geneva for months. However, although plagued by a fearsome catalogue of illnesses, and terribly enfeebled in body from the beginning of the year, his mind had remained sharp and clear, his confidence in God strong and sure. He had worked to the last and, until death came, his concern was for the cause in which he had spent his years and his strength. His final statements on the Christian faith and directions for the Christian Church are in perfect harmony with those which characterise his entire Christian profession and are shot through, not merely with warm devotion to God, but with a driving concern for the good of the whole Reformed constituency and the furtherance of the gospel.

That Calvin was deeply committed to spreading the truths he believed should not seem strange to any of us. What may startle us is the thought that such commitment invites attention to him in the rather unexpected, and largely unexplored, role of evangelist. An upsurge of scholarly interest in this aspect of his work at Geneva has taken place over recent years and has produced some fascinating details of his accomplishments in the sphere of evangelism. The emerging picture kindles a new awareness of his place in the history of Christian missions and exhibits his work in Geneva as one of the finest examples of effective outreach in the history of the Church. This, in turn, calls for a fresh evaluation of his theological perspectives and, in some areas, a radical review of various interpretations and misrepresentations of the man and his actual beliefs.

Calvin's Theology and its Motivation to Mission

The problems with which Calvin had to grapple over the closing months of his life touched many lands, but those of one specific country took particular prominence for him, as they had done for many years. This was France, his own homeland. Right up until the end, Calvin kept receiving information about, and commenting upon, political happenings there. To the end his advice was sought by, and given to, the Protestants of France on how to cope with a situation which, in Church and State, was becoming increasingly intolerant of their life and witness. These concerns of a dying man prompt questions about how they became part of his life and why they weighed so heavily on his mind even in the face of death. The search for an answer leads directly to his theology.

It was in 1536 that the first edition of Calvin's great theological work, *The Institutes of the Christian Religion*, was published. The work provided a clear presentation of Reformed doctrine, linked it back into the writings of the early church fathers, and showed that all its leading tenets were drawn from Scripture. It also carried a powerful apologetic in defence of the historic Christian faith. The apologetic aim is seen in the way Calvin dedicated the book in his introductory preface. It is couched in the form of a powerful plea to the King of France – Francis I – on behalf of the persecuted believers in the land.

With its appearance, French Protestants were given a measured and meticulous exposition of their faith by which to refute misrepresentation and misconception; they were also provided with a handbook from which to evangelise and instruct others in the doctrines of biblical Christianity. The appearance of the book in this format, and at this juncture, alerts us to the fact that Calvin's work, even at this early stage of his life, was already deeply enmeshed with the spiritual welfare of his own countrymen.

This concern for mission has been overlooked in the traditions which have encrusted – and too often calcified around – the study of Calvin's life; mission has far too frequently been assumed to be absent because banished by the force of theological necessity. Dr. P. E. Hughes reflects the position accurately, even if he states it starkly:

> As for Calvin's theology, we are all familiar with the scornful rationalisation that facilely asserts that his horrible doctrine of divine election makes nonsense of all missionary and evangelistic activity.[2]

Here, Dr. Hughes highlights the truth that there has been a long-standing failure to appreciate, far less assess accurately, Calvin's conviction about or his involvement in missions because of a distorted view of his theology.

This failure traces back, in too many instances, to preconceived ideas about the man and his actual teaching. The notion has prevailed, and still does with people who do not read their Calvin

2. P. E. Hughes, 'John Calvin: Director of Missions', in *The Heritage of John Calvin*, J. Bratt, ed. (Grand Rapids 1973); p. 42.

directly, that his theology axiomatically excluded him and his fellow ministers in Geneva from having any concern about, or interest in, a theology of mission. This conception runs counter to the historical facts and to entertain it is to misread both the situation at Geneva and the theology which inspired its circumstances.

Another writer, David B. Calhoun, very cogently summarises the imbalance which has crept into the historical assessment of Calvin's theology and practice at this very point:

> The whole issue has been dismissed at times by the facile assertion that Calvin's doctrine of divine election makes nonsense of all missionary and evangelistic activity. At other times it has been misunderstood or distorted because of lack of a full definition of missions and the failure to study comprehensively both Calvin's missionary teaching and activity.[3]

His assessment is all too factual, and accentuates the need to subject this construction of Calvin's doctrine of election to careful analysis. Is it the case that Calvin construed his theology in such a way as to obviate any necessity of or obligation towards mission, because the elect would be brought into the Kingdom anyway? Careful and sympathetic scrutiny of his own writing, and intimate acquaintance with his enormously energetic activity, should have made it perfectly plain that this was never Calvin's own view of the matter. A systematic theologian *par excellence*, as all historians and theologians who have studied him allow, he is acknowledged as the outstanding systematiser of Reformed theology. His reputation here should alert us to the danger of assuming that he would easily fall into the one-sided view of this central doctrine which has so frequently been credited to him.

The fact is that comprehensive analysis of his own writings compels a very different opinion. For example, they articulate the continual danger of the church, or of individuals, becoming complacent about evangelism precisely because of a wrong conception of this very article of the faith. He teaches that, since no man knows who the elect are, preachers must take it for granted that God wills all to be saved.[4] In practice, that must be the prin-

---

3. *Presbuterion:* Volume V, No. 1, Spring 1979, p. 16.
4. Calvin holds that the gospel call embraces all men, but is made effectual only to the elect. He writes: Did God not, at the very time when he

ciple upon which the ministry of the Word operates.[5] Election
belongs to a special category, the secret purpose of God, not to
the evangelistic activity of the church, which has no way of dis-
tinguishing between elect and reprobate. The church must preach
the gospel to men, not as elect, but as sinners;[6] for it is one's
believing response to the free offer of Christ in the gospel which
reveals one's election.[7] Further, God opens doors before the church

---

is verbally exhorting all to repentance, influence the elect by the secret
movement of his Spirit, Jeremiah would not say, 'Turn thou me, and I
shall be turned; for thou art the Lord my God. Surely after that I was
turned I repented.' ... let us now see whether there by any inconsistency
between the two things – viz. that God, be an eternal decree, fixed the
number of those whom he is pleased to embrace in love, and on whom
he is pleased to display his wrath, and that he offers salvation indis-
criminately to all. I hold that they are perfectly consistent, for all that is
meant by the promise is, just that his mercy is offered to all who desire
and implore it, and this none do, save those whom he has enlightened
(*Institutes*, III: 24:16 and 17; E. T. of H. Beveridge, Vol. 2, p. 256,
London 1957), cf. also his following discussion re the will of God and
his assertion: though to our apprehension the will of God is manifold,
yet he does not in himself will opposites.

5. *Op. cit.* Vol. 2, pp. 221-22. Calvin writes: Some object that God would
be inconsistent with himself, in inviting all without distinction while he
elects only a few. Thus, according to them, the universality of the promise destroys the distinction of special grace .... The mode in which Scripture reconciles the two things – viz. that by preaching all are called to
faith and repentance, and that yet the Spirit of faith and repentance is not
given to all – I have already explained .... How then can it be said, that
God calls while he knows that the called will not come? Let Augustine
answer for me: 'Would you dispute with me? Wonder with me and explain, O the depth! Let us let us both agree in dread, lest we perish in
error.'

6. He draws special attention to, and quotes with approval, Augustine's
telling comment: 'Because we know not who belongs to the number of
the predestinated, or does not belong, our desire ought to be that all may
be saved; and hence every person we meet, we will desire to be with us
a partaker of peace.' *Op. cit.* Vol. 2, p. 238.

7. Calvin writes: In regard to the elect, we regard calling as the evidence
of election. *Op. cit.* III:21:7. Vol. 2 p. 211. The same interconnection

that the gospel might go into all the world so that his elect may hear it and respond in faith.[8]

The paradox between election and the free offer of the gospel – a paradox of which he is, of course, sharply aware – is never an embarrassment to his exegesis and his handling of Scripture. For example, in his comment on John 3:16, he says:

> God has employed the universal term *whosoever*, both to invite all indiscriminately to partake of life, and to cut off every excuse from unbelievers. Such is also the import of the term *world*, which he formerly used; for though nothing will be found in the world that is worthy of the favour of God, yet he shows himself to be reconciled to the whole world, when he invites all men without exception to the faith of Christ, which is nothing else than an entrance into life.[9]

This is typical of the way in which he leaves the free offer completely unfettered. He is utterly confident that the preaching of the gospel will accomplish the divine purpose and that, through the gospel call being made powerful and effective by God, it will bring the elect to saving faith in Christ. However, he normally spells out the obverse implications of effectual calling as well, and his comment on this verse continues:

> Let us remember, on the other hand, that while *life* is promised universally to *all who believe* in Christ, still faith is not common to all. For Christ is made known and held out to the view of all, but the

---

between election and calling is in view, also, when he writes: 'Then, if we doubt whether we are received into the protection of Christ, he obviates the doubt when he spontaneously offers himself as our shepherd, and declares that we are of the number of his sheep if we hear his voice (John 10:3, 16). Let us, therefore, embrace Christ, who is kindly offered to us, and comes forth to meet us: he will number us among his flock, and keep us within his fold' p. 245.

8. '... where an opportunity presents itself of edifying, let us consider that by the hand of God a door is opened to us for introducing Christ there, and let us not withhold compliance with so kind an indication from God' (*Commentary on 2 Corinthians*, E. T. by J. Pringle, Edinburgh, 1849, ch. 2:12; cf. also, his comments on 1 Corinthians 16:9).

9. *Commentary on John*. E. T. Wm. Pringle, The Calvin Translation Society, (Edinburgh. 1847).

elect alone are they whose eyes God opens, that they may seek him
by faith.[10]

This makes clear that vocation harmonises with, and is dictated
by, election but that the latter does not circumscribe the freeness,
nor impugn the integrity, of the gospel invitation to men as sinners. This is, in fact, the force of his comment on the opening
phrase of the next verse, *For God sent not his Son into the world
to condemn the world.*

> He came not to destroy; and therefore it follows that *all who believe*
> may obtain salvation by him. There is now no reason why any man
> should be in a state of hesitation, or of distressing anxiety, as to the
> manner in which he may escape death, when we believe that it was
> the purpose of God that Christ should deliver us from it. The word
> *world* is again repeated, that no man should think himself wholly
> excluded, if he only keep the road of faith.[11]

This fine, biblical, balance runs all through his writings and
his theology of election was held in such a way that he felt bound
to work and witness for the salvation of others with all his strength.
While mission is God's work, it is also ours and we must be faithful in our prosecution of it. The desire for, and opportunity of,
sending preachers into other nations is an argument and pledge of
the love of God:

> Therefore, there is no question but that God doth visit that nation
> where his gospel is preached ... the gospel doth not fall down, and,
> as it were, by chance, like rain out of the clouds, but is brought by
> the hands (and the ministry of men) whither it is sent from above.[12]

Calvin believed that the church must faithfully discharge the
commission to go 'into the world' with the gospel. In one of his
sermons he says:

> ... it is not enough for every man to occupy himself in the service of
> God; but our zeal must extend further, to the drawing of other men

---

10. *Ibid.*
11. *Ibid.*
12. Commentary on Romans; 10:15; E. T. Ed. H. Beveridge (Edinburgh,
1844).

thereto .... We must as much as lieth in us endeavour to draw all men on earth unto God ....[13]

Calvin and his fellow pastors in Geneva had strong convictions about God being the sovereign Creator of all things and these also informed their attitudes towards and promotion of mission. Against the gnostic and mystic strands of teaching which persisted into the sixteenth century, Calvin taught that God had not abandoned creation nor the world he had made. The opposite was true. God loved the work of his own hands and although evil had invaded it he would not absolve himself of concern nor allow it to remain forever alienated from himself. Not only mercy, grace and love but also righteousness, justice and holiness dictated that sin and evil must be dealt with. Calvin's teaching on redemption does have a particularistic and individual orientation: no one can doubt that. But it also has a comprehensive, cosmic thrust that should not be overlooked:

> God will restore the world, now fallen with mankind, into perfection ... let us be content with this simple doctrine, that there shall be such a temperature, and such a decent order, that nothing shall appear either deformed or ruinous.[14]

In the view of Professor Standford Reid, a scholar who has given powerful stimulus to the study of Calvin and mission, this specific ingredient in Calvin's thought had a powerful influence on our theme:

> In order to understand the missionary endeavours of Calvin and the Genevan Church, we must first of all comprehend the theological motivation which lay behind much of their effort to spread as widely as possible the teachings of the reformers. Basic to all their thinking was the doctrine of creation. The sovereign God has made all things, and they are, therefore, his. And although through man's sin, alienation has taken place, it is the responsibility of those who are God's people to bring creation back to him. This is the mission of the church until Christ's return in glory.[15]

---

13. See Calvin's sermon on Deuteronomy 33:18, 19.
14. Commentary on Romans 8:21.
15. W. Stanford Reid, *The Reformed Theological Review*, Vol. 42; No. 3; 1983, p. 65.

Calvin's Preaching and its Inspiration to Mission

Calvin not only taught that God had elected a people who should be saved but that he had also appointed the means by which their salvation would be effected. The focal point of grace was, of course, Christ in the glory of his person and the perfection of his work. But Christ must be made known and the means by which this was to be achieved was, chiefly, by a knowledge of God's Word; men must hear the Word; the gospel must be made known; this was the task of preaching: election, far from making gospel preaching a useless redundancy, ensured that it would lead to the very success at which all true preaching aims, the bringing of others into the kingdom of God and of Christ.

This was why he insisted that the visible church was of the utmost importance to the world and the spread of the gospel and why he asserted the primacy of preaching over against ritual and ceremony in the worship and activity of the church. He himself, of course, gave his strength to preaching as few men have ever done, considering it to be his main business in life.

Holding high views of preaching, it is not strange that he should place a premium upon the training of suitable men for the preaching of the word and the work of evangelism: 'the ordinary method of collecting a church,' he says, 'is by the outward voice of men; for though God might bring each person to himself by a secret influence, yet he employs the agency of men, that he may awaken in them an anxiety about the salvation of each other.'[16] Standford Reid links those emphases in Calvin's teaching with his magnificent achievements in training and sending out ministers and evangelists:

> With this pattern of thought, it is not surprising that Calvin and those with him, looked out upon the world around them with a strong sense of responsibility to the many people in neighbouring lands who were seeking .... Calls were constantly coming in for help ... those who were in the places of leadership in the Genevan church saw them as God's opening of a door before them .... Here was the mission placed at their hand, and to which they were prepared to respond with all their resources, both spiritual and material.[17]

16. Commentary on Isaiah 2:3.
17. *Op. cit.*, p. 66.

Calvin's City and its Contribution to Mission

During the years of Calvin's settled ministry in Geneva (1541-
1564), the Reformation was struggling for its very existence
throughout the lands of Europe. There was compelling need for
providing, and maintaining, properly trained workers to carry on
the task of spreading the gospel in France, the Netherlands, Germany, Hungary, the British Isles and other countries within reach.

Those needs were constantly being brought home to Calvin.
From the early 1540s onward, Geneva became a city of refuge for
the persecuted Protestants of other lands, and they flocked into it.
It is calculated that at some periods during the 40s and 50s, the
population (estimated at between 10,000 and 15,000) probably
doubled. Naturally enough, Calvin, himself a refugee from religious persecution, was tenderly sympathetic to people driven from
their homelands because of their religious beliefs. And of course,
in various ways Geneva benefited from their presence. Says Reid:

> Coming from very different countries and covering a wide social
> spectrum, they brought much new life and activity to Geneva.[18]

Amongst those who fled and found haven in Geneva were crowds
of Calvin's own countrymen. He was thus always deeply aware
of the religious and political situation in France and constant dealings with Christians from there must have whetted his concern
and maintained his aspiration for the nation's religious reform at
a consistently high pitch.

Calvin, however, saw his city as far more than a haven for
refugees. He realised the enormous potential of the situation for
preparing and sending out preachers and evangelists to the needy
lands around him – lands which he regarded, from the spiritual
aspect, as being 'fields white unto harvest'. Commenting on this
P. E. Hughes writes:

> ... it was also a school – 'the most perfect school of Christ which has
> been seen on earth since the days of the apostles,' according to the
> estimate of the great Scottish Reformer John Knox, who himself
> found refuge and schooling in Geneva. Here able and dedicated men,
> whose faith had been tried in the fires of persecution, were trained
> and built up in the doctrine of the gospel at the feet of John Calvin,
> the supreme teacher of the Reformation.[19]

---

18. *Ibid.* p. 67. 19. *Op. cit.*, p. 44.

That Calvin was fully alive to the doors of opportunity opened in this way, we can have no doubt. In a letter to Henry Bullinger, for example, he explicitly links Geneva and evangelistic mission when he writes:

> ... when I consider how very important this corner is for the propagation of the kingdom of Christ, I have good reason to be anxious that it should be carefully watched over ....[20]

This passionate concern that the gospel should reach out to the world from Geneva is reflected in a sermon on 1 Timothy 3:4:

> May we attend to what God has enjoined upon us, that he would be pleased to show his grace, not only to one city or a little handful of people, but that he would reign over all the world; that everyone may serve and worship him in truth.

Geneva was, geographically, superbly situated to be a training centre equipping evangelists for the Reformed Church in France. It was only through Geneva that Protestants could find a reasonably safe entrance into that country, ringed around as it was by Spain, Savoy, Lorraine and the Spanish Netherlands, all firmly under the control of strongly reactionary Romanist leaders.

Politically the city had a powerful military ally, the Republic of Berne, warding off fears of military intervention in its affairs. Within this city Calvin could set to work unhampered by too much outside interference; from it he could keep in touch with the rest of Europe:

> He was probably better informed about the religious and political affairs of his time than anyone else in Switzerland.[21]

At this centre men were trained and sent out into the lands of Europe. Most of the factual information about them, and especially about those trained for the work in France, comes to us from records which are available for only part of the period between 1541 and 1564. R. M. Kingdon, whose work with these

---

20. Bonnet. *Letters of John Calvin*, p. 227.
21. Harro Hopfel, *The Christian Polity of John Calvin* (London 1985), p. 140.

records has opened up this whole field of investigation within the last thirty years or so, says:

> In April 1555 the official Registers of the Company (of Pastors) for the first time listed missionaries formally dispatched.[22]

Obviously, records prior to this time were not retained for reasons of security. On this question of extant records P. E. Hughes reminds us:

> They were restricted, in the main, to the few years between 1555 and 1562 when it was felt that the names of those who were sent out from Geneva as missionaries might be recorded (though not advertised) with some degree of safety.[23]

We know that a very solid programme of education was laid out for these men. One of the catalysts of Reformation had been scholarly study of the Scriptures and so every man training for this ministry was expected to be well equipped for the lifelong task of biblical exegesis and exposition. The maestro himself epitomised the ideal as in his daily lectures and expositions he spoke extemporaneously and directly from the Hebrew or Greek text of the Scripture.

> People today turn up their noses at the many sermons in Geneva and the 'intellectualist' instruction. But we should realise that on this intellectualism depends a great deal of the penetrating power of Calvinism. The Calvinist knows *what* he believes and *why* he believes it.[24]

The source of Protestant power in France, shown by the sudden appearance of organised Huguenot armies in 1560, has always been difficult for historians to explain. The entire movement is expressive of careful organisation and meticulous central planning. It now emerges that a well-instructed people had by then been integrated into a structured church life which, like a spider's web, reached out into all the provinces and yet had sufficient central

---

22. R. M. Kingdom, *Geneva, and the Coming of the Wars of Religion to France* 1555-63, (Geneva 1953), p. 2.
23. *Op. cit.*, p. 45.
24. Karl Hall, quoted by T. H. L. Parker, *John Calvin*, p. 113.

coherence for problems to be discussed, plans to be formulated and, if necessary, unified defensive strategies employed.

There is now, also, a growing awareness that the emergence of this powerfully motivated church has to be traced back to the training at Geneva of a very effective missionary force. And supporting it was the line of direct communication back into Geneva, and the men there who had moulded its beliefs and directed its energies. The missionary thrust inherent in their theology, and the spiritual vision for the salvation of others which it generated, ensured that Calvin – and his ministerial colleagues in Geneva – recognised, in the mountain pathways into France, doors of opportunity for spreading the gospel. The story of how they went through them is, in the words of Professor David B. Calhoun, 'a thrilling chapter in the history of missions'.[25]

Much more could be said on this fascinating subject, but even our brief, outline study illustrates the urgent need to reassess and reinterpret the traditional notions entertained about it. The more recent collations, and interpretations, of the relevant data available to us about Calvin, Geneva and Mission combine to show that he was the person, and it the place, to which one of the finest churches of the Reformation era owed, under God, its life and witness. It was a church which was to stand strong for Christ for more than one hundred years in its own homeland and which, even after its final dispersal in the latter part of the seventeenth century, took its godly witness and its theological heritage out from France to England, Ireland, Holland, America and South Africa.

25. *Op. cit.*, p. 27.